# Restoration Cut Short:

## *The Roman Catholic Eschatology of the Churches of Christ*

## Samuel G. Dawson

Published by:
    SGD Press
    Bowie, Texas

Library of Congress Cataloging in Publications Data.

Dawson, Samuel G., 1943-
Restoration Cut Short: The Roman Catholic Eschatology of the Churches of Christ
252 p.
Includes bibliography and indexes
1.    Eschatology–Religious    aspects–Christianity.    2.
Resurrection–Religious aspects–Christianity. 3. Prophecy–Religious aspects–Christianity. 4. Judgment–Religious aspects–Christianity. 5. Last days–Religious aspects–Christianity.

ISBN 978-1983685958

*Printed and bound in the United States of America*

The *Catechism of the Catholic Church* has the term "end of time" 19 times. The Bible has it not one time. Where do YOU think we got it? And the return of Christ at the end of time? And the judgment at the end of time? And the resurrection at the end of time? And the renewal of the universe at the end of time? Likely from the Roman Catholic Church or a protestant denomination resulting from the Reformation Movement or a number of protestant denominations in the Restoration Movement.

**Other Books by the Author**

**(All available at Amazon.com)**

*Commentary on Job:*
*The Largest Collection of False Doctrine in the Bible*

*Imminent Judgment in the New Testament*

*Revelation Realized: Martyr Vindication*
*from Genesis to Revelation*

*Restoration Cut Short:*
*The Roman Catholic Eschatology of the Churches of Christ*

*The Teaching of Jesus: From Mount Sinai to Gehenna*
*A Faithful Rabbi Urgently Warns Rebellious Israel*

*The Resurrection: Israel's Old Covenant Hope*
*in Chronological Order*

*Fellowship: With God and His People*
*The Way of Christ Without Denominationalism*

*Christians, Churches, & Controversy*
*Navigating Doctrinal & Personal Clashes*

*Marriage, Divorce & Remarriage*
*The Uniform Teaching of Moses, Jesus & Paul*

*How to Study the Bible*
*A Practical Guide to Independent Bible Study*

*Denominational Doctrines*
*Explained, Examined, Exposed*

*Foundations of Faith:*
*Practical Essays on Christian Evidences*

# Personal Background and Purpose in Writing

After 50 years of experience among churches of Christ, I am compelled to address some detrimental tendencies that I've observed becoming increasingly harmful. My experience includes 22 years of full-time preaching; gospel meetings in 16 states and provinces of the United States and Canada; seven books; numerous pamphlets and bulletin articles; debates with atheists, denominational preachers, and brethren; over eight years of live, call-in radio work; and audio cassettes numbering in the hundreds of thousands. All of this was in the propagation and defense of the nondenominational way of Christ.

During my years of preaching, brethren always treated me royally. I still enjoy the confidence of a great many brethren, mostly in North America.

Now retired and at the sunset of my life, I want to candidly describe some deficiencies among most of these churches. I know personally a number of notable exceptions to my observations, both congregationally and individually. However, such congregations are rare, and exceptional Christians are not clustered together to a great degree.

Let me briefly describe how I came to this realization in this introduction, and then I'll address the issues more fully in the remaining chapters.

As a young preacher, I thought that I didn't dare admit I was ignorant of anything, so I read huge books of answers to Bible questions. Later on, I was less concerned about admitting my ignorance and more concerned about the quality of the answers I was giving. As I questioned the teaching of various denominations, I was asking others to be open-minded and critical of their own beliefs. Consistency required that I bind myself, as well, to be open-minded about everything I believed. We all know the word for someone who demands something of others he's not willing to do himself. It starts with an "h" and it's not hippopotamus or hypotenuse. I quickly found that some of my own beliefs did not stand up to careful examination. In some cases, the arguments needed to be made better. In others, the belief had to be abandoned entirely. This dedication to questioning and my background in physics, mathematics, and logic has helped me boil many controversies down to core issues and then to refine them into an easily understood form.

One elder told me, "I really like the way you throw the grain down on the ground so us chickens can get at it and digest it."

In 1988, I tackled a foundation controversy with *Fellowship: With God and His People: The Way of Christ Without Denominationalism.* It exposes many misunderstandings of what the church is or the differences between the universal and local church. Our ignorance in this area has allowed denominational thinking to creep into our own thinking and practice. The danger here is that if we're thinking denominationally, we begin to also act denominationally.

After 40 years of serious Bible study and teaching experience, I published *What Is Wrong with Many Churches of Christ, and How They Can Avoid Extinction.* This volume demonstrates how because of ignorance, lack of independent study, lack of skills for dealing with brethren with whom we disagree, tolerance of high-handed leaders, and codependence, churches of Christ are rapidly approaching extinction.

Some, who are familiar with my work, will recognize many of the topics I raise in that book, perhaps from my recordings or books—or from the teaching of others. In it, excerpts were pulled together into one volume and applied specifically to churches of Christ. I hope that if you've read the eight problems which I identify, that you've ascertained whether my points are correct, and where they are, measure yourself as to whether you're part of the problem, or part of the solution.

My motive in describing the shortcomings I see in these churches is not anger, nor is it to tear down a single one of these churches; but rather, it is to highlight problems most of us have known existed, perhaps for decades. I want to let individual Christians know that scriptural solutions are readily available, and to urge them to make needed reforms in their own lives and in the congregations where they worship. Because of our plea to the world to embrace the way of Christ without denominational allegiance, I can urge no reform larger than that of a local church.

Samuel G. Dawson
SGD Press
Bowie, Texas

# Table of Contents

# Introduction

## Where Churches of Christ Fit in Religious History

Most religious folks are familiar with the Reformation Movement of the 16th century that splintered Roman Catholic Europe. It produced hundreds of denominations that endure to the present day. Prominent leaders of that movement included John Calvin, Martin Luther, John Wycliffe, John Knox, Philipp Melanchthon, William Tyndale, and Huldrych Zwingli, plus a host of other lesser-known figures.

With the colonization of America, many of those denominations came to the new world as well. Beginning in the first half of the 19th century in America, a significant religious phenomenon known as the restoration movement began. Beginning with men such as Thomas Campbell, a Presbyterian minister and his son Alexander, recently arrived from Scotland, a great many religious people started a trek away from the denominational religious division of their day back to the nondenominational way of Christ they found in the Bible. Their mantra was, "We will speak where the Bible speaks and be silent where the Bible is silent." They determined to lay aside their denominational creeds and use just their Bible as their standard of authority, and to persuade others to do the same. While not entirely successful, the movement had stupendous effect in America.

Within a few decades, Campbell would claim that the restoration movement consisted of several thousand congregations and several hundred thousand members. By 1906, David Lipscomb, a later member of the movement, claimed that the churches of Christ, a product of the movement consisted of 18,000 congregation and nearly 3 million members, comprising the third largest religious group in the United States.

Many students of the history of the churches of Christ maintain that the "restoration" stopped about the time of Lipscomb's announcement. One legendary minister illustrated it this way: that in the beginning, people in churches of Christ found the church like a rusted, dented, wagon that needed many repairs, new wheels, new paint, body work, etc. By the early 20th century, most of them felt that the little red wagon had been restored, and that their job now was to ride around in their shiny new wagon. Indeed, most readers will recognize that there's very little restoration work going on among these churches now. As a matter of fact, older Christians remember preachers of their youth issuing a challenge to audiences: "You show us one thing we're doing or teaching wrong from the Bible, and we'll change!" Nowadays, if someone raises a question or concept different from what is commonly taught or practiced, we don't study the matter out publicly, but somehow that person will be silenced. He won't be allowed to teach any more, or somehow, his views will be squelched. The restoration process is over!

Whether or not the restoration movement stopped, our task is not to promulgate the results of their study. If my father arrived at the complete truth of God's word, my task is not to teach what my father taught, but to study for myself and teach what God taught to the utmost of my ability!

At the time of writing of this volume, the churches of Christ are on the wane. As I've documented in my *What Is Wrong with Most Churches of Christ and How They Can Avoid Extinction*, in the fifty years from 1955 to 2005, churches of Christ dwindled from 3.0 million to 1.267 million members and from 18,000 to 12,963 congregations. While the population nearly doubled in the same period of time, membership in churches of Christ declined 58%. At the average rate of decline of 35,000 members or 1.2% per year, churches of Christ will vanish by 2042.

The writer of this volume is one of those who believe the restoration of the New Testament way of Christ has been cut short. This is true on many Bible topics, but in this volume we want to see it on the topic of eschatology, the study of last things. He's going to demonstrate that because of general weakness and lack of teaching of the Old Testament, particularly the prophets, churches of Christ have a view of last things that is not the result of their own independent study, but one which has been handed down to them through the denominations of the reformation movement to our present time without critical examination. The purpose of this volume is to stimulate and initiate that critical examination of the popular view of eschatology in churches of Christ. It can also apply to most denominations as well.

We will first describe the popular view of eschatology, last things, held in churches of Christ. We will then show the origin of this view, surprisingly the Roman Catholic Church. Then we will set forth the Bible's view of eschatology or last things.

The topics will be covered in the following order:

1. Is Sunday the Lord's Day?
2. Does Hebrews 10.25 Require Assemblies in Local Churches?
3. The End of Time
4. The Coming of Christ at the End of Time
5. The Judgment at the End of Time
6. Biological Death as Punishment for Adam's Sin
7. Are Souls Unconditionally Immortal?
8. The Destruction of the Universe at the End of Time
9. The Resurrection of Biological Bodies at the End of Time
10. Eternal Conscious Torment in Hell
11. The Rich Man & Lazarus
12. Immortality & The Afterlife

After these topics are covered, we will offer our conclusions.

## The Popular View of Eschatology

The popular view of eschatology among churches of Christ and most denominations is this:
> 1. Adam and Eve were placed in the Garden of Eden, and told not to eat of the tree of knowledge of good and evil, and that they would die the day they ate.
> 2. They disobeyed God and *begin to die* biologically that day, losing their original immortality and their fellowship with God, being cast from the garden
> 3. God's plan to redeem man worked through history to the coming of his son, who died on the cross to redeem man, and ascended back to heaven.
> 4. At the end of time on earth, Christ will return a second time.

5. At that time, Christ will resurrect the physical bodies of all who have ever lived on earth.

6. Planet earth and the stars will be destroyed by burning, and be replaced by a new heavens and earth.

7. All those resurrected will then appear before the judgment seat of Christ to be judged for the deeds done in their bodies.

8. The righteous will be assigned to heaven eternally, and the unrighteous will be assigned to eternal conscious torment in Hell.

It will surprise many to learn that all of these points have their origin within Roman Catholicism, not the Bible. We will now demonstrate this in the case of each of these topics, and set forth the scriptural truth on them as well.

## A Plea for Open-Mindedness as We Begin

If we strive for open-mindedness and truly want to know what the Bible teaches, the following quotation will help us in our search:

> We do not start our Christian lives by working out our faith for ourselves; it is mediated to us by Christian tradition, in the form of sermons, books and established patterns of church life and fellowship. We read our Bibles in the light of what we have learned from these sources; we approach Scripture with minds already formed by the mass of accepted opinions and viewpoints with which we have come into contact, in both the Church and the world. It is easy to be unaware that it has happened; it is hard even to begin to realize how profoundly tradition in this sense has moulded us. But we are forbidden to become enslaved to human tradition, either secular or Christian, whether it be "catholic" tradition, or "critical" tradition, or "ecumenical" tradition. We may never assume the complete rightness of our own established ways of thought and practice and excuse ourselves the duty of testing and reforming them by Scriptures. (J. I. Packer, *"Fundamentalism" and the Word of God* [Grand Rapids, MI: William B. Eerdmans Publishing Co., 1958], pp. 69-70.)

Of course, Packer just reminds us of Biblical injunctions to test everything proposed for our belief. For example, in II Cor. 13.5, Paul told the Corinthians:

> Try your own selves, whether ye are in the faith; prove your own selves.

Likewise, in Eph. 5.8-10, Paul commanded the Ephesian Christians to be involved in such testing:

> for ye were once darkness, but are now light in the Lord, walk as children of light, proving what is well-pleasing unto the Lord.

In New Testament times, one was only a disciple of Christ when he was willing to examine himself, his beliefs, and everything proposed for his belief as a child of light. Nothing less is required now.

# Chapter 1

# Is Sunday the Lord's Day?

## The Teaching of Roman Catholicism

In article 638 of the *Catechism of the Catholic Church*, we read:

> 2174 Jesus rose from the dead "on the first day of the week" (Cf. Mt. 28:1; Mk. 16:2; Lk. 24:1; Jn. 20:1). Because it is the "first day," the day of Christ's Resurrection recalls the first creation. Because it is the "eighth day" following the sabbath, it symbolizes the new creation ushered in by Christ's Resurrection. For Christians it has become the first of all days, the first of all feasts, the Lord's Day – Sunday

> We all gather on the day of the sun, for it is the first day [after the Jewish sabbath, but also the first day] when God, separating matter from darkness, made the world; and on this same day Jesus Christ our Savior rose from the dead.

In Rev. 1.10, John begins his book with an inaugural vision by saying:

**1:10 I was in the Spirit on the Lord's day, and I heard behind me a great voice, as of a trumpet**

Since John is having this theophany, this inaugural vision, "in the spirit" probably means "under the control of the Spirit."

The Lord's day is generally taken to be the first day of the week, Sunday, but scripture doesn't demand it. It also doesn't define or explain what the Lord's day is. In the author's early years of preaching in the northwest part of the United States, he frequently debated preachers from Sabbath-keeping denominations (Seventh-day Adventists, Seventh-day Church of God, Church of God Seventh-Day, etc.), on whether Christians were to observe the Sabbath commandment. I was happy to deny their affirmatives. On the other hand, when they wanted me to affirm that the Lord's Day was the first day of the week, I always respectfully declined to do so, because I couldn't prove it from the Bible. Over forty years later, I still can't. The term only occurs once in the New Testament, and that instance doesn't equate the Lord's Day with the first day of the week. We can't just assume it's the first day. Many *assume* that since Jesus was raised from the dead on the first day of the week (Mt. 28.1ff), that the Lord's day is the first day of the week. However, that's just another unprovable assumption. Some *assume* that since the Corinthians contributed to their local church treasury on the first day of the week (I Cor. 16.1ff), the Lord's day is the first day of the week. It's still just another unprovable assumption. Many *assume* that since the early church partook of the Lord's supper on the first day of the week, the Lord's day is the first day of the week. Again, it's just another unprovable assumption. (For more discussion on the Sabbath question, please see Chapters 13-15 in the author's *Denominational Doctrines: Explained, Examined, Exposed*, available from Amazon.com.)

F. I . Stanley, a preacher in Churches of Christ and author of a commentary on Revelation, affirms that the term isn't explained or defined in the Bible:

> The term "The Lord's Day" was so well understood by all that it did not need an explanation. Why should it? Every Christian knew the day that belonged to the Lord. They knew the day of their covenant just as well as the Hebrew people know theirs. (F. I. Stanley, *As A Lamb Slain, A Unique Commentary on the Book of The Revelation* (Rogers, AR: F. I. Stanley, 1985, p. 41-43.)

If you wonder if Stanley's take on the covenant day of the Mosaic Law and the New Covenant smacks of the concept that Sunday is the Christian sabbath, your suspicions will prove correct. For now, we merely mention Paul's teaching in Rom. 14.5 that Christians could "esteem every day alike." There are no holy days in the New Testament. This certainly wasn't the case under the Law of Moses!

Obviously, Stanley agrees with my take on the Lord's day, that it's not defined or explained in the Bible. His contention was that it didn't need to be because everyone knew it meant Sunday. Even if that were true, shouldn't we still be prepared to answer non-believer's questions about its meaning? Also, Sabbatarian groups wouldn't assent to Stanley's contention at all. I doubt that he ever debated any of them, nor was he prepared to if he didn't think scripture defined or explained the term.

Stanley continues:

> In fact, it was so well understood that only to mention it was enough for all to understand. To us, it is without question and beyond argument. (*Ibid.*, p, 43.)

This assertion won't set well with one who takes to heart Paul's command to "prove (test, examine) all things, hold fast that which is good, abstain from every form of evil (I Thes. 5.21-22), nor will it with one who is a child of light, for Paul commands in Eph. 5.8, 10:

> 8 For ye were once darkness, but are now light in the Lord: walk as children of light...10 proving what is well-pleasing unto the Lord;

Simply asserting that everyone understood the term "the Lord's day," the way Stanley understood it isn't proving what is well-pleasing to the Lord, and merely accepting such assertions isn't walking as a child of light. I know of no subject the Bible touches upon that is beyond question and argument. Do you?

Stanley then quotes from St. Ignatius, Bishop of Antioch, in a letter to the church at Magnesia. Ignatius died in AD 107, so these words were probably penned in the latter part of the first century:

> Let everyone of you keep the Sabbath after a spiritual manner, rejoicing in meditation on the law, not in relaxation of the body, admiring the workmanship of God, and not eating things prepared the day before, nor using lukewarm drinks and walking within a prescribed space, nor finding a delight in dancing and plaudits which have no sense in them. And after the observance of the Sabbath, let every friend of Christ keep the Lord's Day as a festival, the resurrection day, the queen and chief of all the days...If then those who had walked in ancient practices attained unto newness

of hope, no longer observing sabbaths but fashioning
their lives after the Lord's day, on which our life also
arose through Him and through His death which some
men deny..." (Epistle to the Magnesians, ix, 1.v., p.
63, cited by Stanley, *op. cit.,* p. 44.)

If you think Ignatius makes a murky distinction between the
sabbath and Sunday, again, your suspicions will be proven correct. Of
course, Ignatius' statements that the Lord's day was the resurrection
day and the chief of all the days is language Stanley would like to find
in the Bible, but cannot. This is the very thing lacking in the inspired
text, and is hardly proving what is well-pleasing unto the Lord. It's
what is well-pleasing to Ignatius and Stanley! Stanley then tells us
what weight he assigns to the testimony of Ignatius:

We feel that no greater proof can be given than the
writings of these men who lived and worshipped in the
time of the apostles...Since the Lord's day and the
first day of the week were being used synonymously
by the early Christian fathers during the first century,
we see no reason why it should be questioned here.
(*Ibid.*)

This author couldn't disagree more. Greater proof of the assertion
that the Lord's day was Sunday would be a simple definition or
explanation from scripture, which Stanley has admitted isn't there!

What credence should be attached to Ignatius' testimony? A
simple survey of his doctrinal stands will help. Ignatius affirmed a
single bishop in each city with assistance from the elders in the
congregations of that city:

Take care to do all things in harmony with God, with
the bishop presiding in the place of God, and with the
presbyters in the place of the council of the apostles,
and with the deacons, who are most dear to me,
entrusted with the business of Jesus Christ, who was
with the Father from the beginning and is at last made
manifest" — Letter to the Magnesians 2, 6:1

This in spite of the New Testament's teaching that bishops and
elders referred to the same men (Ac. 20.17, 28).

He also affirmed the infallibility of the bishop:

It is not lawful to baptize or give communion without the consent of the bishop. On the other hand, whatever has his approval is pleasing to God. Thus, whatever is done will be safe and valid." — Letter to the Smyrnaeans 8.

Ignatius' teaching formed a foundation of the Roman Catholic doctrine of apostolic succession, which they view a mark of the true church.

He was also a proponent of the doctrine of transubstantiation, that the bread and fruit of the vine in the communion becomes the literal flesh and blood of Jesus. Speaking of a congregation that didn't agree, Ignatius said:

They abstain from the Eucharist and from prayer because they do not confess that the Eucharist is the flesh of our Savior Jesus Christ, flesh which suffered for our sins and which that Father, in his goodness, raised up again. — Letter to the Smyrnaeans 6:2–7:1.

Ignatius was the first known Christian writer to argue in favor of Christianity's replacement of the sabbath with the Lord's day. Sabbatarians now gleefully quote the Roman Catholic Church's claim that they changed the sabbath from Saturday to Sunday. Those who came out of Roman Catholicism in the Reformation Movement brought Ignatius' concepts with them. Later, those who abandoned their denominational allegiance in the Restoration Movement in the United States, brought Ignatius' concepts with them, as well. One has to ask, "When will those of us striving to be just Christians ever get all the Roman Catholicism out of our teaching?"

## Is the Day of the Lord Equivalent to the Lord's Day?

There is a grammatical distinction between the two phrases, but it's a distinction without a real difference. For example, scripture speaks of the Lord's house and the house of the Lord, but no one thinks those two terms refer to different things. Scripture speaks of the servant of the Lord and the Lord's servant, but again, no one thinks those two things are different. Likewise with the will of the Lord and the Lord's will, the supper of the Lord and the Lord's supper, or the table of the Lord and the Lord's table. Isn't it just an assumption to assume that there's a distinction between the day of the Lord and the Lord's day? Clearly, if we know what the house of the Lord is, we know what the Lord's house is. If we know what a servant of the Lord is, we know what a Lord's servant is. If we know what the will of the Lord is we know what the Lord's will is. If we know what the supper of the Lord is, we know what the Lord's supper is. In exactly the same way, if we know what the Day of the Lord is, we know what the Lord's day is.

Realizing this, when John says "I was in the spirit on the Lord's day," from our knowledge of the day of the Lord, we know what John meant. Likewise, in the rest of Revelation, we'll see further evidence of this same Lord's day. In Rev. 6.15-17, we see:

> 15 And the kings of the earth, and the princes, and the chief captains, and the rich, and the strong, and every bondman and freeman, hid themselves in the caves and in the rocks of the mountains; 16 and they say to the mountains and to the rocks, Fall on us, and hide us from the face of him that sitteth on the throne, and from the wrath of the Lamb: 17 for *the great day of their wrath is come*; and who is able to stand?

From our previous discussion in the introductory chapter of this quotation from Isaiah 2.2, 12, and 20-21," we know that these verses are fulfilling Isaiah's prophecy of the day of the Lord in Old Covenant Israel's last days. Thus, it's also referring to the Lord's day in their last days. In Rev. 16.13-14, when John speaks of the destruction of Jerusalem at "war of the great day of God, the Almighty," this is another reference to the Lord's day. Similarly in Rev. 18.8, when Jerusalem's end finally comes, John will say:

> Therefore *in one day* shall her plagues come, death, and mourning, and famine; and she shall be utterly burned with fire; for strong is the Lord God who judged her.

Surely this "one day" is another reference to the day of the Lord or the Lord's day.

Also on the day of the Lord, in Ac. 2.20, Peter quotes Joel 2.28-32, referring to the destruction of Jerusalem *in the last days of the Mosaic age*, and uses the same apocalyptic language Jesus used in the Olivet Discourse when he says, "The sun shall be turned into darkness, And the moon into blood, Before *the day of the Lord* come, *That great and notable day*." Again, the term is used here of the destruction of Jerusalem when men called on the name of the Lord. In I Cor. 5.5, Paul commanded the Corinthians to withdraw fellowship from an impenitent fornicator, saying, "to deliver such a one unto Satan for the destruction of the flesh, that the spirit may be saved in *the day of the Lord Jesus*." Here, the term is used in the same way as Peter used it in the first gospel sermon, as it is in I Thes. 5.2, where he said: "For yourselves know perfectly that *the day of the Lord* so cometh as a thief in the night." The only day of the Lord we know of in the New Testament is the one coming on the Jews of the first century, and especially in Thessalonians, as avenging the martyrs at the destruction of Jerusalem. In II Thes. 2.2, Paul addressed that event again: "to the end that ye be not quickly shaken from your mind, nor yet be troubled, either by spirit, or by word, or by epistle as from us, as that *the day of the Lord* is *just at hand*."

The KJV and ASV introduce confusion into this verse with the expression "just at hand," which makes it sound like Paul was correcting their misunderstanding about the near coming of Jesus. The phrase translated "just at hand" is actually in the perfect tense. Literally, the phrase is "has already happened." The Thessalonians were not confused because they thought the coming of the Lord was *near*, it was because *they thought it had already occurred*! In essence, they thought the entire Christian age lasted only 20 years, yet as we've seen, the age of the Messiah was to have no end (Isa. 9.6-7 Lk. 1.33). To be sure, as we've already seen in Mt. 16.27-28, Mt. 24.29, 34, Heb. 10.37, Jas. 5.8, and Rev. 22.10, 12, Jesus and his apostles taught that his return was near, but the Thessalonians thought the Lord had come! That's what the text says.

Again, the popular view of the return of Christ, that every eye will see him, the dead will come forth from their graves, a universal judgment will occur, and the planets and stars will be burned up, doesn't fit this text at all. If your preacher announced that the day of the Lord had occurred yesterday, and the Lord had returned, the dead were raised, the earth burned up, and the stars, too, wouldn't you think it was time for the straitjacket to come out? Do you suppose the Thessalonians really believed that Christ had come (though none of them saw him), that the resurrection had taken place (although the cemeteries were all still intact), the judgment had taken place (though none of them had participated), and the planet had burned up (though they were still walking around on it)? They actually believed none of this, yet they thought the Lord had returned. Obviously, their concept wasn't the popular one of today. This alone should convince us that we might need to go back to the drawing board with our concepts of the return of Christ, don't you think? (For a full discussion of the eschatology of Thessalonians, please see Appendix 5, "The Eschatology of Thessalonians" in the author's *Essays on Eschatology: An Introductory Overview of the Study of Last Things.*)

The last New Testament passage containing the day of the Lord is found in II Pet. 3.10, where Peter says:

> But the day of the Lord will come as a thief; in the which the heavens shall pass away with a great noise, and the elements shall be dissolved with fervent heat, and the earth and the works that are therein shall be burned up.

There are three sets of "heavens and earth" in this text, the first before the flood, the one Peter was living under, and the new heavens and earth that was about to replace the one Peter lived under. In no case did the term refer to the planet and stars. We live on the same planet and under the same stars that Peter and Adam did! The term heavens and earth represented a covenantal system. In addition, we popularly take "elements" in this passage to be atomic elements, yet every other time the word (*stoichion*) is used, it refers to the fundamental elements of the law of Moses! For a full discussion of this passage, please see Chapter 5, "II Peter 3: Destruction of the Universe or Jerusalem?" in the author's *Essays on Eschatology: An Introductory Overview of the Study of Last Things.*)

One last usage of the day of Jehovah is found in Zech. 14.1-2, again, in connection with the destruction of Jerusalem:

> 1 Behold, *a day of Jehovah* cometh, when thy spoil shall be divided in the midst of thee. 2 For I will gather all nations against Jerusalem to battle; and the city shall be taken, and the houses rifled, and the women ravished; and half of the city shall go forth into captivity, and the residue of the people shall not be cut off from the city.

All six passages which use the term "day of the Lord" refer to a day of judgment on a city or region on the earth, which is exactly how John is going to describe the harlot Babylon, and its replacement by New Jerusalem. Babylon is identified in Rev. 11.8 as "where the Lord was crucified." In Rev. 18.24, Babylon was destroyed because "in her was found the blood of prophets and of saints, and of all that have been slain upon the earth (*ge*, lit., land—SGD). As we noticed in the introductory chapter of *Revelation Realized: Martyr Vindication from Genesis to Revelation,* our commentary on Revelation, Moses, Isaiah, Jesus, the author of Hebrews, John, and Paul made clear that Jerusalem was going to be held responsible for the blood of all the prophets in his generation! Jerusalem was destroyed to avenge the martyrs on the day of the Lord.

# Chapter 2

# Does Hebrews 10.25 Require Weekly Assemblies in Local Churches?

## The Teaching of the Roman Catholic Church on Hebrews 10.25

From the *Catechism of the Catholic Church*, we see the assertion that Heb. 10.25 taught weekly assemblies of local churches:

> 2178 This practice of the Christian assembly dates from the beginnings of the apostolic age. The Letter to the Hebrews reminds the faithful "not to neglect to meet together, as is the habit of some, but to encourage one another." (p. 525)

Of course, the passage from Hebrews the catechism refers to is Heb. 10.24-27, the subject of this essay:

> ...let us consider one another to provoke unto love and good works; 25 *not forsaking our own assembling together,* as the custom of some is, but exhorting one another; and so much the more, as ye see *the day* drawing nigh. 26 For if we sin wilfully after that we have received the knowledge of the truth, there remaineth no more a sacrifice for sins, 27 but a *certain fearful expectation of judgment,* and a *fierceness of fire* which shall devour the adversaries.

Many will be surprised to learn that the basis of this passage is found in the very important chapter of Deuteronomy 32, where at the beginning of the nation of Old Covenant Israel, God revealed to Moses how that nation would end in Christ's generation.

Just before Moses' death, after he led the first generation of Jews through the wilderness of Sinai, he brought them to the border of their promised land. In Deuteronomy 28-30, he pronounced all the blessings Israel would receive if they were faithful to him, and all the curses they would receive if they were unfaithful. In Dt. 31.19-21, God instructed Moses to write a song, the Song of Moses, and teach it to Israel:

> 19 Now therefore, write this song for yourselves, and teach it to the sons of Israel; put it on their lips, in order that this song may be a witness for Me against the sons of Israel. 20 For when I bring them into the land flowing with milk and honey, which I swore to their fathers, and they have eaten and are satisfied and become prosperous, then they will turn to other gods and serve them, and spurn Me and break My covenant. 21 Then it shall come about, when many evils and troubles have come upon them, that this song will testify before them as a witness (for it shall not be forgotten from the lips of their descendants); for I know their intent which they are developing today, before I have brought them into the land which I swore.

God told Moses that this generation of Jews wasn't going to turn out well. He was to teach the Song of Moses to Israel, so that when they became unfaithful to him and his judgments began to fall on them, this song and their singing of it would be a witness that God told them how they were going to turn out. Future generations of Jews, including the ones whom Jesus taught, knew this song—they had been taught it since childhood. In Dt. 32.29, Moses told Israel:

> 29 For I know that after my death you will act corruptly and turn from the way which I have commanded you; and evil will befall you in the latter days, for you will do that which is evil in the sight of the LORD, provoking Him to anger with the work of your hands.

Moses tells them that punishments from God will befall them "in the latter days," i.e., in their future, because of their involvement with false gods. This would include a variety of punishments, including the

Assyrian and Babylonian captivities. However, in Dt. 32.20-21, Moses became much more specific, foretelling the very end of the nation of Old Covenant Israel:

> 20 Then He said, I will hide My face from them, I will see what their *end* [emphasis mine throughout—SGD] shall be; For they are a *perverse generation*, Sons in whom is no faithfulness. 21 They have made Me jealous with what is not God; They have provoked Me to anger with their idols. So I will make them jealous with those who are not a people; I will provoke them to anger with a foolish nation,

In this passage, which Paul quotes as fulfilled in his time (in Rom. 10.19), God foretold "the end" of Old Covenant Israel, that their last generation will be a perverse generation. Jesus, of course, called his generation of Jews an "unbelieving and perverse generation" in Mt. 12.38, 16.4, and 17.11. In the first gospel sermon, Peter called faithful Jews to "save yourselves from this perverse generation" (Ac. 2.40). Paul also uses this language in Phil. 2.15 of the first century Jewish generation which was about to suffer destruction of their temple, capitol, and nation.

We can know that the generation of Jesus and Peter is the one under consideration in Deuteronomy 32 since Paul quotes Dt. 32.21 in Rom. 10.19 as justification of his taking the gospel to the Gentiles in an attempt to provoke the Jews to jealousy. This was in the early 60s AD, shortly before the end of Old Covenant Israel in AD 70.

Continuing in Dt. 32.28-29, we read:

> 28 They are a nation without sense, there is no discernment in them. 29 If only they were wise and would understand this and discern what their end will be! (NIV)

In Dt. 32.34-36, we have Moses speaking of God's vengeance on Israel:

> 34 Is it not laid up in store with Me, Sealed up in My treasuries? 35 *Vengeance is Mine*, and retribution, In due time their foot (Old Covenant Israel—SGD) will slip; For the day of their calamity is near, And the impending things are hastening upon them. 36 For the LORD will vindicate His people (the faithful of Old

Covenant Israel—SGD), And will have compassion on
His servants; When He sees that their strength is gone,
And there is none remaining, bond or free.

We can know the time element of this judgment, for verse 35 is
quoted in Heb. 10.30a and verse 36 is quoted in Heb. 10.30b as both
are about to be fulfilled:

For we know him that said, *Vengeance belongeth unto
me, I will recompense.* And again, *The Lord shall
judge his people.*

Thus both Moses in Dt. 32 (written 15 centuries before Jerusalem
and the temple were destroyed) and the author of Hebrews (written
several years before) are speaking of the same judgment, that of Old
Covenant Israel by the Romans in AD 70.

Of course, Heb. 10.30 directly follows Heb. 10.23-39, verses that
have been appropriated to urge people to go to church on Sunday:

23 let us hold fast the confession of our hope that it
waver not; for he is faithful that promised: 24 and let
us consider one another to provoke unto love and good
works; 25 *not forsaking our own assembling together*,
as the custom of some is, but exhorting one another;
and so much the more, as ye see the day drawing nigh.
26 For if we sin wilfully after that we have received
the knowledge of the truth, there remaineth no more a
sacrifice for sins, 27 but a certain *fearful expectation
of judgment*, and a *fierceness of fire* which shall
devour the adversaries.

"The day" that was drawing nigh when Hebrews was written was
the day of the Lord we see in the prophets (Isa. 2.12, "the day of
Jehovah" in KJV, ASV, NKJV in Old Covenant Israel's last days, Isa.
2.2). This was the day of judgment coming on Old Covenant Israel
when Jerusalem and the temple were destroyed, as we'll see in detail in
Chapter 5, "The Judgment at the End of Time?". The "assembling" the
author of Hebrews was urging his Jewish listeners not to forsake was
not Sunday assemblies of local churches, but of the gathering the
messiah and John the Baptist were doing of the Jews. Isaiah 11.9-12
foretold the messiah would *gather* Israel and Judah in the last days. Isa.
49.5-7, 56.6-8, and Hos. 1.10-11 foretold the same *gathering*. It was
this *gathering* Jesus referred to when he said in Mt. 23.37:

> O Jerusalem, Jerusalem, that killeth the prophets, and stoneth them that are sent unto her! how often would I have gathered thy children together, even as a hen gathereth her chickens under her wings, and ye would not!

In Mt. 24.31, Jesus referred to this same gathering when he said:

> And he shall send forth his angels with a great sound of a trumpet, and they shall gather together his elect from the four winds, from one end of heaven to the other.

These angels (angelos, messengers) were the apostles who through their preaching were also participating in the gathering of the faithful Jews from among Old Covenant Israel in Jesus' generation (Mt. 24.34) We'll see further indications of the destruction of Jerusalem on the day of the Lord as we proceed further through the prophets.

Notice in Deut. 32.35, 36, 41, and 43 that *vengeance* and *vindication* would take place at the same time. Both the righteous and the wicked will see the same event, the end of Old Covenant Israel (at the hands of the Romans in AD 70) and interpret it entirely differently. The wicked see cruel destruction; the righteous see their salvation from the wicked. This is not unique to their judgment. In the flood of Noah's time, the wicked and righteous again saw the same event entirely differently. The wicked saw its destruction, while the same flood was the salvation of the righteous as the same water that destroyed the wicked carried the righteous to a new world order after the flood. This passage is alluded to in Hebrews 10:30-31 to describe a first century judgment of Old Covenant Israel.

Jesus spoke of this same vengeance of God on Old Covenant Israel in Lk. 21.20-24, when he says:

> But when ye see Jerusalem compassed with armies, then know that her desolation is at hand. Then let them that are in Judaea flee unto the mountains; and let them that are in the midst of her depart out; and let not them that are in the country enter therein. For these are days of vengeance, that all things which are written may be fulfilled. Woe unto them that are with child and to them that give suck in those days! for there shall be great distress upon the land, and wrath unto this people. And they shall fall by the edge of the

sword, and shall be led captive into all the nations: and
Jerusalem shall be trodden down of the Gentiles, until
the times of the Gentiles be fulfilled.

"All things that are written may be fulfilled" would certainly
include the prophecy of God's vengeance on Old Covenant Israel, as
well as the vindication of the righteous and the taking of the gospel to
the Gentiles.

## Conclusion

We've seen that Heb. 10.25 has nothing to do with the first day of
the week nor of congregational assemblies. Other than that we're using
it exactly right, and so is the Roman Catholic church.

# Chapter 3

# The End of Time?

## The Teaching of the Catholic Church

The *Catechism of the Catholic Church* uses the term "end of time" 19 times. It's used at least of the coming of Christ, the judgment, the resurrection, and the destruction of heaven and earth.

## The Teaching of the Bible

The Bible never uses the term "end of time," not a single time, not in reference to the coming of Christ, the judgment, the resurrection, nor the destruction of heaven and earth. Not one time in the Old Testament or the New Testament.

There are two passages that a few translations use the term, mistakenly so as we'll see, but the vast majority of translations do not use the term even in these two passages.

### Daniel 12.4

The closest that the Bible comes to using the term "end of time" is Dan. 12.9 only in the NASV:

> But as for you, Daniel, conceal these words and seal
> up the book until the *end of time*; many will go back
> and forth, and knowledge will increase."

The American Standard version translates it as "the time of the end," as do the KJV, NIV, and the NKJV, among others. *Young's Literal Translation* translates it as "the time of the end."

The expressions "time of the end" and "the end of time" reflect two vastly different concepts. One supposes the end of time itself (on which the popular view of the resurrection is based), and the other speaks of the time of "the end," the end of the Mosaic age. In Daniel's context, the age ends with the destruction of Jerusalem and her temple.

## Rev. 10.5-7

> 5 And the angel that I saw standing upon the sea and upon the earth lifted up his right hand to heaven, 6 and sware by him that liveth for ever and ever, who created the heaven and the things that are therein, and the earth and the things that are therein, and the sea and the things that are therein, that there shall be *delay no longer*: 7 but in the days of the voice of the seventh angel, when he is about to sound, then is finished the mystery of God, according to the good tidings which he declared to his servants the prophets.

The strong angel makes an oath "that there shall be *delay* no longer." The KJV has "there shall be time no more." A favorite hymn of many reads, "When the trumpet of the Lord shall sound and time shall be no more," is obviously taken from this verse, but all newer translations use "delay." There is no statement in the entire Bible correctly translated "end of time" or "time no more." Men have invented the concept of the end of time and moved a lot of events in the Bible off to that imaginary point of no time, including the return of Christ, the judgment, the destruction of universe, and the resurrection, the very topics of this book.

The "delay" spoken of is that issued to the martyrs in Rev. 6.9-10 who wanted immediate vengeance on their persecutors. They were told to rest for *a little time* until some more saints were killed. That little time was used to assure the faithful that they wouldn't be lost in the shuffle, and now the *time is up*. It's time for judgment on their adversaries; *there shall be delay no longer!* The passage doesn't teach that there would be an end of time, just the end of a delay.

## Conclusion

If the *Catechism of the Catholic Church* has the term "end of time" 19 times, and the Bible has it not one single time, just where do you think we got the concept? How about the return of Christ at the end of time? The resurrection at the end of time? The judgment at the end of time? Or the destruction of the universe at the end of time? Obviously, if the Bible knows nothing about the end of time itself, it knows nothing about a coming of Christ, a judgment, a destruction of heavens and earth, a resurrection, or anything else at the end of time! However, we will examine each of those concepts in detail in further chapters.

## What's Ahead

We're going to see very quickly and simply that Jesus and his apostles taught that instead of the end of time or the end of the messianic age, the coming of Christ, the judgment, the resurrection, and the destruction of the old heavens and earth (not the planet and stars), was going to take place at the end of the age, their age, the Mosaic Age (as the Messianic Age has no end, Lk. 1.33, Isa. 9.6-7).

# Chapter 4

# The Coming of Christ—at
# the End of Time?

## Roman Catholic Church on the Coming of Christ at the End of Time

In the *Catechism of the Catholic Church*, we find in section 682:

> When he comes at the end of time to judge the living and the dead, the glorious Christ will reveal the secret disposition of hearts and will render to each man according to his works and according to his acceptance or refusal of grace.

Thus, Roman Catholicism places the coming of Christ at the end of time.

## The Bible's Teaching on the Coming of Christ

We first notice that the Bible teaches only one return of Christ following his ascension into heaven. there are 17 passages that refer to "the coming" or "his coming," that is, there's only one. All these passages refer to the same coming. Again, this is the way we refer to "the moon." When someone says, "Did you see the moon tonight?", we don't have to wonder which moon they're speaking of, and we never have in our entire lives!

However, since the Bible never says anything about the end of time, when did the New Testament say the coming of Christ was to occur? You may be surprised by the answer:

## Mt. 16.27-28

> 27 For the Son of man shall come in the glory of his
> Father with his angels; and then shall he render unto
> every man according to his deeds. 28 Verily I say unto
> you, there are some of them that stand here, who shall
> in no wise taste of death, till they see the Son of man
> coming in his kingdom.

Jesus said his coming would come in glory with his angels while some of his apostles were still alive. Do you believe that? If he didn't fulfill this promise, how was he any different than the false prophet Joseph Smith, who made predictions that didn't come to pass? If you don't believe he came in the lifetime of some of his apostles, don't lay your head on your pillow tonight and tell yourself that you believe Jesus or the Bible. You cannot!

## Mt. 24.30, 34

> 30 and then shall appear the sign of the Son of man in
> heaven: and then shall all the tribes of the earth mourn,
> and they shall see the Son of man coming on the
> clouds of heaven with power and great glory... 34
> Verily I say unto you, This generation shall not pass
> away, till all these things be accomplished.

In these verses, Jesus speaks of his coming as occurring in his generation. Do you believe what Jesus said? If Jesus was a false prophet by making such predictions that didn't come to pass, the Mosaic Law under which he lived and preached demanded his execution (Dt. 18.20, 22).

## I Thes. 5.23

> And the God of peace himself sanctify you wholly;
> and may your spirit and soul and body be preserved
> entire, without blame at the coming of our Lord Jesus
> Christ.

In this passage, Paul prays that the Thessalonians of the first century, not us in the $21^{st}$ century 2000+ years later) would still be alive (their spirit, body, and soul still intact) at the coming of the Lord.

Did the Lord's coming not occur in their time, or was Paul as mistaken and deserving of death as Jesus was?

## Heb. 10.35-37

> 35 Cast not away therefore your boldness, which hath great recompense of reward. 36 For ye have need of patience, that, having done the will of God, ye may receive the promise. 37 For yet a very little while, He that cometh shall come, and shall not tarry.

This passage speaks of a "recompense of reward" in v35, referring to a "payback" in a judgment (cf. Mt. 16.27-28, where Christ would render to every man according to his works while some of his disciples were still alive). In v36, he urges patience because in v37, he says the Lord is coming in a very little while, and shall not tarry. Most think that he hasn't come yet. "Very little while" comes from *hoson hoson micro* (from which we get "microscope, micrometer, etc.), which is literally "a very very tiny time." Was he urging them to be patient for 2000+ years because the Lord has tarried that long? He said that he wouldn't do that, but that he was coming in a very short time, and those people should be patient until then.

## Jas. 5.7-8

> 7 Be patient therefore, brethren, until the coming of the Lord. Behold, the husbandman waiteth for the precious fruit of the earth, being patient over it, until it receive the early and latter rain. 8 Be ye also patient; establish your hearts: for the coming of the Lord is at hand.

James urges his first century readers to be patient till Christ's coming, because it was at hand. It was literally within their reach. Do you think it was about to come in their time, or do you think James was asking them to be patient for 2000+ years? Again, if Jesus didn't fulfill his promise to return in his generation, James was a false prophet, as was his Lord.

Surely we can see that the coming of the Lord wasn't taught to be at the end of time, but in Jesus' generation. If that's not true, why continue to study the Bible, if our Lord and his apostles were that mistaken? Will you continue to think that the Roman Catholic church is right in teaching that the return of Christ will be at the end of time, and that Jesus, Paul, and James were wrong, or will you accept what Jesus, Paul, and James taught, and that Roman Catholicism is wrong with its unscriptural "end of time"?

## Rev. 22.6, 7, 10, 12, 20

At the conclusion of this great book, John gives these time statements concerning the coming of Christ:

> 6 And he said unto me, These words are faithful and true: and the Lord, the God of the spirits of the prophets, sent his angels to show unto his servants the things which must shortly come to pass. 7 And behold, I come quickly. Blessed is he that keepeth the words of the prophecy of this book...12 Behold, I come quickly; and my reward is with me, to render to each man according as his work is...20 He who testifieth these things saith, Yea: I come quickly. Amen: come, Lord Jesus.

"The things which must shortly come to pass" would include the coming of Christ, the resurrection, the judgment, the destruction of the harlot city (where the Lord was crucified, Rev. 11.8), its replacement by New Jerusalem, the destruction of the old heavens and earth, and its replacement by the new heavens and earth. Of course, the imminent coming of Christ is given specifically in v7, 12, and the imminent coming and judgment is given in v12, echoing Mt. 16.27-28.

# Conclusion on the Time of the Coming of Christ

There is no passage saying Christ would come at the end of time. Jesus himself said he would come during the lifetime of some of his disciples, at the end of the age, the Mosaic age, and in his generation. His New Testament writers said he was coming in a very very little time and would not tarry, as well as quickly, and at hand.

Timothy James, in Chapter 13 of his book, *THE MESSIAH'S RETURN, Delayed? Fulfilled? or Double-Fulfillment?,* asks the question: "Why has the Church, for two thousand years taught that Christ's Coming is still in OUR future?" He then makes a suggestion that's worthy of our consideration:

"The belief in the failure of Christ's prophecies stems
from the attempts of a Gentile-dominated church after
A.D. 70 trying to understand Jewish concepts."

This is certainly a plausible reason for the futurist view of the
coming of Christ, the judgment, the passing of the Old Heavens and
Earth, and the resurrection, for two reasons: 1) the Jewish/Gentile
problem was the major church problem in New Testament times and
for centuries thereafter, and 2) Gentile Christians to this day are
generally ignorant of Old Testament concepts on those subjects, as
well as others unrelated to eschatology like marriage and divorce, the
sermon on the mount, etc. Paul said that he didn't teach anything on
the resurrection except what Moses and the Prophets taught on the
subject (Ac. 24.14, 26.22-23). ALL these last days events are based on
the Old Testament's concepts and teaching, and we as a people are
pretty ignorant of the Old Testament, and particularly the prophets. If
you've never heard a sermon on the coming of Christ, the judgment,
and the resurrection from Moses and the Prophets, you're in for a
surprising and interesting study in this volume.

For further study on the coming of Christ, please see the author's
*Essays on Eschatology: An Introductory Overview of the Study of Last
Things, The Teaching of Jesus: From Sinai to Gehenna, A Faithful
Rabbi Urgently Warns Rebellious Israel*, and *Revelation Realized:
Martyr Vindication from Genesis to Revelation*, all available from
Amazon.com.

# Chapter 5

# The Judgment—at the End of Time?

As we saw in Chapter 1, the Bible knows nothing of an "end of time," thus it knows nothing of a judgment (or anything else) at the end of time. However, the popular eschatology of most Churches of Christ believe that's when the judgment will take place, as does Roman Catholicism, which we now document.

## Teaching of Roman Catholicism

In article 682 of the *Catechism of the Catholic Church*, we read:

> 682 When he comes at the end of time to judge the living and the dead, the glorious Christ will reveal the secret disposition of hearts and will render to each man according to his works and according to his acceptance or refusal of grace.

As we've seen in Chapter 2, Roman Catholicism teaches that Christ will return at the end of time, and here they state that he will also judge all men at that same time. In article 1040, the Catechism states the same thing:

> **1040** The Last Judgment will come when Christ returns in glory. Only the Father knows the day and the hour; only he determines the moment of its coming. Then through his Son Jesus Christ he will pronounce the final word on all history. We shall know the ultimate meaning of the whole work of creation and of the entire economy of salvation and

understand the marvelous ways by which his Providence led everything towards its final end. The Last Judgment will reveal that God's justice triumphs over all the injustices committed by his creatures and that God's love is stronger than death.[628]

Thus again, the Churches of Christ and the Roman Catholic Church teach the same thing.

# Introduction to the Bible's Teaching on the Judgment

## Well-Known Verses on the Judgment

There are a number of New Testament passages we in Churches of Christ (and Roman Catholic churches) commonly use to teach about the judgment. We'll mention most of them here.

### Mt. 16.27-28:

27 For the Son of man shall come in the glory of his Father with his angels; and then shall he render unto every man according to his deeds. 28 Verily I say unto you, there are some of them that stand here, who shall in no wise taste of death, till they see the Son of man coming in his kingdom.

We've already noticed this passage where Jesus foretold his coming in the lifetime of some of his disciples, but notice also that he says that when he comes, he will render to every man according to his deeds, that is, he will be coming for the judgment! Notice also that the Catholic catechism quotes the "render unto every man according to his deeds," and says that will occur at the end of time. Jesus said it would occur while some of his apostles were still alive! Either there are some pretty old apostles around, or the Catholic Church missed the time of the judgment entirely.

### Ac. 17.30-31 (Paul at Athens)

30 The times of ignorance therefore God overlooked; but now he commandeth men that they should all everywhere repent: 31 inasmuch as he hath appointed

> a day in which he will (lit., *is about to* judge—YLT)
> judge the world in righteousness by the man whom he
> hath ordained; whereof he hath given assurance unto
> all men, in that he hath raised him from the dead.

So Paul taught that the judgment was imminent in his own time,
not ours!

## II Cor. 5.10

> For we must all be made manifest before the
> judgment-seat of Christ; that each one may receive the
> things done in the body, according to what he hath
> done, whether it be good or bad.

## Mt. 25.31-46

> 31 But when the Son of man shall come in his glory,
> and all the angels with him, then shall he sit on the
> throne of his glory: 32 and before him shall be
> gathered all the nations: and he shall separate them
> one from another, as the shepherd separateth the sheep
> from the goats; 33 and he shall set the sheep on his
> right hand, but the goats on the left. 34 Then shall the
> King say unto them on his right hand, Come, ye
> blessed of my Father, inherit the kingdom prepared for
> you from the foundation of the world:  35 for I was
> hungry, and ye gave me to eat; I was thirsty, and ye
> gave me drink; I was a stranger, and ye took me in; 36
> naked, and ye clothed me; I was sick, and ye visited
> me; I was in prison, and ye came unto me. 37 Then
> shall the righteous answer him, saying, Lord, when
> saw we thee hungry, and fed thee? or athirst, and gave
> thee drink? 38 And when saw we thee a stranger, and
> took thee in? or naked, and clothed thee? 39 And when
> saw we thee sick, or in prison, and came unto thee? 40
> And the King shall answer and say unto them, Verily I
> say unto you, Inasmuch as ye did it unto one of these
> my brethren, even these least, ye did it unto me. 41
> Then shall he say also unto them on the left hand,
> Depart from me, ye cursed, into the eternal fire which
> is prepared for the devil and his angels: 42 for I was

hungry, and ye did not give me to eat; I was thirsty, and ye gave me no drink; 43 I was a stranger, and ye took me not in; naked, and ye clothed me not; sick, and in prison, and ye visited me not. 44 Then shall they also answer, saying, Lord, when saw we thee hungry, or athirst, or a stranger, or naked, or sick, or in prison, and did not minister unto thee? 45 Then shall he answer them, saying, Verily I say unto you, Inasmuch as ye did it not unto one of these least, ye did it not unto me. 46 And these shall go away into eternal punishment: but the righteous into eternal life.

**Heb. 9.27-28:**

27 And inasmuch as it is appointed unto men once to die, and after this cometh judgment; 28 so Christ also, having been once offered to bear the sins of many, shall appear a second time, apart from sin, to them that wait for him, unto salvation.

**Rev. 20.11-15:**

11 And I saw a great white throne, and him that sat upon it, from whose face the earth and the heaven fled away; and there was found no place for them. 12 And I saw the dead, the great and the small, standing before the throne; and books were opened: and another book was opened, which is the book of life: and the dead were judged out of the things which were written in the books, according to their works. 13 And the sea gave up the dead that were in it; and death and Hades gave up the dead that were in them: and they were judged every man according to their works. 14 And death and Hades were cast into the lake of fire. This is the second death, even the lake of fire. 15 And if any was not found written in the book of life, he was cast into the lake of fire.

These verses are certainly familiar ones, and Churches of Christ and Catholics alike are comfortable with them, and they agree that the New Testament speaks of "the" judgment, that is, one judgment of all men at one time. As we've noted, none of these passages (or any others in the entire Bible) speaks of the judgment taking place at the end of time.

# The New Testament Teaching on the Judgment Is Based on the Old Testament

However, many don't realize that the New Testament's teaching on the judgment is based on the Old Testament, a fact that has been widely ignored in both Churches of Christ and Roman Catholicism. Although we'll not have the space to refer to all of it, there's a massive amount of Old Testament teaching on the judgment described in the New Testament.

Anyone with familiarity with the New Testament probably knows that it speaks of a judgment of Old Covenant Israel in connection with the return of the Messiah. John the Baptist and Jesus spoke of such a judgment during their ministries in the Gospels. Other New Testament writers, like Paul, Peter, James, the author of Hebrews, and John, also spoke of a coming judgment in their books. Most of this teaching is mistakenly interpreted in our time as a judgment coming on all men at a supposed end of time. It is our purpose in this essay to survey this teaching, developing it in its proper context.

## The Judgment Foretold in Deuteronomy 32

We now want to notice an extremely important chapter with reference to the Messiah's judgment of Israel, Deuteronomy 32, the Song of Moses. With the aid of several student friends, I've recently come to the conclusion that Deuteronomy 32 may indeed be the most important chapter of the Bible, yet hardly anyone reads it, or appreciates the significance of it. I've taught the Old Testament through five or six times, yet I've missed the importance of this chapter. It's no exaggeration to say that Deuteronomy 32 is the basis of the teachings of the Old Testament prophets, as well as the teaching of John the Baptist, Jesus and his apostles throughout the New Testament.

We began our study of God's foretelling of Old Covenant Israel's end from its beginning by noticing a characteristic of the true God as opposed to idols. In Isa. 46.5-7, God compares himself with idols:

> 5 To whom would you liken Me, And make Me equal and compare Me, That we should be alike? 6 Those who lavish gold from the purse And weigh silver on the scale Hire a goldsmith, and he makes it into a god;

They bow down, indeed they worship it. 7 They lift it upon the shoulder and carry it; They set it in its place and it stands there. It does not move from its place. Though one may cry to it, it cannot answer; It cannot deliver him from his distress.

This is an accurate description of man-made gods. They can't talk, they can't walk, they have to be nailed down so they won't fall over, as they can't stand on their own. In vv9-10, God further says:

9 Remember the former things long past, For I am God, and there is no other; I am God, and there is no one like Me, 10 Declaring the end from the beginning And from ancient times things which have not been done, Saying, My purpose will be established, And I will accomplish all My good pleasure;

Notice in particular that the true God is the one who can declare the end of a matter from its beginning. We now want to notice where God declares the end of Old Covenant Israel from its national beginning, particularly in Deuteronomy 32.

NOTE: The next 2.5 pages are repeated from Chapter 2 so this chapter can stand alone.

Just before Moses' death, after he led the first generation of Jews through the wilderness of Sinai, he brings them to the border of their promised land. In Deuteronomy 28-30, he pronounces all the blessings Israel will receive if they remain faithful to him, and all the curses they will receive if they are unfaithful. In Dt. 31.19-21, God instructs Moses to write a song, the Song of Moses, and teach it to Israel:

19 Now therefore, write this song for yourselves, and teach it to the sons of Israel; put it on their lips, in order that this song may be a witness for Me against the sons of Israel. 20 For when I bring them into the land flowing with milk and honey, which I swore to their fathers, and they have eaten and are satisfied and become prosperous, then they will turn to other gods and serve them, and spurn Me and break My covenant. 21 Then it shall come about, when many evils and troubles have come upon them, that this song will testify before them as a witness (for it shall not be forgotten from the lips of their descendants); for I know their intent which they are developing today,

before I have brought them into the land which I swore.

God tells Moses that this generation of Jews isn't going to turn out good. He is to teach the Song of Moses to Israel, so that when they became unfaithful to him and his judgments began to fall on them, this song and their singing of it would be a witness that God told them how they were going to turn out. Future generations of Jews, including the ones whom Jesus taught, knew this song—they had been taught it since childhood. In Dt. 32.29, Moses told Israel:

> 29 For I know that after my death you will act corruptly and turn from the way which I have commanded you; and evil will befall you in the latter days, for you will do that which is evil in the sight of the LORD, provoking Him to anger with the work of your hands.

Moses tells them that punishments from God will befall them "in the latter days," i.e., in their future, because of their involvement with false gods. This would include a variety of punishments, including the Assyrian and Babylonian captivities. However, in Dt. 32.20-21, Moses becomes much more specific, foretelling the very end of the nation of Old Covenant Israel:

> 20 Then He said, I will hide My face from them, I will see what their end [emphasis mine throughout—SGD] shall be; For they are a perverse generation, Sons in whom is no faithfulness. 21 They have made Me jealous with what is not God; They have provoked Me to anger with their idols. So I will make them jealous with those who are not a people; I will provoke them to anger with a foolish nation,

In this passage, which Paul quotes as fulfilled in his time (in Rom. 10.19), God now foretells "the end" of Old Covenant Israel, that their last generation will be a perverse generation. Jesus, of course, called his generation of Jews an "unbelieving and perverse generation" in Mt. 12.38, 16.4, 17.11, and in the first gospel sermon, Peter called faithful Jews to "save yourselves from this perverse generation" (Ac. 2.40). Paul also uses this language in Phil. 2.15 of the first century Jewish generation.

We can know that the generation of Jesus and Peter is the one under consideration in Deuteronomy 32 since Paul quotes Dt. 32.21 in Rom. 10.19 as justification of his taking the gospel to the Gentiles in an attempt to provoke the Jews to jealousy. This was in the early 60s AD, shortly before the end of Old Covenant Israel in AD 70.

Continuing in Dt. 32.28-29, we read:

> 28 They are a nation without sense, there is no discernment in them. 29 If only they were wise and would understand this and discern what their end will be! (NIV)

Thus, "the end" of Old Covenant Israel was foretold at their beginning in Sinai, verifying that the true God is faithfully called the one who foretells a matter's end from its beginning, in this case, sixteen centuries before!

In Dt. 32.34-36, we have Moses speaking of God's vengeance on Israel:

> 34 Is it not laid up in store with Me, Sealed up in My treasuries? 35 Vengeance is Mine, and retribution, In due time their foot (Old Covenant Israel—SGD) will slip; For the day of their calamity is near, And the impending things are hastening upon them. 36 For the LORD will vindicate His people (the faithful of Old Covenant Israel—SGD), And will have compassion on His servants; When He sees that their strength is gone, And there is none remaining, bond or free.

We can know the time element of this judgment, for verse 35 is quoted in Heb. 10.30a and verse 36 is quoted in Heb. 10.30b:

> For we know him that said, Vengeance belongeth unto me, I will recompense. And again, The Lord shall judge his people.

Thus both Moses in Dt. 32 (written 15 centuries before Jerusalem and the temple were destroyed) and the author of Hebrews (written several years before) are speaking of the same judgment, that of Old Covenant Israel by the Romans in AD 70. Of course, Heb. 10.30 directly follows Heb. 10.25-39. Verse 25 has been appropriated to use to urge people to go to church on Sunday:

23 let us hold fast the confession of our hope that it waver not; for he is faithful that promised: 24 and let us consider one another to provoke unto love and good works; 25 not forsaking our own assembling together, as the custom of some is, but exhorting one another; and so much the more, as ye see the day drawing nigh. 26 For if we sin wilfully after that we have received the knowledge of the truth, there remaineth no more a sacrifice for sins, 27 but a certain *fearful expectation of judgment*, and a *fierceness of fire* which shall devour the adversaries.

"The day" that was drawing nigh when Hebrews was written was the day of the Lord we see in the prophets, the day of judgment coming on Old Covenant Israel when Jerusalem and the temple were destroyed. The "assembling" the author of Hebrews was urging his Jewish listeners not to forsake were not Sunday assemblies of local churches, but of the gathering the messiah and John the Baptist were doing of the Jews. Isaiah 11.9-12 foretold the messiah would gather Israel and Judah in the last days. Isa. 49.5-7, 56.6-8, and Hos. 1.10-11 foretold the same gathering. It was this gathering Jesus referred to when he said in Mt. 23.37:

O Jerusalem, Jerusalem, that killeth the prophets, and stoneth them that are sent unto her! how often would I have gathered thy children together, even as a hen gathereth her chickens under her wings, and ye would not!

In Mt. 24.31, Jesus referred to this same gathering when he said:

And he shall send forth his angels with a great sound of a trumpet, and they shall gather together his elect from the four winds, from one end of heaven to the other.

We'll see further indications of the destruction of Jerusalem on the day of the Lord as we proceed further through the prophets.

Notice in Deuteronomy 32 that vengeance and vindication will take place at the same time. Both groups of people will see the same event, the end of Old Covenant Israel (at the hands of the Romans in AD 70) and interpret it entirely differently. The wicked see cruel destruction; the righteous see their salvation from the wicked. This is not unique to their judgment. In the flood of Noah's time, the wicked and righteous again saw the same event entirely differently. The wicked saw its destruction, while the same flood was the salvation of the righteous as the same water that destroyed the wicked carried the righteous to a new world order after the flood. This passage is alluded to in Hebrews 10:30-31 to describe a first century judgment of Old Covenant Israel.

Jesus speaks of this same vengeance of God on Old Covenant Israel in Lk. 21.20-24, when he says:

> But when ye see Jerusalem compassed with armies, then know that her desolation is at hand. Then let them that are in Judaea flee unto the mountains; and let them that are in the midst of her depart out; and let not them that are in the country enter therein. For these are days of vengeance, that all things which are written may be fulfilled. Woe unto them that are with child and to them that give suck in those days! for there shall be great distress upon the land, and wrath unto this people. And they shall fall by the edge of the sword, and shall be led captive into all the nations: and Jerusalem shall be trodden down of the Gentiles, until the times of the Gentiles be fulfilled.

"All things that are written may be fulfilled" would certainly include the prophecy of God's vengeance on Old Covenant Israel, as well as the vindication of the righteous and the taking of the gospel to the Gentiles.

## The Judgment Foretold in Joel

Joel was an 8th Century BC prophet, who begins his book by foretelling the invasion of Israel by the Assyrians, before they were taken into Assyrian captivity in 722 BC. We notice first in Joel 1.15 where Joel explains the concept of the day of the Lord as a day of destruction from God, although he's using the Assyrians to punish them:

> Alas for the day! For the day of the Lord is near, And it will come as destruction from the Almighty.

Joel continues the concept of the day of the Lord in 2.1f:

1 Blow a trumpet in Zion, And sound an alarm on My holy mountain! Let all the inhabitants of the land tremble, For the day of the LORD is coming; Surely it is near, 2 A day of darkness and gloom...

In v10, we wish to notice the language Joel uses to describe Israel's dark day at the hands of the Assyrians:

10 Before them the earth quakes, The heavens tremble, The sun and the moon grow dark, And the stars lose their brightness.

Joel uses the language of earthquakes, and the dimming of the sun, moon, and stars as we speak of "Black Tuesday" when the stock market crashed, not literally, but to describe the "dark day" when the Assyrians came.

After several verses describing how Israel will be restored after the Assyrian captivity, Joel then describes a future judgment that will befall Old Covenant Israel later on in vv28-32:

28 "And it will come about after this
That I will pour out My
Spirit on all mankind;
And your sons and daughters will prophesy,
Your old men will dream dreams,
Your young men will see visions.
29 "And even on the male and female servants
I will pour out My Spirit in those days.
30 "And I will display wonders in the sky and on the earth,
Blood, fire, and columns of smoke.
31 "The sun will be turned into darkness,
And the moon into blood,
Before the great and awesome day of the LORD comes.
32 "And it will come about that whoever calls on the name of the LORD
Will be delivered;
For on Mount Zion and in Jerusalem
There will be those who escape,
As the LORD has said,
Even among the survivors whom the LORD calls.

These verses are familiar to us because Peter quoted them in the first gospel sermon in Ac. 2.16f and said:

> 16 but this is that which hath been spoken through the prophet Joel: 17 And it shall be in the *last days*, saith God, I will pour forth of my Spirit upon all flesh: And your sons and your daughters shall prophesy, And your young men shall see visions, And your old men shall dream dreams: 18 Yea and on my servants and on my handmaidens in those days Will I pour forth of my Spirit; and they shall prophesy. 19 And I will show wonders in the heaven above, And signs on the earth beneath; Blood, and fire, and vapor of smoke: 20 The sun shall be turned into darkness, And the moon into blood, Before the day of the Lord come, That great and notable day. 21 And it shall be, that whosoever shall call on the name of the Lord shall be saved.

The "last days" Peter quoted from Joel are the last days of Old Covenant Israel, "the end" of Israel we saw in Deuteronomy 32. The rest of the quotation is language that Jesus used to describe the end of Old Covenant Israel in Matthew 24, of the dark days that were coming on Jerusalem at the hands of the Roman armies in Jesus' generation (Mt. 24.34). However, as Jesus gave signs for the Jews in Jerusalem to watch for so they could "flee to the mountains" and escape the unparalleled destruction that was coming upon their city and temple (Mt. 24.15-16). It was unparalleled because during the Roman siege, where 1.1 million Jews perished and another 2.5 million were sold into slavery.

This was the day of the Lord Joel foretold. However, we want to continue into Joel 3.1-2, where we read:

> "For behold, in those days and at that time, When I restore the fortunes of Judah and Jerusalem, 2 I will gather all the nations, And bring them down to the valley of Jehoshaphat. Then I will enter into judgment with them there On behalf of My people and My inheritance, Israel, Whom they have scattered among the nations; And they have divided up My land.

Notice in v1 where Joel gives the time when this judgment would take place: "in those days and at that time" is the same time when Jerusalem and the temple was destroyed. That's the time element of the judgment he's going to describe in the following verses, where he describes how God not only judged the Jews at the Valley of Jehoshaphat, the valley on the East side of Jerusalem, but also the surrounding nations, v4

> Moreover, what are you to Me, O Tyre, Sidon, and all the regions of Philistia? Are you rendering Me a recompense? But if you do recompense Me, swiftly and speedily I will return your recompense on your head.

In 3.12, Joel says:

> Let the nations be aroused
> And come up to the valley of Jehoshaphat,
> For there I will sit to *judge*
> *All the surrounding nations.*

Notice that as Joel 2 is the basis of the judgment language against Jerusalem Jesus used in Matthew 24, Joel 3, which happened at the same time as Joel 2, is the basis of the judgment in Matthew 25, where in v31, Jesus said:

> 31 But when the Son of man shall come in his glory, and all the angels with him, then shall he sit on the throne of his glory:

Of course, as far back as Mt. 16.27-28, we've seen that Jesus said he would come in the glory with his angels and judge the Jews and that he would do it in the lifetime of some of his disciples:

> 27 For the Son of man shall come in the glory of his Father with his angels; and then shall he render unto every man according to his deeds. 28 Verily I say unto you, there are some of them that stand here, who shall in no wise taste of death, till they see the Son of man coming in his kingdom.

So it's at that same time that this judgment takes place. Still in Matthew 25, we read:

> 32 and before him shall be gathered all the nations: and he shall separate them one from another, as the shepherd separateth the sheep from the goats; 33 and

he shall set the sheep on his right hand, but the goats on the left. 34 Then shall the King say unto them on his right hand, Come, ye blessed of my Father, inherit the kingdom prepared for you from the foundation of the world: 35 for I was hungry, and ye gave me to eat; I was thirsty, and ye gave me drink; I was a stranger, and ye took me in; 36 naked, and ye clothed me; I was sick, and ye visited me; I was in prison, and ye came unto me. 37 Then shall the righteous answer him, saying, Lord, when saw we thee hungry, and fed thee? or athirst, and gave thee drink? 38 And when saw we thee a stranger, and took thee in? or naked, and clothed thee?

Notice that this is purely a Jewish judgment, not at the end of time, but at the end of the Mosaic age. There's nothing about obeying the gospel of Christ, nothing about baptism, just a judgment of Jews according to the Law of Moses.

## The Judgment Foretold in Isaiah

Isaiah 2-4 is a messianic passage which begins in 2.2-4 dealing with Old Covenant Israel's last days. Notice in particular the judgment among the nations in the last days.

2 Now it will come about that
*In the last days,*
The mountain of the house of the LORD
Will be established as the chief of the mountains,
And will be raised above the hills;
And all the nations will stream to it.
3 And many peoples will come and say,
"Come, let us go up to the mountain of the LORD,
To the house of the God of Jacob;
That He may teach us concerning His ways,
And that we may walk in His paths."
For the law will go forth from Zion,
And the word of the LORD from Jerusalem.
4 And *He will judge between the nations,*
And will render decisions for many peoples;

Like Joel 3.12, v4 teaches judgment of the nations. Next, notice in v12 the day of the Lord in Israel's last days:

> For there shall be a *day of Jehovah* of hosts upon all
> that is proud and haughty, and upon all that is lifted
> up; and it shall be brought low;

Thus, as Joel had foretold a day of the Lord in Israel's last days, Isaiah does the same thing. Next, notice in v19ff the reaction of the people to this day of judgment:

> 19 And men will go into caves of the rocks,
> And into holes of the ground
> Before the terror of the LORD,
> And before the splendor of His majesty,
> When He arises to make the earth tremble.
> 20 In that day men will cast away to the moles and the
> bats
> Their idols of silver and their idols of gold,
> Which they made for themselves to worship,
> 21 In order to go into the caverns of the rocks and the
> clefts of the cliffs,
> Before the terror of the LORD and the splendor of His
> majesty,
> When He arises to make the earth tremble.

This passage is quoted by Jesus to the women watching his trek to Golgotha in Lk. 23.28-31 as he comments on the coming destruction of Jerusalem:

> 28 But Jesus turning unto them said, Daughters of
> Jerusalem, weep not for me, but weep for yourselves,
> and for your children. 29 For behold, the days are
> coming, in which they shall say, Blessed are the
> barren, and the wombs that never bare, and the breasts
> that never gave suck. 30 Then shall they begin to say
> to the mountains, Fall on us; and to the hills, Cover us.

Likewise, John applies it to the destruction of the harlot city, where the Lord was crucified (Rev. 11.8) in Rev. 6.16:

> 15 And the kings of the earth, and the princes, and the
> chief captains, and the rich, and the strong, and every
> bondman and freeman, hid themselves in the caves
> and in the rocks of the mountains; 16 and they say to
> the mountains and to the rocks, Fall on us, and hide us

from the face of him that sitteth on the throne, and
from the wrath of the Lamb: 17 for the great day of
their wrath is come; and who is able to stand?

Thus the judgment on the nations in Israel's last days was, as Jesus
applied it, the destruction of Jerusalem, just as Joel and Peter had
foretold it in Joel 2.28-30 and Ac. 2.16ff.

Isaiah 4.4 concludes this section of Isaiah's description of
Jerusalem's first century destruction:

When the Lord has washed away the filth of the
daughters of Zion, and purged the bloodshed of
Jerusalem from her midst, by the spirit of judgment
and the spirit of burning.

The author of Hebrews 10.27-30 alludes to Isaiah's description of
the spirit of judgment and burning on this day of the Lord judgment on
Jerusalem, when in Moses' language in Deuteronomy 32, God avenges
the wicked and vindicates the righteous at the same act:

27 but a certain fearful expectation of *judgment*, and a
*fierceness of fire* which shall devour the adversaries.
28 A man that hath set at nought Moses' law dieth
without compassion on the word of two or three
witnesses: 29 of how much sorer punishment, think ye,
shall he be judged worthy, who hath trodden under
foot the Son of God, and hath counted the blood of the
covenant wherewith he was sanctified an unholy thing,
and hath done despite unto the Spirit of grace? 30 For
we know him that said, Vengeance belongeth unto me,
I will recompense. And again, The Lord shall judge
his people.

In Isaiah 24-27, the little apocalypse, we first have the destruction
of Jerusalem in Jesus' generation foretold. We begin in Isa. 24.1-6:

24:1 Behold, the LORD lays the earth (Heb. *eretz*, the
land, not the planet throughout this passage--SGD)
waste, devastates it, distorts its surface, and scatters its
inhabitants. 2 And the people will be like the priest,
the servant like his master, the maid like her mistress,
the buyer like the seller, the lender like the borrower,
the creditor like the debtor. 3 The earth will be

completely laid waste and completely despoiled, for the LORD has spoken this word. 4 The earth mourns and withers, the world fades and withers, the exalted of the people of the earth fade away. 5 The earth is also polluted by its inhabitants, for they transgressed laws, violated statutes, broke the everlasting covenant. 6 Therefore, a curse devours the earth, and those who live in it are held guilty. Therefore, the inhabitants of the earth are burned, and few men are left.

In v10, 12, Isaiah describes Jerusalem's condition:

10 The city of chaos is broken down;
Every house is shut up so that none may enter.
All joy turns to gloom.
The gaiety of the earth is banished...
12 Desolation is left in the city,
And the gate is battered to ruins.

Describing Jerusalem as the city of chaos is particularly appropriate as the three divisions of zealots inside the city during the siege by the Romans actually killed more citizens of the city than the Roman soldiers did! Josephus describes the nightly death tolls in the tens of thousands, with corpses stacked like cordwood, and the mothers deliberating over whose babies they were going to devour from starvation on each particular day.

In 24.23, Isaiah describes the last days judgment on Jerusalem in the same terms Joel (2.28-30), Peter (Ac. 2.16f), and Jesus (Mt. 24.29) did when they spoke of the sun being turned to darkness and the moon to blood on that darkest day of Israel's history:

Then the moon will be abashed and the sun ashamed,
For the LORD of hosts will reign on
Mount Zion and in Jerusalem,

In Isa. 25.2, Jerusalem is described as:

For Thou hast made a city into a heap,
A fortified city into a ruin;
A palace of strangers is a city no more,
It will never be rebuilt.

Of course, there is a city named Jerusalem on the site now, but it's not Zion, God's city, and there's no temple. God's city is New Jerusalem, and it's temple is the messianic temple, not one made with physical stones, but spiritual ones. Note in particular Isa. 25.8:

> *He will swallow up death for all time,*
> *And the Lord GOD will wipe tears away from all*
> *faces,*
> And He will remove the reproach of His people from
> all the earth;
> For the LORD has spoken.

Of course, this verse is quoted as about to be fulfilled in I Cor. 15.54 in connection with the resurrection, which we'll discuss in our chapter on the resurrection.

In Isa. 26.17-21, Isaiah's description of the judgment on Jerusalem continues:

> 17 As the pregnant woman approaches the time to give
> birth,
> She writhes and cries out in her labor pains,
> Thus were we before Thee, O LORD.
> 18 We were pregnant, we writhed in labor,
> We gave birth, as it were, only to wind.
> We could not accomplish deliverance for the earth
> Nor were inhabitants of the world born.
> 19 *Your dead will live;*
> *Their corpses will rise.*
> *You who lie in the dust, awake and shout for joy,*
> *For your dew is as the dew of the dawn,*
> *And the earth will give birth to the departed spirits...*
> 21 For behold, the LORD is about to come out from
> His place
> To punish the inhabitants of the earth for their
> iniquity;
> And the earth will reveal her bloodshed,
> And will no longer cover her slain.

Surely we can see in v17 the same description Jesus gave in Mt. 24.8, when he said that the indications of Jerusalem's judgment were just the "beginning of travail," as of a woman about to give birth.

Notice also in v20, the language of Israel's resurrection and judgment, similar to Dan. 12.2 (fulfilled in v7 at the destruction of the city at the end of Israel's age) and Ezekiel 37. Verse 21's reference to the land no longer covering Jerusalem's slain is alluded to by Jesus in Mt. 23.29-33, where all the righteous blood shed from Abel to Zechariah would be visited on Jesus' generation of Jews. Clearly, the judgment spoken of in Matthew 23-25 on Old Covenant Israel is the same as foretold by Moses, Joel, and Isaiah.

Notice two more points in Isaiah 27. In v9, we're giving the time element of this judgment:

> And this will be the full price of the pardoning of his sin: *When he makes all the altar stones like pulverized chalk stones*;

Of course, the stones of the altar were reduced to chalk stones when Titus burned the temple to the ground.

In Isa. 27.12-13, we see further language of Old Covenant Israel's judgment in the work of John the Baptist:

> 12 And it will come about in that day, that the LORD will start His threshing from the flowing stream of the Euphrates to the brook of Egypt; and you will be gathered up one by one, O sons of Israel. 13 It will come about also in that day that a great trumpet will be blown; and those who were perishing in the land of Assyria and who were scattered in the land of Egypt will come and worship the LORD in the holy mountain at Jerusalem.

John warned the Jews in this harvest language in Mt. 3.10-12:

> 10 And even now the axe lieth at the root of the trees: every tree therefore that bringeth not forth good fruit is hewn down, and cast into the fire. 11 I indeed baptize you in water unto repentance: but he that cometh after me is mightier than I, whose shoes I am not worthy to bear: he shall baptize you in the Holy Spirit and in fire: 12 whose fan is in his hand, and he will thoroughly cleanse his threshing-floor; and he will gather his wheat into the garner, but the chaff he will burn up with unquenchable fire.

In Amos 9.9, God gave his guarantee that even in such a formidable judgment, he would not indiscriminately destroy the righteous along with the wicked:

> And I will shake the house of Israel among all nations
> As grain is shaken in a sieve,
> But *not a kernel will fall to the ground.*

Clearly, Isaiah is describing the judgment in Israel's last days also described by Jesus in Matthew 25.

## The Judgment Foretold in Malachi

In Malachi 3.1-6, we read:

> 1 Behold, I am going to send My messenger, and he will clear the way before Me. And the Lord, whom you seek, will suddenly come to His temple; and the messenger of the covenant, in whom you delight, behold, *He is coming*, says the LORD of hosts. 2 But who can endure *the day of His coming*? And who can stand when He appears? For He is like a refiner's fire and like fullers' soap. 3 And He will sit as a smelter and purifier of silver, and He will purify the sons of Levi and refine them like gold and silver, so that they may present to the LORD offerings in righteousness. 4 Then the offering of Judah and Jerusalem will be pleasing to the LORD, as in the days of old and as in former years. 5 *Then I will draw near to you for judgment*; and I will be a swift witness against the sorcerers and against the adulterers and against those who swear falsely, and against those who oppress the wage earner in his wages, the widow and the orphan, and those who turn aside the alien, and do not fear Me, says the LORD of hosts. 6 For I, the LORD, do not change; therefore you, O sons of Jacob, are not consumed.

At the close of the Old Testament, and before 400 years of silence of prophets between the testaments, Malachi foretells the coming of two messengers. In Mal. 3.1, the first, God's messenger, will prepare the way for the Messiah, and the second will be the Messiah himself, the messenger of the covenant. We know this is true, because in Mt.

11.10-12, Jesus quotes this very verse and says it referred to John the Baptist:

> 10 This is he, of whom it is written, Behold, I send my messenger before thy face, Who shall prepare thy way before thee. 11 Verily I say unto you, Among them that are born of women there hath not arisen a greater than John the Baptist: yet he that is but little in the kingdom of heaven is greater than he.

In Mal. 4.5 (which we'll discuss further momentarily), the first messenger is called Elijah, whom Jesus identifies as John the Baptist (Mt. 11.11-12, 14 and Mt. 17.12) because he (as Gabriel told John's father Zacharias in Lk. 1.17) came in the spirit and power of Elijah. Speaking of the coming of the Messiah in 3.2, Malachi says,

> But who can endure the *day of His coming*? And who can stand when He appears? For He is like a refiner's fire and like fullers' soap.

Refiner's fire and fuller's soap refer to the cleansing from impurities that Old Covenant Israel will undergo at the Messiah's judgment of the nation. Refining fire is a metallurgical term describing the smelting of impurities from metal. A fuller is one who cleaned and thickened freshly woven (usually woolen) cloth. The process involved cleaning, bleaching, wetting, and beating the fibers to a consistent and desirable condition. Fuller's soap was an alkali made from plant ashes which was used to clean and full new cloth. Since fullers required plenty of running water and the natural substances described, a fuller's field was a place where all were available for the fullers to conduct their profession. In Mal. 3.3, Malachi said:

> And He will sit as a smelter and purifier of silver, and He will purify the sons of Levi and refine them like gold and silver, so that they may present to the LORD offerings in righteousness.

In v4, Malachi describes the result the Messiah will have on Old Covenant Israel:

> Then the offering of Judah and Jerusalem will be pleasing to the LORD, as in the days of old and as in former years.

So, a renewed Israel will be produced. At the same time (v5), God says:

> *Then I will draw near to you for judgment*; and I will be a swift witness against the sorcerers and against the adulterers and against those who swear falsely, and against those who oppress the wage earner in his wages, the widow and the orphan, and those who turn aside the alien, and do not fear Me, says the LORD of hosts.

These words describe God's judgment on those of Israel who will not be refined and cleansed from their impurities.

In Malachi 4.1-6, the prophet continues:

> 1 For behold, *the day is coming, burning like a furnace*; and all the arrogant and every evildoer will be chaff; and *the day that is coming will set them ablaze*, says the LORD of hosts, so that it will leave them neither root nor branch. 2 But for you who fear My name the sun of righteousness will rise with healing in its wings; and you will go forth and skip about like calves from the stall. 3 And you will tread down the wicked, for they shall be ashes under the soles of your feet *on the day* which I am preparing, says the LORD of hosts. 4 *Remember the law of Moses My servant*, even the statutes and ordinances which I commanded him in Horeb for all Israel. 5 Behold, I am going to send you Elijah the prophet before the coming of *the great and terrible day of the LORD*. 6 And he will restore the hearts of the fathers to their children, and the hearts of the children to their fathers, lest I *come and smite the land with a curse*.

Verse 1 describes the day of judgment when the Messiah will purify Israel, as he will harvest the nation, thresh the wheat from the chaff, and set the chaff ablaze. Verse 2 shows that the godly will survive the harvest and refining process, while verse 3 shows the destructive effect that the same judgment process will have on the wicked:

And you will tread down the wicked, for they shall be
ashes under the soles of your feet *on the day* which I
am preparing, says the LORD of hosts.

That this is to be seen as a Jewish judgment based on the Mosaic
law is seen in verse 4:

*Remember the law of Moses My servant*, even the
statutes and ordinances which I commanded him in
Horeb for all Israel.

Verse 5 speaks of the coming of Elijah (who Jesus identifies as
John the Baptist) before the coming of the great and terrible day of the
Lord.

The result of John's work is seen in verse 6:

And he will restore the hearts of the fathers to their
children, and the hearts of the children to their fathers,
lest I come and smite the land with a curse.

Thus, John, the messenger of the Messiah, would prepare Old
Covenant Israelites for the Messiah's judgment on the day of the Lord,
when the Messiah would smite the land of Israel with a curse,
destruction.

To summarize Malachi's prophecy of the Messiah's judgment, we
have:

The day of the Lord's coming – 3.2
The day of judgment – 3.5
A day of harvest and smelting – 4.1, 3.2
A judgment of Jews – 4.4
A Great and Terrible Day – 4.5
The Messiah would smite the land with a curse – 4.6

Notice that none of these events occurred during Jesus' earthly
ministry. John fulfilled Malachi's prophecies concerning him (as we're
about to see), but Jesus did not fulfill the prophecies Malachi made
concerning him during his three year ministry. However, we will see
that Jesus foretold that these events would be fulfilled during his
generation.

# John the Baptist Fulfills
# Malachi's Prophecies of Him

In Mt. 3.1-12, we begin to see the fulfillment of Malachi's prophecies of John the Baptist and Jesus. In verse 5, John, who began preaching about six months before Jesus did, attracting stupendous crowds, for in vv5-7 we read:

> 5 Then went out unto him Jerusalem, and all Judaea, and all the region round about the Jordan; 6 and they were baptized of him in the river Jordan, confessing their sins. 7 But when he saw many of the Pharisees and Sadducees coming to his baptism, he said unto them, Ye offspring of vipers, who warned you to flee from the wrath to come?

Here John is preaching the message that Malachi foretold, and that Old Covenant Israel needed to hear, a message of repentance, lest they encounter God's wrath that was (lit.) *about to* come. John doesn't speak of wrath way off in the future, but imminently. The imminence is also shown in verse 10, when John says:

> And even now *the axe lieth at the root of the trees*: every tree therefore that bringeth not forth good fruit is hewn down, and cast into the *fire*.

John points out to his audience that the harvest isn't far off, as the axe is already at hand, at the root of the fruitless tree of Old Covenant Israel, and their end is to be burned, a fiery, refining judgment which will purify Israel.

Notice the use of "fire" in John's preaching. In v10, it's used of the judgment coming on the Jews. In vv 11-12, John says further concerning this fire:

> 11 I indeed baptize you in water unto repentance: but he that cometh after me is mightier than I, whose shoes I am not worthy to bear: he shall baptize you in the Holy Spirit and in *fire*: 12 whose fan is in his hand, and he will thoroughly cleanse his threshing-floor; and he will gather his wheat into the garner, but the chaff he will burn up with unquenchable *fire*.

Notice in verse 12 that John speaks of the Messiah's imminent harvest of Israel. His winnowing fan is already in his hand, and he's going to burn the chaff of Old Covenant Israel with unquenchable fire, fire that cannot he extinguished, or stopped. Notice that "fire" occurs each of verse 10-12. Many read of the Messiah's baptizing in the Holy Spirit and fire to be a blessing, and claim to be fire-baptized. Baptism in the Holy Spirit certainly was a blessing, but baptism in fire was not. Since fire in verses 10 and 12 is speaking of a fiery punishment, undoubtedly baptism in fire in verse 11 was not a blessing, but punishment. Thus, John affirms that the judgment of the Messiah would be a blessing to the godly, but destruction for the ungodly. This is similar to the flood in Noah's day: the same water that destroyed the unrighteous also saved the righteous from earthly destruction. Likewise, when the Roman army besieged Jerusalem in AD 70, their coming provided for the salvation of the righteous Jews (due to their escaping, Mt. 24.16) while the unrighteous who didn't heed Jesus' warning were killed in the tumult.

For now, we merely notice that, as Malachi had foretold, John the Baptist warned of a imminent fiery messianic judgment on Old Covenant Israel.

# Further Indications of Imminent Judgment in the Gospels

## Lk. 11.45-51

In this passage, Jesus has just confronted some Jews for their traditions, and one of their lawyers took umbrage, perhaps thinking Jesus would back off his accusation:

> 45 And one of the lawyers answering saith unto him, Teacher, in saying this thou reproachest us also. 46 And he said, Woe unto you lawyers also! for ye load men with burdens grievous to be borne, and ye yourselves touch not the burdens with one of your fingers. 47 Woe unto you! for ye build the tombs of the prophets, and your fathers killed them. 48 So ye are witnesses and consent unto the works of your fathers: for they killed them, and ye build their tombs. 49 Therefore also said the wisdom of God, I will send unto them prophets and apostles; and some of them

> they shall kill and persecute; 50 that the blood of all
> the prophets, which was shed from the foundation of
> the world, may be required of this generation; 51 from
> the blood of Abel unto the blood of Zachariah, who
> perished between the altar and the sanctuary: yea, I say
> unto you, it shall be required of this generation.

In verse 48, Jesus shows that since these Jews consented with their ancestors' treatment of the prophets, they were actually in fellowship with their evil deeds! Consenting with evil constitutes fellowship with it. Paul, in Rom. 1.32, affirms that even Gentiles were held responsible for such sinful consenting with evildoers, and these were people who didn't even know of God or his revealed will. How much more responsible were God's covenant people for such fellowship with sin. Because of this, Jesus' audience ("this generation") was going to be held responsible for the victims of their wicked ancestors. Later on, in our discussion of Mt. 23.33-36, we'll see that they would be judged *in* their own generation.

## Lk. 12.49-56

This passage foretells a coming judgment on this generation of Jews in their present time.

> 49 I came to cast fire upon the earth [lit., land—SGD];
> and what do I desire, if it is already kindled? 50 But I
> have a baptism to be baptized with; and how am I
> straitened till it be accomplished! 51 Think ye that I
> am come to give peace in the earth? I tell you, Nay;
> but rather division: 52 for there shall be from
> henceforth five in one house divided, three against
> two, and two against three. 53 They shall be divided,
> father against son, and son against father; mother
> against daughter, and daughter against her mother;
> mother in law against her daughter in law, and
> daughter in law against her mother in law. 54 And he
> said to the multitudes also, When ye see a cloud rising
> in the west, straightway ye say, There cometh a
> shower; and so it cometh to pass. 55 And when ye see
> a south wind blowing, ye say, There will be a
> scorching heat; and it cometh to pass. 56 Ye
> hypocrites, ye know how to interpret the face of the

earth and the heaven; but how is it that ye know not
how to interpret *this time* [emphasis mine—SGD]?

Malachi had foretold that the Messiah would bring a curse upon
the land of Israel (4.6). Here Jesus specifies that the curse he will bring
on the land will be fiery. He then upbraids them for being able to
forecast rainy weather, and heat spells, but that they can't see what's to
happen to them *in their own time*, implying that his judgment on the
isn't a long way off, and certainly not at the end of time, but in their
own present time!

## Lk. 13.3

In this passage, Jesus again warns of impending judgment on the
Jews:

> 1 Now there were some present at that very season
> who told him of the Galilaeans, whose blood Pilate
> had mingled with their sacrifices. 2 And he answered
> and said unto them, Think ye that these Galilaeans
> were sinners above all the Galilaeans, because they
> have suffered these things? 3 I tell you, Nay: but,
> except ye repent, ye shall all in like manner perish. 4
> Or those eighteen, upon whom the tower in Siloam
> fell, and killed them, think ye that they were offenders
> above all the men that dwell in Jerusalem? 5 I tell you,
> Nay: but, *except ye repent, ye shall all likewise perish.*

Many religious folks believe that great suffering on the part of
God's people is an indicator of great sin. Job's three friends, when they
heard of his suffering, suspected that Job was a great sinner, although
God had said in Job 1 that he was an upright man. However, since
Job's friends thought that his great suffering indicated that he was a
great sinner, when they came to encourage him, could not because they
didn't want to be endorsing his sin. The Jews in Jesus' audience
evidently thought the same way, as Jesus questions why they thought
some Galileans that Pilate had killed, or others who had suffered at the
collapse of a tower were terrible sinners. He then denied that they were
worse sinners that the Jews to whom he spoke, and asserted that unless
they repented, they would suffer similar destruction. They would be
judged shortly in the end of Old Covenant Israel, foretold by Moses,
Malachi, John the Baptist, and now by the Messiah himself.

With absolutely no regard for the context, this passage has often been used to teach people who would become Christians to repent. Jesus wasn't telling them what to do to become Christians, for there were none yet, and he certainly wasn't giving instruction for us to use to evangelize the lost.

## Lk. 13.6-9

> 6 And he spake this parable; A certain man had a fig tree planted in his vineyard; and he came seeking fruit thereon, and found none. 7 And he said unto the vinedresser, Behold, these three years I come seeking fruit on this fig tree, and find none: cut it down; why doth it also cumber the ground? 8 And he answering saith unto him, Lord, let it alone this year also, till I shall dig about it, and dung it: 9 and if it bear fruit thenceforth, well; but if not, thou shalt cut it down.

The author, raised in the Texas panhandle where trees are so scarce that there hardly is one that wasn't planted by a white man, treasured any tree that could give shade from the Texas heat. Our lord isn't that desperate. He expected fruit from his trees, and deemed worthless those that are fruitless. In the Old Testament, he had depicted Israel as his choice tree, from which he expected fruit. This parable depicts Old Covenant Israel as his tree, from which he had expected fruit, but found none. Jesus' parable teaches that if Israel didn't finally produce the fruit of righteousness, it would be destroyed, as a warning of upcoming judgment on their nation.

## Mt. 13.24-30, 36-42 – Parable of the Tares

> 24 Another parable set he before them, saying, The kingdom of heaven is likened unto a man that sowed good seed in his field: 25 but while men slept, his enemy came and sowed tares also among the wheat, and went away. 26 But when the blade sprang up and brought forth fruit, then appeared the tares also. 27 And the servants of the householder came and said unto him, Sir, didst thou not sow good seed in thy field? whence then hath it tares? 28 And he said unto them, An enemy hath done this. And the servants say unto him, Wilt thou then that we go and gather them up? 29 But he saith, Nay; lest haply while ye gather up

the tares, ye root up the wheat with them. 30 Let both grow together until the harvest: and in the time of the harvest I will say to the reapers, Gather up first the tares, and bind them in bundles to burn them; but gather the wheat into my barn.

This harvest is the same theme foreseen by Malachi and John the Baptist. The imminence of it comes in Jesus' teaching when his disciples ask him further about this parable in vv. 36-42:

36 Then he left the multitudes, and went into the house: and his disciples came unto him, saying, Explain unto us the parable of the tares of the field. 37 And he answered and said, He that soweth the good seed is the Son of man; 38 and the field is the world; and the good seed, these are the sons of the kingdom; and the tares are the sons of the evil one; 39 and the enemy that sowed them is the devil: and *the harvest is the end of the world* [*aionios*, lit., age—SGD]; and the reapers are angels. 40 As therefore the tares are gathered up and burned with fire; so shall it be in the end of the world [*aionios*, lit., age—SGD]. 41 The Son of man shall send forth his angels, and they shall gather out of his kingdom all things that cause stumbling, and them that do iniquity, 42 and shall cast them into the furnace of fire: there shall be the weeping and the gnashing of teeth.

Jesus says that the harvest he's speaking of will be at the end of the age, not the end of time nor the end of the planet. The Jews to whom he spoke recognized two ages (and Jews still do): the age in which they lived, the Mosaic age, and the Messiah's age. Jews who don't recognize Jesus as the Messiah believe they are still in the Mosaic age, and when the Messiah comes, his age will begin.

Jesus respected the Jewish usage of these terms in Mt. 12.31-32 when he said:

31 Therefore I say unto you, Every sin and blasphemy shall be forgiven unto men; but the blasphemy against the Spirit shall not be forgiven. 32 And whosoever shall speak a word against the Son of man, it shall be forgiven him; but whosoever shall speak against the Holy Spirit, it shall not be forgiven him, neither in this

world [*aionios*, lit., age—SGD] nor in that which is to come.

"This age" would be the Mosaic age; Jesus says that blaspheming the Holy Spirit wouldn't be forgiven in the Mosaic age, nor in the age to come, the Messianic (or Christian) age.

Likewise, in Lk. 20.27-35, when responding to the question from the Sadducees concerning marriage in the resurrection, Jesus used this same distinction:

> 27 And there came to him certain of the Sadducees, they that say that there is no resurrection; 28 and they asked him, saying, Teacher, Moses wrote unto us, that if a man's brother die, having a wife, and he be childless, his brother should take the wife, and raise up seed unto his brother. 29 There were therefore seven brethren: and the first took a wife, and died childless; 30 and the second: 31 and the third took her; and likewise the seven also left no children, and died. 32 Afterward the woman also died. 33 In the resurrection therefore whose wife of them shall she be? for the seven had her to wife. 34 And Jesus said unto them, The sons of this world [*aionios*, lit., age—SGD] marry, and are given in marriage: 35 but they that are accounted worthy to attain that world [*aionios*, lit., age—SGD], and the resurrection from the dead, neither marry, nor are given in marriage:

In the Mosaic age, in which every character in this conversation lived, citizens of the kingdom were produced by marriage and procreation. In the case of the woman involved, she had no children after five marriages. This was of utmost seriousness in the Mosaic age, as children of the kingdom were produced solely by physical procreation. Eunuchs, for example, could produce no heirs in the kingdom, and they were regarded as inferior citizens because of this.

However, Jesus says, that won't be the case in the Messiah's age. Children of God will not be produced by physical procreation, but by teaching the gospel. Now, in the Messiah's age, we know that to be the case. Christians are produced by evangelism, not procreation. Imagine the effect this teaching would have on eunuchs (such as the Ethyopian in Acts 8) or unmarried people now: they can produce citizens and heirs of God's kingdom as well as anyone else!

Where both Roman Catholics and members of Church of Christ have missed proper interpretation of the coming of Christ, the judgment, and the resurrection is that they have moved those events down to the end of time or the end of the Christian age, both unknown to scripture, and have ignored their proper scriptural time, the end of the age in which Jesus lived.

## The Age of Christ Has no End

We next notice that the Messianic age has no end. In the Messianic prophecy of Isa. 9.6-7, God foretold:

> 6 For a child will be born to us, a son will be given to us; And the government will rest on His shoulders; And His name will be called Wonderful Counselor, Mighty God, Eternal Father, Prince of Peace. 7 There will be *no end to the increase of His government or of peace*, On the throne of David and over his kingdom, To establish it and to uphold it with justice and righteousness From then on and forevermore. The zeal of the LORD of hosts will accomplish this.

This prophecy of the Messiah also says that there will be no end to the increase of his government or of peace. The increase of the Messiah's government takes place, again, through preaching the gospel, and it has no end.

Similarly in Lk. 1.28-33, we find the angel Gabriel appearing to Mary, saying:

> 28 And he came in unto her, and said, Hail, thou that art highly favored, the Lord is with thee. 29 But she was greatly troubled at the saying, and cast in her mind what manner of salutation this might be. 30 And the angel said unto her, Fear not, Mary: for thou hast found favor with God. 31 And behold, thou shalt conceive in thy womb, and bring forth a son, and shalt call his name JESUS. 32 He shall be great, and shall be called the Son of the Most High: and the Lord God shall give unto him the throne of his father David: 33 and he shall reign over the house of Jacob for ever; and *of his kingdom there shall be no end*.

Again, the kingdom of the Messiah will never end. One had just as well talk about the end of eternity as the end of the Messiah's rule. It will never end!

Hence, the Age of Christ or the Messiah's age has no end. The Mosaic age did. The Messiah's age has no last days, last day, nor last hour. The Mosaic age had all of those, and they are spoken of repeatedly. Thus, when these parables speak of the end of the age, they're not speaking of the end of the Christian age, which has no end, but the end of the Mosaic age, the age in which Jesus' audience lived. The harvest and judgment of which Jesus spoke to his countrymen would occur at the end of the Mosaic age.

## Mt. 13.47-50 – Parable of the Net

We see this same teaching in the parable of the net in Mt. 13.47-50:

> 47 Again, the kingdom of heaven is like unto a net, that was cast into the sea, and gathered of every kind: 48 which, when it was filled, they drew up on the beach; and they sat down, and gathered the good into vessels, but the bad they cast away. 49 So shall it be in the end of the world [*aionios*, lit., age—SGD] the angels shall come forth, and sever the wicked from among the righteous, 50 and shall cast them into the furnace of fire: there shall be the weeping and the gnashing of teeth.

Here again Jesus speaks of a judgment between good and bad in God's kingdom at the end of the age, with the bad to be cast away in a fiery destruction. This is precisely what is going to happen to the unbelievers in Old Covenant Israel.

## Mk. 9.1, Mt. 16.27-28

In Mk. 9.1, Jesus says concerning his kingdom:

> And he said unto them, Verily I say unto you, There are some here of them that stand by, who shall in no wise taste of death, till they see the kingdom of God come with power.

This is a verse frequently and comfortably used in churches of Christ of the author's background. It shows that the kingdom of Christ was coming during the lifetimes of those in his Jewish audience. Did that happen, or do we have some mighty old disciples around? Or, was Jesus mistaken, a false prophet? We're comfortable emphasizing that if the Messiah's kingdom didn't happen during his disciples' lifetimes, then Jesus was a false prophet, and he deserved to be put to death according to the Mosaic Law under which he lived. In short, we're extremely confident in our use of this verse.

Are we as comfortable with its parallel in Matthew? In Mt. 16.27-28, Jesus said:

> 27 For the Son of man shall come in the glory of his Father with his angels; and then shall he render unto every man according to his deeds. 28 Verily I say unto you, there are some of them that stand here, who shall in no wise taste of death, till they see the Son of man coming in his kingdom.

Here, Jesus says he would come in the glory of his father with the angels while some of his disciples were still alive, and that he would judge, rendering to every man according to his deeds in the same time frame.

Did this happen? Or do we have some awfully old disciples around? Or, was Jesus mistaken, a false prophet? Are we as confident that if this wasn't fulfilled as Jesus said, that he was a false prophet, justifying his crucifixion? If this wasn't fulfilled, Jesus was a false prophet, no better than the Mormon prophet Joseph Smith, and deserved to be put to death.

"But wait," someone will say, "that was speaking of the transfiguration, the next event we read of in Matthew 17." Yet there's no marvel that some of Jesus' disciples would still remain alive after only 6 days (Mt. 17.1). Also, there was no element of judgment in the Transfiguration, or at Pentecost, where most believe that Mk. 9.1 was fulfilled.

No, this is the same coming in judgment we began with in Malachi, of which John the Baptist warned, and which Jesus foretold in terms of imminence. Not at the "end of time," nor at the "end of the planet," but at the end of the Mosaic age.

Jesus said that he would come in the glory of his father, that is, the glory that his father had come with many times in the Old Testament, though the father had never come physically, nor bodily. For example, in Isa. 19.1 we read:

The oracle concerning Egypt. Behold, the LORD is riding on a swift cloud, and is about to come to Egypt; The idols of Egypt will tremble at His presence, And the heart of the Egyptians will melt within them.

Here is God coming on a cloud down to Egypt, not speaking of God coming physically, bodily, or geographically to Egypt, but through his instruments Assyria and Babylon.

We see a similar example in Jer. 4.13, where Jeremiah warns of God's coming in judgment on Judah using Babylon's horses:

Behold, he goes up like clouds, And his chariots like the whirlwind; His horses are swifter than eagles Woe to us, for we are ruined!"

In Mic. 1.3, 6 we see a similar example of God coming against Samaria:

3 For behold, the LORD is coming forth from His place. He will come down and tread on the high places of the earth 6 For I will make Samaria a heap of ruins in the open country,

Jesus affirmed that he would be coming in the same way his father had come, in glory, on clouds of judgment, on Old Covenant Israel.

## Mt. 21.33-45 – Parable of the Vineyard

33 Hear another parable: There was a man that was a householder, who planted a vineyard, and set a hedge about it, and digged a winepress in it, and built a tower, and let it out to husbandmen, and went into another country. 34 And when the season of the fruits drew near, he sent his servants to the husbandmen, to receive his fruits. 35 And the husbandmen took his servants, and beat one, and killed another, and stoned another. 36 Again, he sent other servants more than the first: and they did unto them in like manner. 37 But afterward he sent unto them his son, saying, They will reverence my son. 38 But the husbandmen, when they saw the son, said among themselves, This is the heir; come, let us kill him, and take his inheritance. 39 And they took him, and cast him forth out of the vineyard,

and killed him. 40 When therefore the lord of the vineyard shall come, what will he do unto those husbandmen? 41 They say unto him, He will miserably destroy those miserable men, and will let out the vineyard unto other husbandmen, who shall render him the fruits in their seasons. 42 Jesus saith unto them, Did ye never read in the scriptures, The stone which the builders rejected, The same was made the head of the corner; This was from the Lord, And it is marvelous in our eyes? 43 Therefore say I unto you, The kingdom of God shall be taken away from you, and shall be given to a nation bringing forth the fruits thereof. 44 And he that falleth on this stone shall be broken to pieces: but on whomsoever it shall fall, it will scatter him as dust. 45 And when the chief priests and the Pharisees heard his parables, *they perceived that he spake of them* [emphasis mine—SGD].

He spake of *them*, not just anyone, not us, not just theoretical teaching, but he spake of *them*. They had killed the prophets. They were going to kill the son, Jesus himself. They will be miserably destroyed and the vineyard will be given to others, Gentiles.

## Mt. 22.1-14 – Parable of the Wedding Feast

And Jesus answered and spake again in parables unto them, saying, 2 The kingdom of heaven is likened unto a certain king, who made a marriage feast for his son, 3 and sent forth his servants to call them that were bidden to the marriage feast: and they would not come. 4 Again he sent forth other servants, saying, Tell them that are bidden, Behold, I have made ready my dinner; my oxen and my fatlings are killed, and all things are ready: come to the marriage feast. 5 But they made light of it, and went their ways, one to his own farm, another to his merchandise; 6 and the rest laid hold on his servants, and treated them shamefully, and killed them. 7 *But the king was wroth; and he sent his armies, and destroyed those murderers, and burned their city*. 8 Then saith he to his servants, The wedding is ready, but they that were bidden were not worthy. 9 Go ye therefore unto the partings of the highways, and as many as ye shall find, bid to the marriage feast. 10 And those servants went out into the highways, and gathered together all as many as they found, both bad and good: and the wedding was filled with guests. 11 But when the king came in to behold the guests, he saw there a man who had not on a wedding-garment: 12 and he saith unto him, Friend, how camest thou in hither not having a wedding-garment? And he was speechless. 13 Then the king said to the servants, Bind him hand and foot, and cast him out into the outer darkness; there shall be the weeping and the gnashing of teeth. 14 For many are called, but few chosen.

Notice that after the king vented his wrath and destroyed their city, he went right on with the wedding. This is what we see in Revelation 18-19. Chapter 18 describes the destruction of the harlot city, Old Covenant Jerusalem (Rev. 11.8 – where their Lord was crucified), and chapter 19 proceeds with the wedding feast.

## Mt. 23.29-36

In Mt. 23.29-36, Jesus prosecutes the case against Old Covenant Jerusalem for killing the prophets, and foretells her imminent punishment in his generation:

29 Woe unto you, scribes and Pharisees, hypocrites! for ye build the sepulchres of the prophets, and garnish the tombs of the righteous, 30 and say, If we had been in the days of our fathers, we should not have been partakers with them in the blood of the prophets. 31 Wherefore ye witness to yourselves, that ye are sons of them that slew the prophets. 32 Fill ye up then the measure of your fathers. 33 Ye serpents, ye offspring of vipers, how shall ye escape the judgment of hell? 34 Therefore, behold, I send unto you prophets, and wise men, and scribes: some of them shall ye kill and crucify; and some of them shall ye scourge in your synagogues, and persecute from city to city: 35 that upon you may come all the righteous blood shed on the earth, from the blood of Abel the righteous unto the blood of Zachariah son of Barachiah, whom ye slew between the sanctuary and the altar. 36 Verily I

say unto you, *All these things shall come upon this generation.*

## Conclusion on the Judgment

The New Testament doctrine of the judgment is based squarely on the prophets' teaching in the Old Testament. It was to occur not at the end of time, but in the last days of Old Covenant Israel, as is made clear in both the Old and New Testaments. It took place at the destruction of Jerusalem in AD 70. A full discussion of this judgment is given in my *Essays on Eschatology: An Introductory Overview of the Study of Last Things, The Teaching of Jesus: From Sinai to Gehenna, A Faithful Rabbi Urgently Warns Rebellious Israel* and *Revelation Realized: Martyr Vindication from Genesis to Revelation.*

# Chapter 6

# Is Biological Death the Punishment for Adam's Sin? Is Immortality Innate or Conditional?

## The Teaching of Roman Catholicism

In section 366 of the *Catechism of the Catholic Church*, we read:

> The Church teaches that every spiritual soul is created immediately by God—it is not "produced" by the parents—and also that it is immortal: it does not perish when it separates from the body at death, and it will be reunited with the body at the final Resurrection.

In section 1018 we find:

> As a consequence of original sin, man must suffer "bodily death, from which man would have been immune had he not sinned" (GS § 18).

Is it true that biological death occurred because of Adam's sin in the Garden of Eden? Was man created with an immortal spirit? Is that what the Bible teaches?

## Bible Teaching on Biological Death

Is it true, as Roman Catholicism teaches, that man was created with an immortal spirit, and that he died physically or biologically only because he sinned? I'm afraid we'll see that is not true. Let's notice the Biblical record in Genesis.

In Gen. 2.16-17, we know God commanded Adam saying:

> From any tree of the garden you may eat freely; but from the tree of the knowledge of good and evil you shall not eat, for *in the day that you eat from it you shall surely die.*

Question: Did Adam die that day or not? Satan offered Eve a simple alternative in Gen. 3.4:

> You surely shall not die!

Obviously, either God or Satan was mistaken on the coming death of Adam. Who should we believe, God (for whom it is impossible to lie, Heb. 6.18), or Satan (the father of lies Jn. 8.44)?

**Immortality: Innate or Conditional?**

Is immortality unconditional? We generally hear that God created Adam immortal, not subject to death. Then because of Adam's sin, he died physically, as did his descendants.

But was Adam created immortal, not subject to physical death? It appears not. Let's briefly review the Bible's teaching concerning man being a living soul. The word *soul* in the Old Testament comes from the Hebrew *nephesh,* which fundamentally refers to man's animal life, i.e., the life he shares with all animals. Hence, in Genesis 2.7, we read:

> And Jehovah God formed man of the *dust* of the ground, and breathed into his nostrils the *breath* of life; and man became a *living soul.*

Here, Adam consisted of (1) a physical body, composed from the earth, which was not living. However, when God gave this body (2) the breath of life, Adam was a living soul (Heb., *nephesh*). Interestingly, that same creation chapter applies the term *nephesh* to animals many times. For example, Gen. 1.20 says: "Let the waters swarm with swarms of living creatures (*nephesh*)." In Gen, 1.21, the same word is translated *living creature:* "And God created the great sea-monsters, and every *living creature* that moves wherewith the water swarmed." In Gen. 1.24, it's translated *living creatures:* "And God said, Let the earth bring forth *living creatures* after their kind, cattle, and creeping things, and beasts of the earth." In Gen. 1.30, it's rendered *life:* "And to every beast of the earth, and to every bird of the heavens, and to everything that creeps upon the earth, wherein there is *life.''* Hence, the term *a living soul* is applied to animals as well as to man. They are all *living souls.*

Not only were Adam and all the living creatures *living souls* before Adam sinned, but they also were all subject to death before he sinned. After his creation, God placed Adam in the garden and gave him access to the tree of life *to sustain his life.* This fact alone tells us he wasn't immortal, but subject to death before he sinned. Some suggest the fact Adam had to eat at all (much less of the tree of life), showed he was mortal (as are all other living creatures who eat to survive). Would he have starved to death if he had not eaten, like all the other living creatures? If not, why did he need a stomach with a complete digestive system? When he sinned, he lost access to the tree of life, "lest he stretch out his hand, and take also from the tree of life, and eat, and live forever" (Gen. 3.22).

God forbade Adam to eat of the tree of the knowledge of good and evil, saying in Gen 2.16-17:

> From any tree of the garden you may eat freely; but from the tree of the knowledge of good and evil you shall not eat, *for in the day that you eat from it you shall surely die.*

We take the phrase "the day" as God had already used it in Genesis, of a 24-hour day. In Gen. 1.14, we read, "...lights to separate *the day* from the night," Gen. 1.16, "the greater light to govern *the day*," and Gen. 1.18, "rule over *the day* and over the night." Genesis 2.4 speaks of "the account of the heavens and the earth when they were created, in *the day* that the LORD God made earth and heaven." After our verse, Gen. 2.17, we have Gen. 3.5, where Moses wrote:

> For God knows that in the day you eat from it your eyes will be opened, and you will be like God, knowing good and evil.

Did "the day" refer to a long period of time, say, nine hundred years until Adam died physically? Was that how long they took to learn good and evil? I submit they knew good and evil the day they ate, not an extended time, even years, later. This knowledge led to their being afraid, ashamed, and needing to hide from God.

In Gen 3.5-7, we learn further what happened that day:

> "For God knows that *in the day you eat from it your eyes will be opened, and you will be like God, knowing*

*good and evil."* When the woman saw that the tree
was good for food, and that it was a delight to the
eyes, and that the tree was desirable to make one wise,
she took from its fruit and ate; and she gave also to her
husband with her, and he ate. Then the eyes of both of
them were opened, and they knew that they were
naked; and they sewed fig leaves together and made
themselves loin coverings.

Adam didn't die physically the day he ate from the tree of
knowledge. Instead, he died in the sense of being separated from God
by his sin the day he ate, and he knew it. Suddenly, his relationship
with God changed. He reacted with fear of approaching God, and
attempted to hide from him. This was Adam's sin-death. His
relationship with God was broken. This is the death we're concerned
with–a death that affects one's relationship with God. Physical death
does not. We may or may not be in fellowship whether we're
physically dead or alive.

Again, we ask: Was Adam immortal? Notice some conclusions
thus far. *First*, Adam didn't die physically because of sin. The physical
death of Adam and his descendants was not a punishment for Adam's
sin, any more than the physical death of any other *living creature* was
punishment for Adam's sin. Like all others of Adam's descendants,
you and I will die physically, but not because of Adam's sin. Our
physical death is not a curse for sin. Surely, the serpent was cursed, as
was the ground. Likewise, painful childbirth and toilsome labor
resulted from Adam's sin, but we die physically for the same reason
Adam did. We're mortal, as was he, and we lack of access to the tree
of life, as did he.

## Is Immortality an Innate Quality of the Soul or Spirit, or Is It Conditional?

It appears that immortality is promised only to the righteous, for
we read in Rom. 2.4-10:

4 Or do you think lightly of the riches of His kindness
and forbearance and patience, not knowing that the
kindness of God leads you to repentance? 5 But
because of your stubbornness and unrepentant heart
you are storing up wrath for yourself in the day of
wrath and revelation of the righteous judgment of

God, 6 who will render to every man according to his
deeds: 7 to those who by perseverance in doing good
seek for glory and honor and *immortality*, eternal life;
8 but to those who are selfishly ambitious and do not
obey the truth, but obey unrighteousness, wrath and
indignation. 9 There will be tribulation and distress for
every soul of man who does evil, of the Jew first and
also of the Greek, 10 but glory and honor and peace to
every man who does good, to the Jew first and also to
the Greek.

Notice that Paul speaks of the coming judgment as the day of
wrath, when God will render to every man according to his deeds.
Jesus had said in Mt. 16.17-28 that he would come and render such
judgment during the lifetime of some of his disciples Paul then said
that those who did good would receive glory, honor, and immortality,
eternal life, but those who did evil would receive wrath, indignation,
tribulation, and distress..

Immortality here is from the same word used in II Tim. 1.10:

...Jesus, who abolished death, and brought life and
immortality to light through the gospel...

and it was only the righteous who would receive immortalilty. As
we've seen, man wasn't born with immortality even in the garden, and
they wouldn't receive it in the judgment.

# Chapter 7

# The Destruction of the Universe—at the End of Time?

## The Teaching of Roman Catholicism on the New Heavens and Earth

The *Catechcism of the Catholic Church* teaches:

> 1042 At the end of time, the Kingdom of God will come in its fullness. After the universal judgment, the righteous will reign for ever with Christ, glorified in body and soul. The universe itself will be renewed:

This chapter offers a brief study of II Peter 3. Although for many years the author, along with most Bible students now, believed this chapter dealt with a final advent of Christ at the end of time, he now believes it deals with the destruction of Jerusalem by the Roman General Titus in AD 70. This, however, does not make his position right, but he hopes you will at least examine this position to see if it doesn't deal with the text more accurately than his previously held, and the more popular, position.

## Introduction to II Peter

II Peter is, of course, the second of two books written by the apostle Peter shortly before the destruction of Jerusalem. Scholars generally date the books about 66-67 A.D. The theme of I Peter is hope, i.e., it was written to instill hope in Christians who were undergoing severe Jewish persecution in those years. The theme of II Peter is knowledge, the knowledge to combat certain false teachers of the time. II Peter 1 deals with the importance of knowledge, II Peter 2 with the character of the false teachers, and II Peter 3 with the character of their false teaching. The false teachers were denying the coming of Christ, and it is about this coming we now concern ourselves. Was Jesus coming in the person of the Roman army to destroy Jerusalem in AD 70, as he foretold in Matthew 24, or was he coming at the end of time?

Actually, the Bible nowhere uses the expression "end of time." The closest passage might be Dan. 12.4, which the only the NASV mistakenly translates as "the end of time." The ASV translates it as "the time of the end," as do the KJV, NIV, and the NKJV, among others. The expressions "time of the end" and "the end of time" reflect two vastly different concepts. One supposes the end of time itself, and the other speaks of the time of "the end," the end of the age. In Daniel's context, the age ends with the destruction of Jerusalem and her temple.

II Peter 3 is a more detailed account of the imminent judgment Peter had already touched upon in I Pet. 4.7-19. In the context of I Peter, Peter said, "the end of all things is at hand," (verse 7). He spoke of "the fiery trial among you, which cometh upon you to prove you," (verse 12). He spoke of the "revelation of his (Jesus') glory," (verse 13). This corresponds to Jesus telling his disciples in Mt. 16.27-28 that he would be coming in glory and for judgment *while some of them were still alive*:

> For the Son of man shall come in the glory of his Father with his angels; and then shall he render unto every man according to his deeds. Verily I say unto you, there are some of them that stand here, who shall in no wise taste of death, till they see the Son of man coming in his kingdom.

Peter's context from I Peter also corresponds to Mt. 24.30, where Jesus had described the destruction of Jerusalem as a coming in glory, which would occur in that generation (Mt. 24.34). As part of that same discourse, Matthew 25 also portrays the judgment to take place in Jesus' generation (See our essay on The Olivet Discourse for detailed treatment of Matthew 25). Peter also said, "for the time is come for judgment to begin at the house of God," (verse 17). In verse 18 he asked, "And if the righteous is scarcely saved, where shall the ungodly and sinner appear?" In verse 19 he said, "Wherefore let them also that suffer according to the will of God commit their souls in well-doing unto a faithful Creator." Thus, I Peter deals with an imminent judgment that would seriously affect the children of God. II Peter occurs in this same context of imminent judgment. Does it deal with the same judgment as I Peter, the destruction of Jerusalem, or does it deal with a totally new subject, an advent of Christ at "the end of time?" Does it describe the end of the Mosaic Covenant, as discussed in Matthew 24, or does it describe the end of the planet and astronomical heavens, as we so often hear it portrayed? We want to investigate the answers to these questions.

## Brief Commentary on II Peter 3

We now give a brief verse-by-verse commentary on this chapter.

**Verse 1: "This is now, beloved, the second epistle that I write unto you; and in both of them I stir up your sincere mind by putting you in remembrance;"**

This verse shows how we know this is the second letter. Peter stated the purpose: to stir up their minds, to keep their thinking on the right track. Since he was *reminding* his first century readers (not us) of the Lord's imminent coming, II Peter was written to the same disciples. Consider that had you and I been among those first century disciples, we wouldn't have viewed our Lord's imminent coming in judgment nearly as casually as if we thought it was at least twenty centuries in the future as is popularly believed. We would have been as watchful and eager as they were.

Then Peter proceeded to admonish Christians to study:

**Verse 2: "that ye should remember the words which were spoken before by the holy prophets, and the commandment of the Lord and Saviour through your apostles:"**

Here Peter commanded Christians to be serious students of the holy prophets—the Old Testament, as well as the teaching of the apostles—the New Testament. If someone now denied that Christians should study the teaching of the apostles, the commandment of the Lord and Saviour, we would surely take issue. Do we argue as vigorously if someone says Christians today don't need to study seriously the holy prophets who spoke before? Usually not, hence our problems with interpreting much of the New Testament—we don't know nearly enough about the Old Testament! In verse 8, Peter quoted Ps. 90.4; in verse 13, he quoted from Isaiah concerning the new heavens and new earth. Without familiarity with these Old Testament prophets, we're not the caliber of Christians to whom this letter was written originally. That makes us apt to fall for just about any interpretation offered to us.

Peter made three great statements about a Christian's relation to the Old Testament. In I Pet. 1.12, he implied the Old Testament was written more for Christians than for the Old Testament people themselves. In II Pet. 1.19 he commanded Christians to study it, and here in II Pet. 3.2, he again commanded Christians to study the Old Testament. This lack of in-depth understanding of the holy prophets is probably one important way we don't imitate New Testament Christians. Thus, our ignorance makes it easy for us to jump to false conclusions that the Christians of Peter's day wouldn't have embraced.

The Old Testament prophets taught many times about the destruction of Jerusalem by the Romans. In one of the most amazing chapters of the Bible, Deuteronomy 32, Moses foretells Israel's final end. Malachi spoke of the destruction of Jerusalem in chapters 3 and 4. John the Baptist did in Mt. 3.10-11. Peter spoke of it as the fulfillment of Joel's last days prophecy in the first gospel sermon (Ac. 2.17-21). Thus, the coming of the Lord of which Peter spoke may easily be seen to be the Lord's coming spoken of by Jesus in his generation (Mt. 24.34), i.e., the destruction of Jerusalem discussed by the Old Testament prophets.

Peter then warned of false teachers coming in the last days:

**Verse 3: "knowing this first, that in the last days mockers shall come with mockery, walking after their own lusts,"**

What does "last days" mean? Many times, we hear it applied to the entire period of time beginning at the first Pentecost after the resurrection of Christ until "the end of time." In Ac. 2.17, Peter said that what happened on Pentecost was what Joel wrote about when he wrote about the last days. Have we now had about two thousand years of last days, i.e., the time of the Messiah's rule, or were these the last days of the Mosaic Covenant?

This is even more easily seen when we realize that the age of Christ has no last days. Jesus' disciples, including even modern Jews, recognized two ages, the Mosaic age, and the age to come, i.e., the age of the Messiah. Jesus even spoke of "this age" and "the age to come" (Mt. 12.31-32, Mk. 10.29-31, Lk. 20.34-35).

Though we many times think "the end" Paul spoke of refers to the end of the Christian age; in reality, *the Christian age has no end.* For example, in Isa. 9.6-7, Isaiah prophesied the endlessness of the Messiah's rule:

> For a child will be born to us, a son will be given to us; And the government will rest on His shoulders; And His name will be called Wonderful Counselor, Mighty God, Eternal Father, Prince of Peace. There will be *no end to the increase of His government* or of peace, On the throne of David and over his kingdom, To establish it and to uphold it with justice and righteousness From then on and forevermore. The zeal of the LORD of hosts will accomplish this.

Likewise, in Lk. 1.31-33, Gabriel told Mary of the endlessness of the Messiah's reign:

> And behold, thou shalt conceive in thy womb, and bring forth a son, and shalt call his name JESUS. He shall be great, and shall be called the Son of the Most High: and the Lord God shall give unto him the throne of his father David: and *he shall reign over the house of Jacob for ever; and of his kingdom there shall be no end.*

Thus, the term "end of the age" in Jesus' teaching never referred to the end of the Christian age, which has no end. Instead, it foretold the end of the Mosaic age. Similarly, the term "last days" never refers to the last days of the Christian age; again, because the Christian age has no end; it has no last days. However, the last days of the Mosaic age certainly did exist. Jesus spoke of it here, and all the Jews understood, that it was the end of the Mosaic age.

Hebrews 9.26 used the same expression, when the writer said:

> ...else must he often have suffered since the foundation of the world: but now once at the *end of the ages* [emphasis mine—SGD] hath he been manifested to put away sin by the sacrifice of himself.

First, the expression "at the end of the ages," which referred to the first coming of Christ, comes from the same Greek expression used in Mt. 24.3. It means, literally, "the consummation of the age." Christ was offered at his first coming as the completion or consummation of the plan of God through all the ages to redeem humanity.

Second, Paul used the same expression in I Cor. 10.11. He spoke of the value of the Old Testament scriptures to New Testament Christians:

> Now these things happened unto them by way of example; and they were written for our admonition, upon whom the ends of the ages are come.

Thus, the last days spoken of in the New Testament are the last days of the Mosaic Covenant, i.e., the time from the coming of John the Baptist to the destruction of Jerusalem in AD 70. For example, see I Pet. 1.20 where God's son was manifested in the flesh in the last days. He wasn't manifested after his rule began, but in the last days of the Mosaic Covenant. In Heb. 1.2, Jesus fully and finally spoke in the last days. Again, this is not after Pentecost, but in the last days of the Mosaic Covenant. In Isa. 2.2 and Dan. 2.28-45, prophets said the kingdom of the Messiah would begin in the last days and during the Roman Empire. This is easily seen to be the last days of the Mosaic Covenant, not the two thousand years since Pentecost. *The last days of the Mosaic age aren't longer than the Mosaic age itelf!* In Heb. 9.16, 26, Christ's blood was to ratify the New Covenant in the last days. This is the last days of the Mosaic Covenant, not the time following Pentecost. In Joel 2.28 and Ac. 2.17, the Spirit was to be poured out in the last days, i.e., during the last days of the Mosaic Covenant, not throughout the Messiah's rule since Pentecost. Peter warned of the false teachers of his day, whose character he had just described in II Peter 2. In Dan. 9.24-27, 12.4, 13, Mt. 24.3, 13f, and Ac. 2.19-21, we see that the last days were when Jerusalem was to fall totally. Thus, the last days are the last days of the Mosaic Covenant, not the unending age of the Messiah's reign since Pentecost.

Peter said that in the last days of the Mosaic Covenant, the time when he was writing this very letter, that mockers would come. A mocker plays like children, or trifles with something, as opposed to engaging in serious argument or debate. Peter continued with an example of the mockery:

**Verse 4: "and saying, Where is the promise of his coming? for, from the day that the fathers fell asleep, all things continue as they were from the beginning of the creation."**

These men were Jewish scoffers, their fathers were the Jewish fathers. Christ had promised an imminent return in Mt. 10.23, 16.28,

26.64, and Lk. 21.27-33 in which he would judge Israel and destroy Jerusalem. He said this coming would come to pass in that generation, Mt. 24.34. Stephen confirmed this coming, Ac. 6.4 ("we heard him say that this Jesus of Nazareth shall destroy this place"), and so did the author of Hebrews in 10.37 ("For yet a very little while, He that cometh shall come, and shall not tarry"). Even James in Jas. 5.7-11 taught it ("coming," verse 7, "at hand," verse 8, "the judge standeth before the doors," verse 9, so "be patient and wait for the lord's coming," (verse 7).

If first century disciples weren't expecting an imminent return of Christ, why would they be mocked about a delay of thirty-five years? Why would they be mocked about a return at least twenty centuries in the future, as most view Christ's return? These Jewish scoffers now said, "It's been thirty-five years since Jesus made the promise. Jesus preached it; the apostles did; we've been preaching this; we've been waiting; and things keep going right on. Since he hasn't come in thirty-five years, *he won't come!*" These men were not looking for something far off, the way we many times use the passage, but for something in their generation.

In Mt. 24.5, 10, Jesus forewarned of false prophets who would arise and lead many believers astray, plainly foretelling an apostasy in his generation. In Mt. 24.11, he foretold that the majority of believers would apostatize. These scoffers in II Peter 3 are some of those Jesus had warned of. Also in the Olivet Discourse, Jesus described the evil of these men when, in the parable of the faithful and unfaithful servants, Jesus said in Mt. 24.48-51:

> 48 But if that *evil servant* shall say in his heart, My lord *tarrieth*; 49 and shall begin to beat his fellow-servants, and shall eat and drink with the drunken; 50 the lord of that servant shall come in a day when he expecteth not, and in an hour when he knoweth not, 51 and shall cut him asunder, and appoint his portion with the *hypocrites*: there shall be the weeping and the gnashing of teeth.

Notice that Jesus pronounced the servant who said the master was tarrying, when Jesus promised he would not (Heb. 10.37 – "for in a very very little while he that cometh shall come, and will not tarry...") as an evil servant.

Thus, Jesus says that such a servant is not only evil, but he's a hypocrite! He claims to be a faithful servant, but he specifically denies his master's teaching. The word hypocrite means a play actor—he's playing the part of a faithful servant, he's not a real one.

If Jesus spoke of false teachers and brethren who said he delayed the judgment of Matthew 24 as evil and hypocritical when they upheld a thirty-five year delay, what in the world would he think of futurists of our day who claim he has delayed fulfillment for 2000+ years?

Peter next showed the fallacy of their position:

**Verse 5: "For this they willfully forget, that there were heavens from of old, and an earth compacted out of water and amidst water, by the word of God;"**

This verse illustrates the free will of man. These men exercised free will by working and striving to forget. They were willing to forget the heavens and earth from of old which were to pass away. Notice: this is the heavens and earth that existed before the flood of Noah's day.

**Verse 6: "by which means the world that then was, being overflowed with water, perished:"**

The old world perished by the same means by which God created it—by God's word. Notice that the world that then perished, the old heavens and earth was not the globe and sky. They were still there as Peter wrote, but he spoke of the old world order. Likewise, the planet and stars Peter lived on and under were the same planet and stars Noah lived on and under. Accordingly, the earth and heavens that passed away were not the planet and stars, but the corrupt pre-flood order or world. The planet and stars Peter lived on and under are the same planet and stars we live on and under. Consequently, the earth and heavens that are about to pass away in II Peter 3 are not the planet and stars, but the religious order Peter was living under, i.e., the Mosaic Covenant.

## Old Heavens and Earth vs.
## New Heavens and Earth

Old Testament writers used the passing of an old heavens and earth and the coming in of a new heavens and earth to speak of the passing away of one social order and the bringing in of another.

For instance, notice Isa. 51.15-16:

But I am the Lord thy God that divided the sea, whose waves roared: The Lord of hosts is His name. And I have put My words in thy mouth, and I have covered thee in the shadow of Mine hand, that I may plant the *heavens*, and lay the foundations of the *earth*, and say unto Zion, Thou art My people.

Notice that as God spoke of the creation of the nation of Israel, he divided the Red Sea, and put his words in their mouths by giving them the Mosaic Covenant. This was so "that I may plant the heavens and lay the foundations of the earth." He couldn't have been speaking of the planet and stars, because they had already been created. This heavens and earth was created when they became his people, at Sinai.

A similar use of heaven and earth is found in Lev. 26.19-20, where, at Sinai, God warned them of the consequences if they disobeyed him: "And I will also break down your pride of power; I will also make *your sky* like iron and *your earth* like bronze. And your strength shall be spent uselessly; for your land shall not yield its produce and the trees of the land shall not yield their fruit."

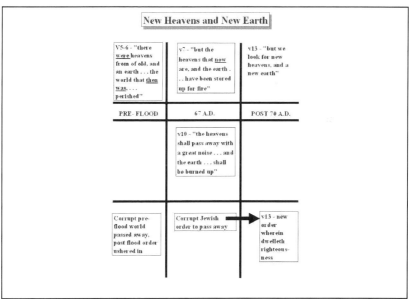

Likewise, sky and earth are not the planet and stars, but Israel's sky and earth. When they disobeyed God, the planet and stars didn't turn to bronze and iron, but their world order was judged. Their condition became much harder, more difficult.

Flavius Josephus, a priest, then a Jewish General who fought and was defeated by the Roman Emperor Vespasian, then a historian, referred to the Mosaic system as Israel's heavens and earth, especially in reference to the tabernacle or temple:

> Now the room within those pillars was the most holy place; but the rest of the room was the tabernacle, which was open for the priests. However, this proportion of the measures of the tabernacle proved to be *an imitation of the system of the world*; for that third part thereof which was within the four pillars, to which the priests were not admitted, is, as it were, *a heaven*, peculiar to God. (*Antiquities of the Jews*: Book III, Chapter 6, Section 4.)

Speaking of the veil at the holy of holies, Josephus says:

> This veil was very ornamental, and embroidered with all sorts of flowers which *the earth* produces; and there were interwoven into it all sorts of variety that might be an ornament, excepting the forms of animals. (*Antiquities of the Jews*: Book III, Chapter 7, Section 7.)

Similarly, in Isa. 34.1-4, Isaiah used the expression of Edom's world. For Edom, the old heavens and earth passed away, and a new world came in when Edom was destroyed. In Isa. 51.4-7, Isaiah said the same of Israel. God took away the order with which they were familiar, and brought in a new one, restored, purified Israel. In Isa. 65.16-17, physical Israel would pass away, and a new order beyond the first coming of Christ, the Messiah's rule over Christians, would come. Haggai 2.6f contains the same language, which Heb. 12.27 quotes as fulfilled in the late 60s when Hebrews was written—the same time II Peter was written! II Peter 3.1-14 depicts the same change of order. Revelation 21 depicts the passing of the old order of Christians persecuted to the new order of Christians enthroned as described in Revelation 21-22, the reward of the martyrs.

The judgment in Noah's day was typical of the judgment on Jerusalem in the first century. Both were escapable judgments. Jesus even paralleled the two judgments, Mt. 24.37ff. Both judgments destroyed the wicked, and delivered the righteous. Both were worldwide events, for Jews from all over the world were in Jerusalem when it fell, because the city was besieged at the time of the Passover (Josephus, *Wars*, 6, 9, 3.)

Peter continued by saying:

**Verse 7: "but the heavens that now are, and the earth, by the same word have been stored up for fire, being reserved against the day of judgment and destruction of ungodly men."**

When Peter spoke of the heavens and earth that "are" to him in 66-67 AD, he lived on the same globe and under the same sky as Noah, as we do. He spoke of the old order of The Mosaic Covenant. The three "heaven and earth" systems of which Peter spoke are illustrated in the chart above.

Malachi foretold that Jerusalem was stored up for fire (chapters 3-4), as did John the Baptist (Mt. 3.10-11), and Jesus (Matthew 24-25). God would not use a flood to destroy the order of Peter's day. It would be burned up with unquenchable fire.

That the old order of The Mosaic Covenant was stored up for fire meant its national overthrow. In Isa. 33.14, speaking of the destruction of Assyria by Babylon, God used terms like "consuming fire" and "everlasting burning." In Jer. 4.4, God spoke of the destruction of Israel when he said she would "burn with none to quench it," i.e., unquenchable fire. Amos 5.6 describes the destruction of Israel by Assyria in the same terms. See also Isa. 66.24, where Isaiah described the church victorious over its enemies in the same terms.

Thus, fire was to be the Jews' fate, as Peter described it. It was so preached in the first gospel sermon in Ac. 2.17ff, when Peter quoted from Joel: "blood, fire, and columns of smoke." John the Baptist spoke of it (Mt. 3.10-11). Jesus himself said, "I came to bring fire on the earth (land)," Lk. 12.49. James 5.3 and I Thes. 2.16 say the same thing. Last, the fiery fate of Sodom was also a type of Jerusalem's fate, Lk. 17.29f. History confirms that Jerusalem was burned to the ground.

This was the day of judgment for Israel. Peter had so spoken of it in his first epistle, I Pet. 4.12-17. In Mt. 16.27-28, Jesus said this judgment would take place while some of his apostles were still alive. Jesus spoke of the destruction of Jerusalem as a day of judgment, Mt. 25.32. (Read a detailed discussion of Matthew 24-25 in "The Olivet Discourse," a chapter in the author's *Teaching of Jesus, from Sinai to Gehenna: A Faithful Rabbi Urgently Warns Rebellious Israel* or *Essays on Eshcatology: An Introductory Overview of the Study of Last Things*, available from Amazon.com)

**Verse 8: "But forget not this one thing, beloved, that one day is with the Lord as a thousand years, and a thousand years as one day."**

When Peter said that one day is with the Lord as a thousand years, he didn't say you can substitute one thousand years for one day wherever you want to. One might say one day equals one thousand years. Consequently, two days equal two thousand years, and 365 days equal 365,000 years. Therefore, one year equals 365,000 years, which also equals one day! You can't have it both ways, literally. Peter spoke as the Psalmist in Ps. 90.4, when he said:

> For a thousand years in thy sight are like yesterday
> when it passes by, or as a watch in the night.

A watch in the night was generally three hours. The psalmist said one thousand years to God is like three hours, i.e., God doesn't view time as we do. If I borrow twenty dollars from you, and after thirty-five years, I still haven't paid you back, you would probably write the debt off. Peter said these false teachers had better not do that with the promise is Christ's coming in their generation. Peter told why in the next verse:

**Verse 9: "The Lord is not slack concerning his promise, as some count slackness; but is longsuffering to you-ward, not wishing that any should perish, but that all should come to repentance."**

Peter explained that the reason Christ hadn't come and destroyed Jerusalem was not because God was slack, i.e., he was not loitering around, or "goofing off." He hadn't forgotten his promise. The reason Christ hadn't come was because he's longsuffering.

Paul, in Rom. 2.4, said that the longsuffering of God works repentance. If God destroyed us immediately when we sinned, none of us would be alive. If He waited five minutes after we sinned to destroy us, we still wouldn't be alive. We want longer, unless of course, someone sins against us, then perhaps we don't want so long! Why does God wait at all? He wants people to change their minds, not because He forgot.

Peter said that God didn't want any to perish. This is the same perishing of which Jesus spoke in Lk. 13.3, "Except ye repent, ye shall all in like manner perish." There, he warned the Jews of his day: "He will avenge them speedily."

**Verse 10: "But the day of the Lord will come as a thief: in the which the heavens shall pass away with a great noise, and the elements shall be dissolved with fervent heat, and the earth and the works that are therein shall be burned up."**

Peter said the day of the Lord *would* come. The false teachers were wrong; it would come. The Old Testament, with the exception of the sabbath day, uses the term "day of the Lord" nearly exclusively of national judgment. In Isa. 13.6-9, Babylon received "destruction from the Almighty" on such a day. In Ezk. 30.3, 10 Egypt did. In Joel 1.15, Israel was to see just such a day, just twenty years off. In Joel 2.1, Israel was to see a day of the Lord, the very one of which John the Baptist, Jesus, and Peter spoke. In Obadiah 1.5, Edom was to see such a day. In Zeph. 1.14f, Judah would see "the great day of the Lord," when Babylon destroyed her in 586 B.C. So was the upcoming destruction of Jerusalem a "day of the Lord," as Peter said in Ac. 2.17ff (cf. Joel 2.31f, 3.14-17), and our Lord himself in Mt. 24.27, 30.

Saying that the day of the Lord would "come as a thief," Peter recognized thieves don't send cards saying, "I plan to be in your neighborhood at 10:00 p.m. Tuesday night. Please have everything ready." Though we don't know when the next thief is coming, that doesn't mean we can't have everything ready! The thief's coming will not be by invitation or announcement. Peter said the Lord's coming would not be by invitation or announcement, either. Jesus gave the same warning about the destruction of Jerusalem in Mt. 24.43 and Lk. 21.34-36.Lk. 21.34-36

When Peter said the heavens would pass away, he used language common in the Old Testament to speak of the overthrow of political powers. In Isa. 14.12f, the fall of the ruler of Babylon was spoken of as a falling star. In Isa. 13.10, 13, 19, Isaiah used such language to describe the fall of Babylon; in Isa. 34.4, the fall of Edom. In Isa. 51.6, the nation of Israel would so fall. In Joel 3.16, the fall of Jerusalem after the Messiah was foretold in such words. Peter said it would be so with the destruction of Jerusalem. Peter had said the same thing in Ac. 2.19ff, when he quoted Joel 2.28-32 in the first gospel sermon. Haggai used the same language in Hag. 2.6, *quoted in Heb. 12.26-28 to speak of the imminent destruction of Jerusalem.* Jesus used the same language in Mt. 24.39-42 and Lk. 21.26, 11.

When Peter said "the elements shall melt with fervent heat," we quickly think of the atomic elements, and that Peter spoke of the conflagration of our whole universe. The word *elements* is given for the Greek word *stoicheion,* which occurs seven times in the New Testament. In Heb. 5.12 it stands for the rudiments of the law, as seen in Heb. 6.4-6. In Gal. 4.3, it depicts the rudiments of the world, for those under the Law of Moses, the rudiments of the Mosaic Covenant. In Gal. 4.9, it represents the weak and beggarly rudiments, identified as the days, months, seasons, and years of the Mosaic Covenant. In Col. 2.20, it denotes the rudiments of the world, possibly Gnostic borrowing from Judaism. In none of these passages does anyone think of atomic elements. Then Peter used it in II Pet. 3.10, 12, where the idea comes nearly automatically to mind. No, it's the rudimentary principles of the Mosaic Covenant again, the priesthood, the temple, it's sacrifices, the city of Jerusalem, and the genealogies. All were swept away in the destruction, which was imminently to occur.

Peter said they would be dissolved. Dissolved here comes from *luo*, used in Eph. 2.14, "*broken down* the middle wall" between Jews and Gentiles, again speaking of the destruction of the Mosaic Covenant's constraints between Jews and Gentiles. It's also the word used in I Jn. 3.8, where John said that Christ was "manifested to *destroy* the works of the devil."

When Peter said the earth (that then was) and the works (that were therein) were to be burned up, he spoke of the same refining of Israel that John the Baptist had announced in Mt. 3.10-12, the burning up of the chaff. Malachi foretold this refining process in Mal. 3.2-5, 4.1-6. "Earth" here may also be "land." See, for example, Lk. 21.23, 26 where the same term means the land of Israel.

Next Peter turned his attention to the lessons that could be learned from the heavens and earth passing away:

**Verse 11: "Seeing that these things are thus all to be dissolved, what manner of persons ought ye to be in all holy living and godliness,"**

Peter here spoke of the dissolving (literally, tearing up, breaking down) of these things, i.e, the earth and the works that then were. The message was: *Be prepared!* He asked, "What manner of persons ought you to be?" He used a word that literally means "of what country should you be?" We might ask this same question in this way, "If the United States is about to wipe out Cuba, of what country should you be?" Not Cuba! Likewise, the Jews to whom Peter wrote had better not be of physical Israel, of Judaism, for God would destroy it.

Likewise, the author of Hebrews mentioned the faithful father of the Jews, who were "strangers and pilgrims on the earth." Paul also reminded Christians in Phil. 3.20 that "our citizenship is in heaven; whence also we wait for a saviour, the Lord Jesus Christ." This is the manner of person Peter said they ought to be in all holy living and godliness. In other words, both their actions and their attitudes should be prepared. Peter continued his admonition:

**Verse 12: "looking for and earnestly desiring the coming of the day of God, by reason of which the heavens being on fire shall be dissolved, and the elements shall melt with fervent heat?"**

This "looking for and earnestly desiring the day of God" is the same as Jesus' exhortations to watchfulness in Mt. 24.44ff. The day of God has to be the destruction of Jerusalem rather than a final advent for two reasons: First, they couldn't look for a final advent of Christ, for there are no signs given of a final advent at the end of time. Second, the final advent wasn't near in Peter's day! However, Peter's audience could look for the destruction of Jerusalem, for Jesus had given signs, Mt. 24.3-15, 32-45 and Lk. 12.56, 21.28. In Heb. 10.25, the author of Hebrews also said his Jewish readers could see the day drawing nigh!

Peter then mentioned that the heavens being on fire would be dissolved. These were the old heavens of Peter's day, the old heavens and earth, the old order. Peter said it would be on fire, and be dissolved. These were expressions similar to those already used to describe the change from the old order to the new, like Edom and physical Israel in the Old Testament.

Peter then described the new order which would replace the old which was about to pass away:

**Verse 13: "But, according to his promise, we look for new heavens and a new earth, wherein dwelleth righteousness."**

This new heavens and new earth were not a new planet and skies, any more than the new heavens and earth after Noah were a new planet and skies. Peter spoke of the new order of things after the destruction of Jerusalem, the victorious church having weathered Jewish persecution, victorious Christians withstanding potential eradication by Jews.

This new heavens and earth had been prophesied in Isa. 65.17:

> For behold, I create a *new* heavens and earth; And the
> former shall not be remembered or come to mind. But
> be glad and rejoice forever in what I create; For be-

hold, I create *Jerusalem* (the new Jerusalem of Heb. 12.22) as a rejoicing, and her people a joy.

Hebrews 12.22 tells us this new Jerusalem was the New Testament church victorious. Isaiah 66.22 also spoke of new Jerusalem, telling of the days of the work of the apostles, Ac. 3.18-24. Peter told Christians of his day to look for this new order, not implying that Christ did not yet rule, but that his rule had not been completely confirmed by the destruction of the old order. Thus, in Dan. 7.18, 22, under persecution in the Roman Empire, Christians were in the kingdom before the enemy was destroyed, but when the enemy was finally destroyed, then they fully possessed a vindicated kingdom. It was not only prophesied that the kingdom was unshakable, but also that it would be proven.

Peter then made the application to the lives of his readers:

**Verse 14: "Wherefore, beloved, seeing that ye look for these things, give diligence that ye may be found in peace, without spot and blameless in his sight."**

Again, these instructions could not refer to an advent of Christ at an end of time the Bible never speaks of, for there was nothing pertaining to that event that first-century Christians could "look for." However, in Matthew 24-25, with its parallel passages, as well as in I Peter, many instructions to watchfulness had been given concerning the destruction of Jerusalem.

Peter continued the application to the lives of his readers:

**Verse 15: "And account that the longsuffering of our Lord is salvation; even as our beloved brother Paul also, according to the wisdom given to him, wrote unto you;"**

The imminent judgment Peter spoke of was indeed written of by Paul. For example, in Rom. 2.6 Paul warned of a "day of wrath" coming on the Jews of his day. In Rom. 13.11-12, he said, "The day is at hand," when speaking of their imminent judgment. In I Corinthians, Paul warned of a coming judgment on Jews in 1.7, 3.15, 4.5, 5.5, 7.29-31, and 10.11. In Phil. 4.5, Paul warned, "The Lord is at hand." Modernists oftentimes think Paul (and even Jesus) were mistaken about how imminent Jesus' coming in judgment was. No, the modernists are mistaken. John the Baptist, Jesus, Paul, and Peter all warned of a coming conflagration which would wipe out the Jewish religion for its apostasy. Peter affirmed that he wasn't teaching anything that Paul hadn't taught already.

Peter then commented on the quality of Paul's teaching:

**Verse 16: "as also in all his epistles, speaking in them of these things; wherein are some things hard to be understood, which the ignorant and unstedfast wrest, as they do also the other scriptures, unto their own destruction."**

We can take heart from this comment. If the apostle Peter thought Paul's writing contained some difficulties, we ought not to be surprised if some of them seem difficult to us.

Peter concluded with exhortations to faithfulness in view of the coming imminent judgment on the Jewish nation:

**Verse 17: "Ye therefore, beloved, knowing these things before-hand, beware lest, being carried away with the error of the wicked, ye fall from your own stedfastness."**

**Verse 18: "But grow in the grace and knowledge of our Lord and Saviour Jesus Christ. To him be the glory both now and for ever. Amen."**

## Conclusion

As we've seen, the purpose of Peter's words in this chapter was to warn faithful people of his time concerning the approaching physical judgment so they could escape it. Eusebius, a third-century historian, wrote of the early Jerusalem church:

> The whole body, however, of the church at Jerusalem, having been commanded by a divine revelation given to men of approved piety therefore before the war removed from the city and dwelt at a certain town beyond the Jordan, called Pella. (Pamphilus Eusebius, *The Ecclesiastical History,* translated by C. F. Cruse [Philadelphia: J. B. Lippincott and Company, 1869], lib. 3, chapter 6.)

So, in a siege of Jerusalem where 1.1 million Jews perished and another 2.5 million were taken into slavery, not one faithful individual who heeded the warnings of John the Baptist, Jesus, Paul and Peter perished.

Thus, both the harmony of Old Testament passages with the New Testament and history, indicate that II Peter 3 refers to the destruction of Jerusalem. To use these passages to teach about the destruction of the universe at the end of time is to rip them out of their context, not only in Jesus' and Paul's teaching, but also the whole Bible.

# Chapter 8

# The Resurrection—at the End of Time?

## The Teaching of Roman Catholicism on the Resurrection at the End of Time

Under the Glossary entry, JUDGMENT, the *Catechism of the Catholic Church* says:

> **JUDGMENT**: The eternal retribution received by each soul at the moment of death, in accordance with that person's faith and works ("the particular judgment") (1021-1022). The "Last Judgment" is God's triumph over the revolt of evil, after the final cosmic upheaval of this passing world. **Preceded by the resurrection of the dead, it will coincide with the second coming of Christ in glory at the end of time**, disclose good and evil, and reveal the meaning of salvation history and the providence of God by which justice has triumphed over evil (677-679, 1021, 1038)

Thus Roman Catholicism teaches that the coming of Christ, the judgment, and the resurrection will all occur at the end of time. Of course, as we've seen, the Bible knows nothing of the end of time, so it can't possibly teach a resurrection at the end of time.

# Does the Roman Catholic Church Preach Like Paul on the Resurrection?

It will surprise many to learn that Paul's preaching on the resurrection was not based upon the New Testament but the old! To Felix, Paul said in Ac. 24.14-15:

> 14 But this I confess unto thee, that after the Way which they call a sect, so serve I the God of our fathers, believing all things which are according to the law, and which are written in the prophets; 15 having hope toward God, which these also themselves look for, that there shall be a resurrection both of the just and unjust.

To Agrippa, Paul said in Ac. 26.22-23:

> 22 Having therefore obtained the help that is from God, I stand unto this day testifying both to small and great, saying nothing but what the prophets and Moses did say should come; 23 how that the Christ must suffer, and how that he first by the resurrection of the dead should proclaim light both to the people and to the Gentiles.

When Paul stated that he taught nothing on the resurrection other than what Moses and the prophets, he had already written Thessalonians and Corinthians. Thus, those letters don't teach anything on the resurrection other than what Moses and the prophets taught. So, let's see what the Old Testament taught about the time of the resurrection.

## The Bible's Teaching on the Time of the Resurrection

### Ezekiel's Teaching about the Time

We'll begin with the Old Testament's teaching on the time of the resurrection, then proceed through the New Testament's teaching. In Ezekiel 37, we have the famous Dry Bones vision of Ezekiel. The chapter consists of three sections:

vv1-14 – The Resurrection of Old Covenant Israel
vv15-23 – The Restoration of Old Covenant Israel
vv24-28 – The Messianic Hope of Israel

## vv1-14 - The Resurrection of Old Covenant Israel

In the first section, Ezekiel is shown a valley of dry bones, and when Ezekiel prophesies over them, they come to life, i.e., a resurrection. In v11, God explains to Ezekiel:

> Then He said to me, "Son of man, these bones are the whole house of Israel; behold, they say, 'Our bones are dried up, and our hope has perished. We are completely cut off.'

Thus the dry bones didn't represent literal fleshly bodies of human beings, but Old Covenant Israel. That nation was in Babylonian captivity at the time, thus they were off the land that had been promised to Abraham, and they had no hope. In v12, God continues:

> Therefore prophesy, and say to them, 'Thus says the Lord GOD," Behold, I will open your graves and cause you to come up out of your graves, My people; and I will bring you into the land of Israel.

Again, God uses resurrection language to speak of his raising Old Covenant Israel from spiritual death, their lack of fellowship with God in Babylon, as bringing them out of their graves. In vv13-14, God gives a clue as to when this resurrection would take place:

> 13 "Then you will know that I am the LORD, when I have opened your graves and caused you to come up out of your graves, My people. 14 "And I will put My Spirit within you, and you will come to life, and I will place you on your own land. Then you will know that I, the LORD, have spoken and done it," declares the LORD.' "

Thus, in connection with the resurrection of Israel in the Messiah's time, God said he would put his Spirit within Israel. A similar promise of the Spirit given to Israel at the same time was given in Joel 2.28-30, which Peter quoted as fulfilled in Ac. 2.15-17:

> For these are not drunken, as ye suppose; seeing it is but the third hour of the day. but this is that which hath been spoken through the prophet Joel: And it shall be in the last days, saith God, I will pour forth of my Spirit upon all flesh: And your sons and your daughters shall prophesy, And your young men shall see visions, And your old men shall dream dreams: Yea and on my servants and on my handmaidens in those days Will I pour forth of my Spirit; and they shall prophesy.

Both Ezekiel and Joel promised to Israel the coming of the Spirit. The gifts of the spirit in Acts 2 and I Corinthians were the result of those promises to Israel.

**vv15-23 - The Restoration of Old Covenant Israel**

In vv16ff, Ezekiel is told to take two sticks, label one for Ephraim (representing the Northern kingdom) and one for Judah (representing the Southern kingdom), and make them one stick to represent the reuniting of the two kingdoms in the Messiah's time.

**vv24-28 - The Messianic Hope of Israel**

In v24, God speaks of the Messiah, the son of David:

> 24 "And My servant David will be king over them, and they will all have one shepherd; and they will walk in My ordinances, and keep My statutes, and observe them. 25 "And they shall live on the land that I gave to Jacob My servant, in which your fathers lived; and they will live on it, they, and their sons, and their sons' sons, forever; and David My servant shall be their prince forever. 26 "And I will make a covenant of peace with them; it will be an everlasting covenant with them. And I will place them and multiply them, and will set My sanctuary in their midst forever. 27 "My dwelling place also will be with them; and I will be their God, and they will be My people.

So again, the resurrection of Old Covenant Israel would take place at the time of the Messiah's new, everlasting covenant. In II Cor. 6.16, Paul quotes this passage as fulfilled in his time. Thus, all three sections of Ezekiel 37 establish the time of the resurrection as the first century, in Old Covenant Israel's last days.

## Daniel's Teaching about the Time

The short chapter of Daniel 12 has a great deal of information about the resurrection. In v1, we have:

> Now at that time Michael, the great prince who stands guard over the sons of your people, will arise. And there will be a time of distress such as never occurred since there was a nation until that time; and at that time your people, everyone who is found written in the book, will be rescued.

"At that time" refers to the time of 11.40-45, where the prince of the Roman empire enters the Beautiful Land, Palestine, and pitches the tents of his royal pavilion between the seas and the beautiful Holy Mountain, i.e., the time when Rome had invaded Palestine to besiege Jerusalem.

The phrase depicting "a time of distress such as never occurred since there was a nation until that time" is quoted directly by Jesus himself in Mt. 24.21 as about to be fulfilled in his generation:

> ...for then shall be great tribulation, such as hath not been from the beginning of the world until now, no, nor ever shall be.

In v2, Daniel is told:

> And many of those who sleep in the dust of the ground will awake, these to everlasting life, but the others to disgrace and everlasting contempt.

Notice that at the time of the unique distress, which Jesus himself tied to the destruction of Jerusalem by Titus, is also the time of the resurrection including both the righteous and unrighteous. In v3, Daniel says concerning the righteous:

> And those who have insight will shine brightly like the brightness of the expanse of heaven, and those who lead the many to righteousness, like the stars forever and ever.

This verse is quoted by Jesus in Mt. 13.38-43 as he explains the parable of the tares to his disciples:

> ...the tares are the sons of the evil one; 39 and the enemy who sowed them is the devil, and *the harvest is the end of the age*; and the reapers are angels. 40 Therefore just as the tares are gathered up and burned with fire, so shall it be at the end of the age. 41 The Son of Man will send forth His angels, and they will gather out of His kingdom all stumbling blocks, and those who commit lawlessness, 42 and will cast them into the furnace of fire; in that place there shall be weeping and gnashing of teeth. 43 Then the righteous will shine forth as the sun in the kingdom of their Father. He who has ears, let him hear.

Note that our savior said "the harvest is the end of the age," i.e., the Mosaic age, when Jerusalem and the temple were destroyed, also the time of the resurrection, per Dan. 12.3.

Then Daniel is told in v4:

> But as for you, Daniel, conceal these words and seal up the book until the end of time; many will go back and forth, and knowledge will increase.

We established in chapter 1 that the Bible nowhere uses the expression "end of time," and that includes this verse, where the NASB mistakenly translates the term "end of time." As the KJV, NKJV, ASV and others translate it, it should be "the time of the end," an entirely different concept. Time of the end correctly refers to the end of the Mosaic age, while the end of time refers to the termination of time itself.

Daniel is told to seal up the book because its fulfillment is far off, approximately 500 years in the future. In vv5-6, Daniel asked the men in the vision when these things would occur, and in v7, the answer was given:

> And I heard the man dressed in linen, who was above the waters of the river, as he raised his right hand and his left toward heaven, and swore by Him who lives forever that it would be for a time, times, and half a time; and *as soon as they finish shattering the power of the holy people, all these events will be completed.*

Only Daniel and Revelation use the expression "time, times, and half a time," and in both cases, it refers to the time of persecution by rebellious Jews of Christians in the first century church. Note that Daniel is told, that *all* [NOTE: not some, not most, but all] these events of Daniel 12 would be fulfilled. This includes the unique distress (v1), the resurrection (v2), the judgment (v2), the insightful shining brightly (v3), "as soon as they finish shattering the power of the holy people," which refers to the destruction of the temple in Jerusalem. Daniel then says in v8:

> 8 As for me, I heard but could not understand; so I said, "My lord, what will be the outcome of these events?" 9 And he said, "Go your way, Daniel, for these words are concealed and sealed up until the end time.

Again, the time of the end, 500 years in the future. Further, in v13 Daniel is told:

> But as for you, go your way to the end; *then you will enter into rest and rise again for your allotted portion at the end of the age.*

Thus Daniel is explicitly promised he will rise again at the end of the age, the Mosaic age.

Summarizing the Old Testament's teaching on the time of the resurrection thus far, we see it's in Old Covenant Israel's last days, when the Spirit is poured out, when Israel is reunited under the Messiah, when the Roman prince is encamped in Palestine, at Israel's unique time of distress, and at the end of the Mosaic age, when Jerusalem and the temple were destroyed.

We'll have a little more to say about the Old Testament's teaching on the time of the resurrection in Isaiah and Hosea in the following chapter.

## New Testament Teaching on the Time of the Resurrection

In Ac. 24.14-15, Paul said to Felix, the governor of Judea:

> 14 But this I confess unto thee, that after the Way which they call a sect, so serve I the God of our

fathers, believing all things which are according to the law, and which are written in the prophets; 15 having hope toward God, which these also themselves look for, that there shall be (lit., *about to be*) a resurrection both of the just and unjust.

The only other passage in the Bible that speaks of the resurrection of the just and unjust is Dan. 12.2, which we've just seen was going to occur at the end of the Mosaic age, shortly after Paul made his defense to Felix in the early 60s AD.

To King Agrippa, Paul said in Ac. 26.6-8:

6 And now I stand here to be judged for the hope of the promise made of God unto our fathers; 7 unto which promise our twelve tribes, earnestly serving God night and day, hope to attain. And concerning this hope I am accused by the Jews, O king! 8 Why is it judged incredible with you, if God doth raise the dead?

We've seen the promise of the resurrection made to Paul's Jewish fathers in Ezekiel 37 and Daniel 12, a resurrection that would take place when the Spirit had been poured out, and in their last days, at the end of the Mosaic age.

The next time indicator we notice is in I Cor. 15.20:

But now hath Christ been raised from the dead, the *firstfruits* of them that are asleep.

The terms firstfruits is an agricultural term used in the Old Testament. At harvest time, God instructed the Jews to present the firstfruits of a crop to him, then he would allow them to have the rest of the harvest, the harvest of that same crop, not a crop 2000+ years later, as a harvest or resurrection in our future would be. Again, in I Cor. 15.23, Paul refers to the firstfruits again:

But each in his own order: Christ the firstfruits; then they that are Christ's, at his coming.

Here, Paul refers to the rest of the harvest would occur at Christ's coming, which we saw in Chapter 2 was stated to be in Jesus' own generation, at the end of the age, the Mosaic age.

The next time indication of the resurrection is found in I Cor. 15.34:

> Then cometh the end, when he shall deliver up the kingdom to God, even the Father; when he shall have abolished all rule and all authority and power.

The "end" referred to isn't the end of time nor the end of the Christian age, which has no end, but again to the end of the Mosaic age. Likewise, in Mt. 24.3, we're told:

> And as he sat on the mount of Olives, the disciples came unto him privately, saying, Tell us, when shall these things be? and what shall be the sign of thy coming, and of the end of the world (lit., age)?

When? At the end of the age, in his generation, Mt. 24.34.

In I Pet. 4.7, Peter, writing very near the end of the Mosaic age, probably even later than Revelation was written, said:

> But the end of all things is at hand: be ye therefore of sound mind, and be sober unto prayer:

The end of all things was the end of everything foretold in Moses and the prophets as seen in Mt. 5.17-18, Rev. 10.7, and Lk. 21.20-22, where Jesus said, in speaking of the destruction of Jerusalem:

> 20 But when ye see Jerusalem compassed with armies, then know that her desolation is at hand. 21 Then let them that are in Judaea flee unto the mountains; and let them that are in the midst of her depart out; and let not them that are in the country enter therein. 22 For these are days of vengeance, that all things which are written may be fulfilled.

Peter said the end of all things was at hand, within their reach. In I Jn. 2.18, John refers to the same event when he says:

> Little children, it is the last hour: and as ye heard that antichrist cometh, even now have there arisen many antichrists; whereby we know that it is the last hour.

The last hour also refers to the end of the Mosaic age, which had an end, a last day, and last days. The Messianic age, which has no end (Isa. 9.6-7, Lk. 1.33), has none of those.

The last New Testament passage giving an indication of the time of the resurrection is Rev. 20.11-12, where John says:

11 And I saw a great white throne, and him that sat upon it, from whose face the earth and the heaven fled away; and there was found no place for them. 12 And I saw the dead, the great and the small, standing before the throne; and books were opened: and another book was opened, which is the book of life: and the dead were judged out of the things which were written in the books, according to their works.

The earth and the heaven that fled away preceding the resurrection and judgment, was not the passing of the planet and stars, but to the passing of the Mosaic age, as we saw in the previous chapter in our study of II Peter 3.

Having seen that the judgment of Rev. 20.11 is of Old Covenant Israel, the old heavens and earth, we now see the same judgment in v12.

**Verses 12: And I saw the dead, the great and the small, standing before the throne; and books were opened: and another book was opened, which is the book of life; and the dead were judged out of the things which were written in the books, according to their works.**

At the passing of the old heavens and earth, the destruction of the Mosaic order at the destruction of Jerusalem, we now see the dead standing! Obviously, they've been raised for judgment. Jesus had foretold this judgment in the Olivet Discourse, as well as his prior teaching in the gospels, and subsequently in Acts through Revelation.

As we just saw in our discussion of II Peter 3 in the previous chapter, as well as I Corinthians 15 in the introductory chapter, John's teaching is completely in harmony with Peter's and Paul's as they all have the resurrection and judgment occurring at the passing of Old Covenant Israel.

Thus Revelation 20 is patently about the fulfillment of Daniel 12, that predicted the resurrection, i.e. the judgment of the dead, at the end of the Mosaic age, the rewarding of the prophets, when the power of the holy people would be completely shattered. Virtually every element of Daniel 12 is in Revelation 20.

This judgment is also the one foretold in Mt. 16.27-28, where Christ spoke of his return and judgment in the lifetime of his disciples, one of whom was John, the author of Revelation. It's also the coming and judgment in Jesus' generation of Matthew 24-25.

Thus Mt. 16.27-28, Matthew 24-25, II Peter 3, and Revelation 20 all speak of the same coming of Jesus and judgment in the first century.

## Since the Resurrection was Foretold in the Old Testament, It Had to Occur by the Time of the Destruction of Jerusalem

One last observation we wish to make to establish the time of the resurrection is this: if the resurrection was foretold in the Old Testament, it had to be fulfilled by the destruction of Jerusalem. In Mt. 5.17-18, Jesus said:

> 17 Think not that I came to destroy the law or the prophets: I came not to destroy, but to fulfil. 18 For verily I say unto you, Till heaven and earth pass away, one jot or one tittle shall in no wise pass away from the law, till all things be accomplished.

Does this statement not teach that none of the law and the prophets would pass away before heaven and earth passed away? Yet we all believe that the Mosaic Law has passed away. All futurist eschatologies (premillennial, postmillennial, and amillennial) believe at least some of the Mosaic Law has passed away. If we believe that any of the Mosaic Law has passed away, we must believe that all things foretold in the Old Covenant have been fulfilled.

We should also note in I Cor. 15.54-55, that Paul concludes his chapter on the resurrection by quoting from Isa. 25.8 and Hos. 13.14, saying that at the resurrection, those two passages would be fulfilled! Realizing that fact is what demanded that the author take another look at the time of the resurrection. If Jesus knew what he was talking about in Mt. 5.17-18, those prophecies had to be fulfilled and the resurrection had to take place before one molecule of the law of Moses could pass away.

> 54 But when this corruptible shall have put on incorruption, and this mortal shall have put on immortality, then shall come to pass the saying that is written, Death is swallowed up in victory. 55 O death, where is thy victory? O death, where is thy sting?

We'll have more to say about those passages in the next chapter on the nature of the resurrection.

# Chapter 9

# The Resurrection—of Biological Bodies?

## Roman Catholic Teaching

From the *Catechism of the Catholic Church we have:*

> 990 The term "flesh" refers to man in his state of weakness and mortality.536 The "resurrection of the flesh" (the literal formulation of the Apostles' Creed) means not only that the immortal soul will live on after death, but that even our "mortal body" will come to life again.537

Thus, the Roman Catholicism teaches that the resurrection will be one of fleshly or biological bodies. Sadly, this is not the teaching of the Bible.

## Bible Teaching

Simply put, the Bible teaches what most of us, including Roman Catholics, tacitly believe in this sense, that the resurrection is the remedy for our death, and Adam's in the Garden. Most of us think that was biological death, but we've already seen in Chapter 4 that biological death was not punishment for, nor a consequence of sin, Adam's or anyone else's. Thus, this chapter investigates the nature of the resurrection.

## Nature of the Resurrection Foretold in the Old Testament

We closed the previous chapter by noticing that Paul concluded his material on the resurrection in I Cor. 15.54-55 by quoting from Isa. 25.8 and Hos. 13.14, saying those prophecies would be fulfilled at the resurrection. We begin our study on the nature of the resurrection that took place at the destruction of Jerusalem by looking closer at Hos. 13.14:

> Shall I ransom them from the power of Sheol?
> Shall I redeem them from death?
> O Death, where are your thorns?
> O Sheol, where is your sting?
> Compassion will be hidden from My sight.

Sheol is the Hebrew equivalent of the Greek Hades, meaning unseen. This verse that Paul quotes in his discussion of resurrection says that it's concerned with redemption of man's spirit from Hades or Sheol, i.e., it's apparently a spiritual resurrection, not a biological one. In Hos. 13.1-2, we see the context of the death Hosea and Paul were speaking of:

> 1 When Ephraim spoke, there was trembling.
> He exalted himself in Israel,
> *But through Baal he did wrong and died.*
> *2 And now they sin more and more,*
> And make for themselves molten images,
> Idols skillfully made from their silver,
> All of them the work of craftsmen.
> They say of them, "Let the men who sacrifice kiss the calves!"

Note the sin that the northern kingdom committed that caused their death—"through Baal he did wrong and died, and now they sin more and more." Could this possibly be biological death? Do people who die biologically *ever* sin more and more? This is spiritual death in this context, isn't it?

What death do you think Paul had in mind when he quoted from Hosea 13? If he wasn't speaking of spiritual death, he was misusing the passage, was he not? Hosea certainly wasn't speaking of biological death, when the dead ones kept sinning more and more.

Many passages in Acts tell us that Paul went into the synagogues every sabbath and persuaded the Jews from the scriptures (Ac. 14.19, 17.4, 18.4, 19.26, etc.). What would have happened had they asked, "Paul, how can you give meanings to Hosea, Daniel, Isaiah, Ezekiel, etc., that they simply did not give us?" Had Paul responded, "The Holy Spirit gave me this fresher, fuller meaning that isn't in the prophets!" do you think his Jewish audience would have accepted Paul's new teaching? Of course not. They would have sent him down the road or killed him.

We'll see momentarily that Paul told the Jews on the resurrection that he taught nothing but what Moses and the prophets said would come to pass. *Nothing.* How could he have said that if he was giving newer revelation on the resurrection than was contained in their Old Testament scriptures?

Until we realize how Paul and the Berean Jews used the Old Testament scriptures, we can't understand the chapter like Paul did, and we won't teach on the subject like Paul did. That's the purpose of this essay, to show the Old Testament background of Paul's teaching on the hope of Israel and the resurrection.

In Ezekiel 37, the resurrection of the whole house of Israel wasn't biological, but spiritual, brought about by God putting the Spirit back into them.

In Daniel 12, the resurrection following the unique distress (quoted by Jesus and applied to the destruction of Jerusalem) certainly wasn't biological, but spiritual, as it was fulfilled at the end of the Mosaic age. Likewise, Daniel's resurrection at the end of the age wasn't biological, but spiritual.

Thus, the Old Testament's teaching on the nature of the resurrection was spiritual, not biological bodies out of holes in the ground:

## Nature of the Resurrection Foretold in the New Testament

In I Cor. 15.21-22, Paul says:

> 21 For since by man came death, by man came also the resurrection of the dead. 22 For as in Adam all die, so also in Christ shall all be made alive.

As we saw in Chapter 4, Adam didn't die biologically the day he sinned, but spiritually; he lost his fellowship with God. Adam didn't bring physical death; he was created mortal; if he didn't eat, he died, and he wasn't even the first person to die, Abel was, yet Paul didn't say that "in Abel all die." Likewise, we descendants of Adam don't die biologically because of Adam's sin, but we die spiritually like Adam did the day he sinned, when that very day he was humiliated, estranged, condemned, and banished. Paul affirms that in the same manner that all die like Adam, in Christ we are made alive, spiritually, not biologically.

In Rom. 5.12, Paul said:

> Therefore, as through one man sin entered into the world, and death through sin; and so death passed unto all men, for that all sinned:

Thus, spiritual death doesn't pass to all men because one man sinned, but because all men sin. Back in I Cor. 15.22, Paul affirms that Christ's resurrection was the sign that his death remedied Adam's spiritual death. Each of us makes the same choice to sin that Adam did.

In Rom. 6.23, Paul taught that the wages of sin is death. If this is physical death, and we're forgiven, why do we still die physically? What more needs to be paid than what Christ paid, if physical death is the subject? What did Christ accomplish if he paid for our sins, yet we still pay our own way? What kind of substitutionary death is that? Why do we still have to pay our own wages by dying physically if Christ paid for our sins? The answer, of course, is that Paul didn't speak of physical death, but the death we suffer like Adam did: spiritual death, the death of his fellowship with God the day he ate of the forbidden tree.

Notice also that Christ was the first to be raised from the dead. In Paul's eschatology, he was. However, Christ wasn't the first to be raised from biological death. Lazarus (along with others both in the Old and New Testaments) was raised from biological death before Christ was, so this isn't speaking of Christ's physical resurrection.

Someone may say, "Yes, but Jesus was the first one to be raised from the dead never to go back again!" To which we say, "Yes, *but is that what Paul said?* Or, did he say Christ was the firstfruits from the dead?" Did Paul say "never to go back again"? Also, Lazarus wasn't raised from the death of Adam four days after he died biologically. Christ was the first to be raised from the death of Adam.

Paul's point was that the resurrection under discussion solved the problem Adam brought upon himself. Adam's biological death was never the problem, or curse for sin, nor was the problem restoration from physical death. Adam, not being created immortal, was destined to die physically before he was created. The real problem was Adam's spiritual death, and being restored from it.

The resurrection of Israel at the destruction of her temple evidently was not a cataclysmic physical event either, but a spiritual event that reversed the spiritual death experienced by Adam. Like Adam's death was an opening of his eyes to the death of his fellowship with God, Paul said the resurrection of I Cor. 15.51 was similar:

> Behold, I tell you a mystery. We shall not all sleep, but
> we shall all be changed in a moment, in the twinkling
> of an eye, at the last trump.

That is, at the resurrection, the Old Covenant faithful would be taken from the "unseen" Hadean state into the presence of Christ in the twinkling of an eye. They would, as a body, in this eye-opening experience, be restored to the relationship Adam had with God before his fellowship was broken. They would be in the presence of Christ himself.

Then after the resurrection of spiritual Israelites at the destruction of Jerusalem, Christians who die physically, don't go to a Hadean warehouse to wait for a massive simultaneous judgment, but straight to their heavenly reward, Rev. 14.13, another spiritual event. This means you and I, and our loved ones, go straight to be with Christ when we die if we've lived a faithful life—no warehousing for thousands of years. Truly a message of Good News! As John heard:

> And I heard the voice from heaven saying, Write,
> *Blessed* [lit., happy] are the dead who die in the Lord
> from henceforth: yea, saith the Spirit, that they may
> *rest* from their labors; for their works follow with
> them.

Thus, ever since the resurrection of Israel at the destruction of Jerusalem and its temple, saints are not raised from physical death, but go to be with Christ at death, where they receive happiness and rest.

I Cor. 15.35ff contains some extremely revealing teaching concerning the nature of the resurrection body:

> But some one will say, How are the dead raised? and
> with what manner of body do they come?

When we read or discuss I Corinthians 15, we usually speak of "bodies" coming from holes in the ground. Second, we often read, "And with what kind of body do they come?" and wonder: Will they have broken bodies, aborted bodies, drowned bodies, mangled bodies, baby bodies, or wrinkled bodies? Since circumcision was such an important issue in the New Testament, will they be circumcised or uncircumcised bodies? Will they be male and female bodies? Will some be the bodies of amputees? Do you notice the shift we make from "body" to "bodies"? Paul said "body," and we think "bodies."

Paul never used "bodies" in this chapter. He spoke of the resurrection of one body, the Old Covenant faithful who were being transformed into the body of Christ. The question had to do with how Jewish and Gentile saints were going to be in that one body, along with Old Covenant saints who didn't even see or obey Christ. Paul had already said that those who deny the resurrection of the Old Testament dead ones must also deny the resurrection of Christ. Christ died for them because of promises made to the fathers, yet some in the Paul Party denied the resurrection of those for whom Christ died according to promise.

Literally, "the dead ones," is plural, while "body" is singular. "They" are in a single body. Paul did not speak of "bodies" coming out of holes in the ground, but of "the body" of Old Testament saints.

NOTE: As Paul said, his words were based on prophecies by Ezekiel, Isaiah, Hosea, and Daniel about a coming resurrection of Israel. Notice that Paul never uses the word "bodies" in the entire chapter, but he speaks of one body being raised.

In I Cor. 15.36, Paul says:

> Thou foolish one, that which thou thyself sowest is not
> quickened except it die:

NOTE: The sequence Paul gave was sowing, dying, and then rising. Jesus gave the same sequence in Jn. 12.24:

> Verily, verily, I say unto you, Except a grain of wheat
> fall into the earth and die, it abideth by itself alone; but
> if it die, it beareth much fruit.

The teaching of neither Jesus' nor Paul's teaching fits physical death, burial, and resurrection, does it? Is that what we do, sow someone in the ground, then he dies, and then he rises? Do we really sow someone before he dies? Is that what's going to happen to you? Jesus speaks of a seed being planted in the earth and dying, then much fruit arises. Paul illustrates sowing a live seed, then a death, and then rising. We've read Paul for years and thought death, then burial, and then rising. Certainly, I'd be nervous if anyone around me couldn't see that difference when I'm near death! I want to be dead before I'm buried!

This is like someone preparing to shoot a pistol whose plan is "Ready, fire, aim!" We wouldn't want to stand close by, would we, if he knew no more about shooting than that! Something is seriously wrong with his concept! How long have we read this verse without noticing it's not speaking of physical death, burial, and resurrection? It doesn't make me proud, either. We've been taught this for so long, our minds just automatically flip the order to death before burial.

In I Cor. 15.54, Paul says:

> But *when* this corruptible shall have put on incorruption, and this mortal shall have put on immortality, *then* shall come to pass the saying that is written, [lit., the] Death is swallowed up in victory.

Paul said this is *when* death (spiritual death suffered by Adam) was swallowed up in victory, a direct quotation from Isa. 25.8:

> He will swallow up death for all time, And the Lord GOD will wipe tears away from all faces, And He will remove the reproach of His people from all the earth; For the LORD has spoken.

Thus, it happened *when* Isaiah 25.8 was fulfilled, which Paul quoted. No serious student of the prophets believes a physical resurrection of a physical body is depicted in Isaiah 25. Yet, ignoring the significance of Paul's quotation of this verse in I Corinthians 15, we think it's a physical resurrection out of the dirt, although we can't read that interpretation back into Isaiah. If we do, remember Paul asserted that he didn't preach anything except what Moses and the prophets taught on the subject; but popularly, we make him do the very thing he denied. In actuality, Paul gave an inspired interpretation of these prophets on the hope of Israel.

If we let Isaiah define the death in Isa. 26.19, we'll know what death Paul taught:

> Your dead shall arise. Your dead will live; *Their corpses will rise.* You who lie in the dust, awake and

shout for joy, For your dew is as the dew of the dawn,
And the earth will give birth to the departed spirits.

The resurrection of those lying in the dust sounds identical to Dan.
12.2:

And many of those who sleep in the dust of the ground
will awake, these to everlasting life, but the others to
disgrace and everlasting contempt.

In Daniel 12, Daniel was told in v5 that the fulfillment would be
*when the power of the holy people was completely shattered*, and in
v12 that it would occur at the time *when the abomination of desolation
would be set up and the regular sacrifice is abolished*. Most of us
know Jesus referred to this same prophecy in Matthew 24, and said it
would occur in his generation. It couldn't possibly be any later than
that, as there has been no regular sacrifice, no priesthood, nor temple
since the Romans destroyed Jerusalem! Paul wrote of the present
fulfillment of the same in his lifetime in the Corinthian letter.

While no one takes Daniel 12 as a resurrection of physical bodies,
we often take Paul's teaching in I Corinthians 15 as a biological
resurrection *still in our future*. We cannot read it back into the
prophets, whose teaching Paul said was the only thing he preached.

Dispensational premillennialists, who also believe the second
coming of Christ is still future, at "the end of time" (a phrase nowhere
found in the Bible), work feverishly to see the Al Aqsa Mosque
demolished on the temple mount in modern Jerusalem, so they can
build the third temple. They also strive to restore the Levitical
priesthood (*sans* genealogies, which the Romans destroyed, so that no
Jew today knows his lineage). They train young men, they suppose to
be Levites, along with craftsmen to build the temple utensils and sew
Levitical garments. Herdsmen genetically breed red heifers to use in
their temple worship as they prepare to offer animal sacrifices all over
again. They do this *all because they don't believe the resurrection of
Israel took place when Daniel said it would*. (For more detail on these
efforts, please see seven chapters on dispensational premillennialism in
the author's *Essays on Eschatology: An Introductory Overview of the
Study of Last Things*.

Amillennial futurists of the author's background in churches of
Christ have nothing to do with these activities, which they rightly
abhor. However, they base their view of I Corinthians 15 on the same
futurism as dispensationalism. Sam Frost, in *Misplaced Hope,* shows

conclusively that historically, from just before the destruction of Jerusalem until about AD 125, the belief prevailed that the coming of Christ, the judgment, and the resurrection, were to occur imminently. The futurist view of all three of these events began to take hold down through Roman Catholicism to our present time.

In verse 21 (of Isaiah 26), Isaiah said:

> For behold, the LORD is about to come out from His place to punish the inhabitants of the earth for their iniquity; And the earth will reveal her bloodshed, And will no longer cover her slain.

Did Jesus give us a time when the blood of the martyrs was going to be avenged? In Mt. 23.34-36, he said:

> Therefore, behold, I send unto you prophets, and wise men, and scribes: some of them shall ye kill and crucify; and some of them shall ye scourge in your synagogues, and persecute from city to city: that *upon you may come all the righteous blood shed on the earth,* from the blood of Abel the righteous unto the blood of Zachariah son of Barachiah, whom ye slew between the sanctuary and the altar. Verily I say unto you, *All these things shall come upon this generation.*

"Earth" (*ge*) is more properly translated "land." It can easily mean soil, country, region, or a part or whole of the planet. The context usually indicates how it should be translated. When we read of a seed falling into the *ge*, it denotes soil. When it is used of the *ge* of Israel, it's the land promised to Abraham.

Thus, the time of the avenging of the blood of the martyrs is the time of the resurrection that Isaiah, Daniel, Ezekiel (chapter 37), and Paul all spoke of.

Speaking of the resurrection as the restoration of Israel at the last trump at the same time in Isa. 27.12-13, Isaiah said:

> And it will come about in that day, that the LORD will start His threshing from the flowing stream of the Euphrates to the brook of Egypt; and you will be *gathered up* one by one, O sons of Israel. It will come about also in that day that a *great trumpet will be blown;* and those who were perishing in the land of Assyria and who were scattered in the land of Egypt

will come and worship the LORD in the holy mountain at Jerusalem.

This served as the basis in the prophets for what Jesus said in Mt. 24.31 about sending out his angels to gather his elect (faithful Israel, including all the Old Testament saints, along with first-century Jewish and Gentile Christians) from the four winds of the earth in his generation. In Paul's view, Israel was the focus of his (and of Moses and the prophets) concept of the resurrection.

The words "when" and "then" reveal an important time statement. They connect with verses 23-24, where Paul spoke of *the end* at Christ's *coming* (in his generation), with verse 52, the time of *the last trump*, and with when Isaiah 25 and Hosea 13 were to be fulfilled. However, neither Isaiah nor Hosea spoke of physical death. Certainly, if Paul taught the resurrection of physical bodies, he misused Hosea and Isaiah while he claimed to preach only what Moses and the prophets said on the hope of Israel. He didn't change the definition of death, nor resurrection, which those prophecies focused on. If Paul changed those concepts, we can't believe one syllable of the Bible; and we can make it teach absolutely anything we want.

Thus, at the last trump, which Jesus said would occur in his generation (Mt. 24.31, 34), death, Adam's spiritual death, was completely defeated by the resurrection.

So Isaiah, Hosea, Ezekiel, and Daniel (and others) spoke of a resurrection and judgment of Israel. Hardly any scholar on earth takes these words as teaching resurrection of physical bodies, as we think Paul taught in I Corinthians 15. In context, Israel was dead, destroyed, and went into captivity because of their sin. If Israel were going to be saved, there needed to be a resurrection, which would occur when God destroyed Jerusalem, when he redeemed the righteous from death, and destroyed the impenitent when he shattered the power of the holy people.

# Chapter 10

# Eternal Conscious Torment in Hell at the End of Time?

*"Don't you know that hell is just something the Catholic Church invented to scare people into obedience?"*

I was righteously indignant when, a number of years ago, a caller uttered these words on a call-in radio show I was conducting. Perturbed by his haphazard use of Scripture, I pointed out to him and the audience, that hell couldn't possibly be something invented by Catholic theologians because Jesus talked about it. I forcefully read some of the passages where Jesus did, and concluded that hell couldn't possibly be the invention of an apostate church.

I now believe that hell is the invention of Roman Catholicism; and surprisingly, most, if not all, of our popular concepts of hell can be found in the writings of Roman Catholic writers like the Italian poet Dante Alighieri (1265-1321), author of *Dante's Inferno.* The English poet John Milton (1608-1674), author of *Paradise Lost,* set forth the same concepts in a fashion highly acceptable to the Roman Catholic faith. *Yet none of our concepts of hell can be found in the teaching of Jesus Christ!* We get indignant at the mention of purgatory—we know that's not in the Bible. We may also find that our popular concepts of hell came from the same place that purgatory did—Roman Catholicism. The purpose of this study is to briefly analyze Jesus' teaching on hell (more correctly *Gehenna,* the Greek word for which hell is given), to see whether these popular concepts are grounded therein.

## Roman Catholic Teaching on Hell

Section 1035 of the *Catechism of the Catholic Church* states

"The teaching of the Church affirms the existence of hell and its eternity. Immediately after death the souls of those who die in a state of mortal sin descend into hell, where they suffer the punishments of hell, 'eternal fire.' The chief punishment of hell is eternal separation from God, in whom alone man can possess the life and happiness for which he was created and for which he longs".

This is the commonly-held view of hell: eternal conscious torment in the spiritual realm, that is, without the physical body, since one is assigned her immediately after death, while his spirit is in his death bed. Is this Bible teaching?

## Hell vs. *Sheol* and *Hades*

We begin by eliminating the problem the King James Version of the Bible introduced to this study by indiscriminately supposedly translating three different words in the Bible as hell: *sheol, hades,* and *gehenna.*

Once we understand the origin of the King James Version, we'll know why the translation "hell" for all of these words, and that none of them should have been, or were, translated "hell." The King James translators are well known: all 48 of them were in the hierarchy of the Church of England, that part of the Roman Catholic Church that King Henry VIII confiscated from the Pope because the Pope wouldn't let him divorce his wife and marry Ann Boleyn. Hence the King James Version was essentially a Roman Catholic translation. Most of us wouldn't touch a translation with all the translators from the same denomination with a ten-foot pole. In this study, we'll see that the concept of hell was substituted for the Greek word Gehenna, which is what the Roman Catholic Church had done the previous century.

Hell, a theologically loaded word that carried with it the concept of eternal torment in the spiritual realm, was substituted for the proper name Gehenna, a word not meaning eternal conscious torment in the spiritual realm at all. Had it not been for such substitutions, none of us would have concluded that Jesus ever taught anything about eternal conscious torment in a spiritual state.

The Jews of Jesus' audience well knew of the destruction that had taken place there in 586 BC by the Babylonian Nebuchadnezzar. In Jesus' time, Gehenna was a proper name for a valley located on the South and East of Jerusalem. It didn't need translating any more than Bethlehem did, and it didn't mean hell any more than Bethlehem did.

Those scholars had a bad habit of that sort of thing. They translated *presbuteros* (elders) as *priests*, *pascha* (Passover) as *Easter* (once), and *baptizo* (dip, plunge, immerse) as *baptism* (to slip their sprinkling and pouring for baptism into the Bible), and substituted the "divine pronouns" (thee, thou, and thine) for us rather than translating consistently. In each case, they substituted theologically-loaded words for the originals.

To be fair, Catholics aren't the only ones to pull such stunts. In Ac. 8.20, where Peter said to Simon the sorcerer, "thy silver perish with thee," *Today's English Version* has him telling Simon to "go to hell." The word *hell* is not there in your Bible; the translators just substituted it, and that's just the point. *Hell's* not in any of them. It was just substituted for *Gehenna* in Bibles with Roman Catholic influence.

### Sheol, Hades, Used of Anything Unseen

We begin with the word *hades*, a word for which hell is given in the King James Version. Its root meaning is "unseen," which occurs only eleven times. The King James Version translates the word "hell." However, the correct translation is *hades*, or the unseen. The Bible doesn't use *hades* exclusively for a place of punishment. Luke 16 pictures righteous Lazarus there. Acts 2.27, 31 says Jesus went there. In I Cor. 15.15, Paul used the same word when he said, "O *grave*, where is thy victory?" In Rev. 1.18, Jesus said he had the controlling keys of death and *hades*, the unseen, and in Rev. 6.8, death and *hades* followed the pale horse. Finally, in Rev. 20.13, 14, death and *hades* gave up the dead that were in them, and were then cast into the lake of fire. These verses illustrate that *hades* refers to anything that is unseen.

*Hades*, a Greek word, and *Sheol*, a Hebrew word, are generally regarded as synonyms. This is confirmed in the *Septuagint*, the Greek translation of the Old Testament Hebrew Bible, where Sheol is translated as Hades.

W. E. Vine, in his *Expository Dictionary of Biblical Words* says:

> Hades corresponds to 'Sheol' in the OT and N.T., it has been unhappily rendered 'Hell.' It never denotes the grave, nor is it the permanent region of the lost; in

point of time it is, for such, intermediate between decease and the doom of Gehenna, the signification of the temporary destiny of the doomed." (pp. 517-518)

In the Old Testament, the word for which hell is given in the King James Version is *sheol.* The King James Version translates *sheol* as "hell" 31 times, "the grave" 31 times (since someone in the grave is unseen), and "the pit" three times.

Yet in the Old Testament *sheol* was not exclusively a place of punishment, for faithful Jacob was there (Gen. 37.35, 42.38, 44.29, 31). Righteous Job also longed for it in Job 14.13. David spoke of going to *sheol* in Ps. 49.15, and Jesus went there, Ps. 16.10 and Acts 2.24-31. In all these cases, these men were "unseen" because they were dead.

## *Sheol* Used of National Judgments

Many times the Bible uses the word *sheol* of national judgments, i.e., the vanishing of a nation. In Isa. 14.13-15, Isaiah said Babylon would go to *Sheol*, and she vanished. In Ezek. 26.19-21, Tyre so vanished in *sheol.* Likewise, in the New Testament, in Mt. 11.23, 12.41, Lk. 10.15, and 11.29-32, Jesus said that Capernaum would so disappear. These nations and cities didn't go to a particular location, but they were going to disappear, and they did. They were destroyed. Thus, *sheol* is used commonly of national judgments in both the Old and New Testaments.

## Hades Used of National Judgments

Like its companion word in the Old Testament, *hades* was also plainly used of national judgments in the New Testament. In Mt. 11.23 and Lk. 10.15, Jesus said Capernaum would go down into *hades,* i.e., it was going to vanish.

About *hades* in Greek mythology, Edward Fudge said:

In Greek mythology Hades was the god of the underworld, then the name of the nether world itself. Charon ferried the souls of the dead across the rivers Styx or Acheron into this abode, where the watchdog Cerberus guarded the gate so none might escape. The pagan myth contained all the elements for medieval eschatology: there was the pleasant Elyusium, the gloomy and miserable tartarus, and even the Plains of Asphodel, where ghosts could wander who were suited for

neither of the above...The word *hades* came into biblical usage when the Septuagint translators chose it to
represent the Hebrew *sheol,* an Old Testament concept
vastly different from the pagan Greek notions just out-
lined. *Sheol,* too, received all the dead...but the Old
Testament has no specific division there involving either punishment or reward. (Edward William Fudge,
*The Fire That Consumes* [Houston: Providential Press,
1982], p. 205.)

We need to make sure that our ideas concerning *hades* come from
the Bible and not Greek mythology. We have no problem using *sheol*
the way the Old Testament used it, or *hades* as the New Testament
used it. Both refer to the dead who are unseen, and to national judgments.

## Tartarus Is Also Translated *Hell* In the King James Version

In II Pet. 2.4, we read:

For if God spared not angels when they sinned, but
cast them down to hell, and committed them to pits of
darkness, to be reserved unto judgment;...

The Greek word translated "pits of darkness" here, the only time
it's used in the Bible, is *tartarus.* Again, the KJV gave us *hell* for free,
there being no reason to translate it so. The passages speak of angels
that were being punished when II Peter was written, to show that God
knew how to treat disobedience among angels. It says nothing about
fire, torment, pain, punishment of anyone else, or that it will last forever. It simply doesn't pertain to our subject.

# The Popular Concept of Hell Unknown to the Old Testament

Before we move to the gospel's teaching on hell, we want to think
further concerning that the word *gehenna* (popularly mistranslated hell,
as we'll see) didn't occur in the Greek Old Testament, the *Septuagint.*
Let's take a few paragraphs to let the significance of that fact soak in.
In previous editions of this material, I merely remarked that prominent
Old Testament characters like David and Abraham never heard the

term or its equivalent. They were never threatened with eternal torment in hell or heard anything like our popular concept now. However, *Gehenna's* absence in the Old Testament is a much more serious omission than that. It shows that the Jews of Jesus' time didn't associate Gehenna with or as being an other-worldly place! (The concepts in this section are suggested by Thomas B. Thayer in his 1855 Edition of *Origin and History of the Doctrine of Endless Punishment.)*

## Before the Mosaic Law

### Adam and Eve in the Garden

When God placed Adam and Eve in the Garden of Eden, he never mentioned the concept of eternal torment to them. Read for yourself–it's just not there. Don't you think it strange that as human history began on this planet, while God explained which tree they could not eat of, that he didn't give the parents of all mankind some kind of warning about eternal punishment, if there was potential for it to be in their future, and the future of all their posterity?

Most think eternal torment will engulf the vast majority of mankind, nearly all of Adam and Eve's descendents, yet here's a father, God, who didn't warn his children of the potential of what might befall them. What would you think of a father who told his young child not to ride his bike in the street, and if he did, he would get a spanking. Suppose he also planned to roast him over a roaring fire for fifty years? After he spanked him, would you think him a just father for not warning his child? Can you think of an apology or a defense for him? Yet to Adam and Eve, the father of all mankind failed to mention a much greater punishment than the death they would die the day they ate of the forbidden tree. Was this just a slip of the mind on God's part, to not mention at all the interminable terrible woes that lay ahead for the vast majority of their descendants? No, God announced to them a tangible present punishment the very day they committed the sin: "In the day thou eatest thereof thou shalt surely die." They found that the wages of sin was death.

### Cain and Abel

The same is true with Cain and Abel, a case of murder of a brother. Surely, we would think that God might roll out the threat of eternal torment that Cain was to receive as a warning to all future generations. In the whole account, there's not a hint, not a single word on the subject. Instead, Cain is told, "And now art thou cursed from the earth...When thou tillest the ground, it shall not henceforth yield unto thee her strength; a fugitive and a vagabond shalt thou be in the earth." Again, Cain received an immediate, tangible physical punishment administered, with absolutely no warning of future eternal torment. Like Adam, Cain heard none of the dire warnings preached from pulpits of the fiery wrath of God, tormenting his soul throughout eternity.

Now, if Cain were to receive such punishment from God without warning, would God be a just lawgiver and judge to impose additional, infinitely greater punishment with no word of caution whatsoever? In Gen. 4.15, God said, "Therefore, whosoever slayeth Cain, vengeance shall be taken on him seven-fold." If, with no warning, Cain was going to receive eternal fiery torment, would those who killed him receive seven times endless fiery torment?

I'm not making light of endless torment, I'm just pointing out that it's remarkable that God hadn't said a word about it thus far in the Bible story.

### Noah and the Flood

When we come to Noah and the flood, God noted that "every thought of man's heart was only evil continually," and that "the earth was filled with violence, and all flesh had corrupted his way upon the earth." If not before, wouldn't this be the ideal time to reveal eternal torment ahead for nearly all inhabitants of the earth? If any circumstances warranted such punishment, this would be the time, would it not? However, Noah, "a preacher of righteousness," didn't threaten endless punishment to evildoers. If warnings of such punishment serve to turn man aside from his evil way, surely this would have been the time to have revealed it, but there's nary a whisper of it. Instead, they were destroyed by the flood, a physical, tangible punishment for their sin, with absolutely no warning of endless torment. Nor was there such a warning when mankind inhabited the earth again after the flood. One word from God might have set the world on an entirely different course. Surprisingly no such word was given.

### Sodom and Gomorrah

We could go on with the story of Sodom and Gomorrah, the physical destruction of the cities and their inhabitants, with not even a rumor of endless future torment that we probably think they unknowingly faced. What would we think if our government passed a new law with a huge fine as the punishment, but when a guilty party was found, he paid the fine, but also had to serve endless torment that the citizens had no warning of? What kind of judge explains the law and known penalty, while carefully concealing a much more awful penalty? What would the penalty of a few thousand dollars matter in a case where he was also going to be tormented horribly and endlessly? Yet the popular concept is that the Sodomites were sent into such a judgment.

We could go through the accounts of the builders of the tower of Babel, the destruction of Pharoah and his armies, and Lot's wife, yet we would notice the same thing. All these received a temporal physical punishment, with no mention of an infinitely greater torturous punishment awaiting them in the future.

Was this teaching deliberately excluded from the record, or did it never belong? We know that it isn't there. Neither the word *gehenna* nor the concept of endless torment was given in the millennia before the giving of the Law of Moses. From the creation to Mt. Sinai, there was simply no insinuation of it in the entirety of human history up to that time. By the conclusion of this study, we'll see that God never had a plan of inflicting such dreadful torment on the people of his own creation.

## Under the Mosaic Law

Most of us are familiar with the blessings and cursings Moses pronounced upon the Israelites in Deuteronomy 28-30 before they entered the promised land. If the Jews were disobedient to God, he promised them every conceivable punishment: he would curse their children, their crops, their flocks, their health, the health of their children, the welfare of the nation, etc. He foretold that they would even go into captivity, and would have such horrible temporal physical judgments to drive them to eat their own children. Among such an extensive list of punishments that would come upon his disobedient people, God uttered not even a whisper of endless torment upon them in any case of rebellion. All these physical, temporal judgments would take place in this life.

We could multiply such cases of temporal punishments for rebellion, corruption, and idolatry under Moses. He spelled them out in minute detail. The writer of Hebrews (in 2.2) said: "...the word spoken through angels (the Mosaic Law) proved stedfast, and *every transgression and disobedience received a just recompense of reward...*" As we've seen, the punishment was physical and temporal with no promise of endless torment whatsoever. Endless torment was simply unknown under the Law.

The question now arises, did every transgressor and disobedient Jew receive just punishment, or not? If they did, will their punishment continue to be just if in the future, they will also receive endless torment in "hell" that they were never told of and knew nothing of? If so, will eternal torment on top of their just physical temporal punishment still be just? It cannot be, can it? How can adding infinite torture in the future that they knew nothing of to a just punishment they received in the past under the Old Testament still be just?

In summary, the popular concept of hell is not found anywhere in the Old Testament. The word *gehenna* is not even contained in the Greek Old Testament; endless conscious torment is nowhere to be found in its pages.

## Where Did the Concept of Endless Torment Originate?

As we've seen, it most certainly did not originate in the Old Testament, either before or during the Mosaic Law. A great deal of evidence (more than we'll give here) suggests that it originated in Egypt, and the concept was widespread in the religious world. Augustine, commenting on the purpose of such doctrines, said:

> This seems to have been done on no other account, but as it was the business of princes, out of their wisdom and civil prudence, to deceive the people in their religion; princes, under the name of religion, persuaded the people to believe those things true, which they themselves knew to be idle fables; by this means, for their own ease in government, tying them the more closely to civil society. (Augustine, *City of God, Book IV*, p. 32, cited by Thomas B. Thayer, *Origin & History of the Doctrine of Endless Punishment,* [Boston: Universalist Publishing House, 1855] p. 37)

Contriving doctrines to control people? Who would have believed it? Well, the Greek world did, the Roman world did, and evidently between the testaments, the Jews got involved, as well, as the concept of endless torment began appearing in the apocryphal books written by *Egyptian Jews.*

Thayer wrote further:

> Polybius, the historian, says: "Since the multitude is ever fickle, full of lawless desires, irrational passions and violence, there is no other way to keep them in or-

der but by the fear and terror of the invisible world; on which account our ancestors seem to me to have acted judiciously, when they contrived to bring into the popular belief these notions of the gods, and of the infernal regions. B. vi 56. .

Livy, the celebrated historian, speaks of it in the same spirit; and he praises the wisdom of Numa, because he invented the fear of the gods, as "a most efficacious means of governing an ignorant and barbarous populace. *Hist., I 19.*

Strabo, the geographer, says: "The multitude are restrained from vice by the punishments the gods are said to inflict upon offenders, and by those terrors and threatenings which certain dreadful words and monstrous forms imprint upon their minds...For it is impossible to govern the crowd of women, and all the common rabble, by philosophical reasoning, and lead them to piety, holiness and virtue-but this must be done by superstition, or the fear of the gods, by means of fables and wonders; for the thunder, the aegis, the trident, the torches (of the Furies), the dragons, &c., are all fables, as is also all the ancient theology. These things the legislators used as scarecrows to terrify the childish multitude." *Geog., B., I*

Timaeus Locrus, the Pythagorean, after stating that the doctrine of rewards and punishments after death is necessary to society, proceeds as follows: "For as we sometimes cure the body with unwholesome remedies, when such as are most wholesome produce no effect, so we restrain those minds with false relations, which will not be persuaded by the truth. There is a necessity, therefore, of instilling the dread of those *foreign* torments: as that the soul changes its habitation; that the coward is ignominiously thrust into the body of a woman; the murderer imprisoned within the form of a savage beast; the vain and inconstant changed into birds, and the slothful and ignorant into fishes."

Plato, in his commentary on Timaeus, fully endorses what he says respecting the fabulous invention of these foreign torments. And Strabo says that "Plato and the Brahmins of India invented fables concerning the future judgments of hell" (Hades). And Chrysippus blames Plato for attempting to deter men from wrong by frightful stories of future punishments.

Plutarch treats the subject in the same way; sometimes arguing for them with great solemnity and earnestness, and on other occasions calling them "fabulous stories, the tales of mothers and nurses."

Seneca says: "Those things which make the infernal regions terrible, the darkness, the prison, the river of flaming fire, the judgment seat, &c., are all a fable, with which the poets amuse themselves, and by them agitate us with vain terrors." *Sextus Empiricus* calls them "poetic fables of hell;" and *Cicero* speaks of them as "silly absurdities and fables" (*ineptiis ac fabulis*).

Aristotle. "It has been handed down in mythical form from earliest times to posterity, that there are gods, and that the divine (Deity) compasses all nature. All beside this has been added, after the mythical style, for the purpose of persuading the multitude, and for the interests of the laws, and the advantage of the state." *Neander's Church Hist.*, I, p. 7. (*Origin & History*, 41-43.)

Mosheim, in his legendary *Institutes of Ecclesiastical History,* described the permeation among the Jews of these fables during the period between the testaments:

Errors of a very pernicious kind, had infested the whole body of the people (the Jews—SGD). There prevailed among them several absurd and superstitious notions concerning the divine nature, invisible powers, magic, &c., which they had partly brought with them from the Babylonian captivity, and partly derived from the Egyptians, Syrians, and Arabians who lived in their neighborhood. The ancestors of those Jews who lived in the time of our Savior had brought from Chaldaea and the neighboring countries many extravagant and idle fancies which were utterly unknown to the original founders of the nation. The conquest of Asia by Alexander the Great was also an event from which we may date a new accession of errors to the Jewish system, since, in consequence of that revolution, the manners and opinions of the Greeks began to spread among the Jews. Beside this, in their voyages to Egypt and Phoenicia, they brought home, not only the wealth of these corrupt and superstitious nations, but also their pernicious errors and idle fables, which were imperceptibly blended with their own religious doctrines. (Mosheim's *Institutes of Ecclesiastical History,* Century I pt. I chap. ii.)

A similar statement is made in an old *Encyclopedia Americana,* cited by Thayer:

The Hebrews received their doctrine of demons from two sources. At the time of the Babylonish captivity, they derived it from the source of the Chaldaic-Persian magic; and afterward, during the Greek supremacy in Egypt, they were in close intercourse with these foreigners, particularly in Alexandria, and added to the magician notions those borrowed from this Egyptic-Grecian source. And this connection and mixture are seen chiefly in the New Testament. It was impossible to prevent the intermingling of Greek speculations. The voice of the prophets was silent. Study and inquiry had commenced. The popular belief and philosophy separated; and even the philosophers divided themselves into several sects, Sadducees, Pharisees, and Essenes; and Platonic and Pythagorean notions, intermingled with Oriental doctrines, had already unfolded the germ of the Hellenistic and cabalistic philosophy. This was the state of things when Christ appeared. [*Encyclopedia Americana,* art. "Demon, " cited by Thayer (*Origin & History,* p. 120].

Note that Luke wrote in Ac. 7.22 that "Moses was learned in all the wisdom of the Egyptians," yet knowing the Egyptian concepts, he gave not a whiff of endless torment in any of his writings.

Thus, we see that the concept of endless torment after life was not found in the Old Testament. It evidently crept in among some Jews during the period between the testaments.

Thayer summarizes the intertestamental period on this subject in the following words:

> The truth is, that in the four hundred years of their intercourse with the heathen, during which they were without any divine teacher of message, Pagan philosophy and superstition had, so far as regarded the future state, completely pushed aside the Law of Moses and the Scriptures of the Old Testament, and set up in place of them their own extravagant inventions and fables respecting the invisible world. (*Ibid.,* p. 53)

In the 16th century, Roman Catholicism substituted the word hell for Gehenna. Strangely, the word originally carried no connotation of eternal conscious torment in the spiritual realm. The word meant "a cover." Our word helmet came from this word, and farmers would use "a cover" over their potatoes to protect them from freezing in the winter.

## The First Use of *Gehenna*

Most of our modern translations no longer translate *hades* and *sheol* with the word "hell." Additionally, modern translations are no longer substituting the word "hell" for the proper noun Gehenna. We now want to examine the 12 passages where the remaining Greek word, *gehenna,* that is still commonly rendered "hell." (We will further discuss whether this is an appropriate translation near the end of this study.) As we look at these 12 passages, notice if the passage mentions anything about eternal conscious torment in the spiritual realm, or does that meaning occur to us because of the substitution of the theologically-loaded word hell that Roman Catholicism inserted to produce that very result? Notice the first occurrence of this word in the Bible in Mt. 5.21-22. In the Sermon on the Mount, Jesus said:

> Ye have heard that it was said to them of old time, Thou shalt not kill; and whosoever shall kill shall be in danger of the judgment: but I say unto you, that every one who is angry with his brother shall be in danger of the judgment; and whosoever shall say to his brother,

Raca, shall be in danger of the council; and whosoever
shall say, Thou fool, shall be in danger of the hell (*gehenna*—SGD) of fire.

When Jesus used the term "hell" in these verses, he actually used
the Greek word *gehenna* for the first time in inspired writing. Notice
carefully that Jesus didn't say what Gehenna was. He said nothing
about eternal conscious torment in the spiritual realm. He just said that
certain folks were in danger of the Gehenna of fire, which is what the
Jews and I understood: a fiery judgment coming on Jerusalem, whose
rubble would end up in Gehenna. Yet most of us, when reading these
verses, take those traditional concepts from it simply because the theologically-loaded word hell is there. It was loaded with concepts not
found in the word gehenna by our Roman Catholic friends.

Scholar Ed Stevens has said that "these twelve verses
demonstrated that gehenna refers primarily (if not exclusively) to
the place in the unseen spiritual realm where the souls of the un-
redeemed will be consciously punished forever." (*Fulfilled! Vol.
XI, No. 2,* Summer 2016 issue, pp. 10-11) It's very easy to see if
this claim is true. We'll just keep reading the twelve passages
and see if we see eternal conscious torment in the spiritual realm
in even a single one of them.

We want to begin with this first occurrence of *gehenna* and then
study all of its occurrences in the New Testament. In this way, we can
determine the totality of the Bible's teaching on what is now commonly called hell.

## The Message of John the Baptist and Jesus

To understand Jesus' first use of *gehenna* in the Sermon on the
Mount, we must first have his ministry, and that of his contemporary,
John the Baptist, in their proper contexts. We saw there that Malachi
prophesied the coming of John the Baptist, and that Jesus confirmed
that fulfillment by John. John's preaching consisted of announcements
of an imminent ("the axe lieth at the root of the tree") fiery judgment
on Israel if she didn't repent. This was the same fiery judgment of
which Malachi had spoken, and said that John would announce. With
this idea of imminent fiery judgment in the context, John continued in
Mt. 3.11-12:

> I indeed baptize you in water unto repentance: but he
> that cometh after me is mightier than I, whose shoes I
> am not worthy to bear: he shall baptize you in the Ho-
> ly Spirit and in fire: whose fan is in his hand, and he
> will thoroughly cleanse his threshing-floor; and he will
> gather his wheat into the garner, but the chaff he will
> burn up with unquenchable fire.

Al Maxey, a serious student of these matters, has noticed the following about the word translated "burn up" here:

> This is the Greek word *katakaio* which means "to burn
> up; consume." It signifies to completely, utterly, total-
> ly destroy with fire. It is enlightening, in the context of
> this study, to note that this word is used in the LXX
> (Septuagint) in Exodus 3:2 where Moses beholds a
> burning bush --- "The bush was burning with fire, yet
> the bush was NOT consumed. (Al Maxey, "The Con-
> suming Fire, Examining the Final Fate of the Wicked
> in Light of Biblical Language," *Reflections #46*, June
> 6, 2003.)

Hence John and Jesus said the wicked would be consumed with
unquenchable fire, yet we popularly read it to mean they will not be
consumed, thinking folks in hell will no more be consumed than the
burning bush was!

Remember this "unquenchable fire." It will figure in our study
throughout. It is the fire spoken of by Malachi, John, and Jesus.

## Old Testament Background of *Gehenna*

Gehenna, the word hell is given for (NOTE: I'm not saying "hell"
is a translation for Gehenna, for it's not, as we'll soon demonstrate) in
the New Testament, is rooted in an Old Testament location. It is generally regarded as derived from a valley nearby Jerusalem that originally
belonged to a man named Hinnom. Scholars say the word is a translit-
eration of the Valley of the Sons of Hinnom, a valley that had a long
history in the Old Testament, all of it bad. Hence, *Gehenna* is a proper
name like the Rio Grande Valley of Texas and New Mexico. This being true, the word should never have been translated "hell," for as we'll
see, the two words have nothing in common.

We first find Hinnom in Josh. 1.8 and 18.16, where he is mentioned in Joshua's layout of the lands of Judah and Benjamin. In II K. 23.10, we find that righteous King Josiah "defiled Topheth in the valley of the children of Hinnom, that no man might make his son or his daughter to pass through the fire to Molech." Josiah, in his purification of the land of Judah, violated the idolatrous worship to the idol Molech by tearing down the shrines. Topheth (also spelled Tophet) was a word meaning literally, "a place of burning." In II Chron. 28.3, idolatrous King Ahaz burnt incense and his children in the fire there, as did idolatrous King Manasseh in II Chron. 33.6. In Neh. 11.30, we find some settling in Topheth after the restoration of the Jewish captives from Babylon. In Jer. 19.2, 6, Jeremiah prophesied calamity coming upon the idolatrous Jews there, calling it the valley of slaughter, because God was going to slaughter the Jews there, using Nebuchadnezzar, King of Babylon. In Jer. 7.32, Jeremiah prophesied destruction coming upon the idolatrous Jews of his day with these words:

> Therefore, behold, the days come, saith the Lord, that
> it shall no more be called Tophet, nor the valley of the
> son of Hinnom, but the valley of slaughter; for they
> shall burn in Tophet, till there be no peace.

Notice the mention of Topheth, "the place of burning," again. Isaiah also spoke of Topheth this way in Isa. 30.33, when he warned the pro-Egypt party among the Jews (i.e., those trusting in Egypt for their salvation from Babylon rather than God) of a fiery judgment coming on them. In Jer. 19.11-14, Jeremiah gave this pronouncement of judgment by Babylon on Jerusalem at the valley of Hinnom:

> And the houses of Jerusalem, and the houses of the
> kings of Judah, shall be defiled as the place of Tophet,
> because of all the houses upon whose roofs they have
> burned incense unto all the host of heaven, and have
> poured out drink offerings unto other gods.

From these passages we can see that, to the Jews, the valley of Hinnom, or Topheth, from which the New Testament concept of *Gehenna* arose, came to mean a place of burning, a valley of slaughter, and a place of calamitous fiery judgment. Thus, Thayer in his *Greek-English Lexicon of the New Testament,* said, concerning *Gehenna:*

Gehenna, the name of a valley on the S. and E. of Jerusalem...which was so called from the cries of the little children who were thrown into the fiery arms of Moloch, i.e., of an idol having the form of a bull. The Jews so abhorred the place after these horrible sacrifices had been abolished by king Josiah (2 Kings xxiii.10), that they cast into it not only all manner of refuse, but even the dead bodies of animals and of unburied criminals who had been executed. And since fires were always needed to consume the dead bodies, that the air might not become tainted by the putrefaction, it came to pass that the place was called *Gehenna.*

Actually, since *Gehenna* was a proper name of a valley, it would have been called *Gehenna* whether or not any idolatry, burning, or dumping of garbage had ever occurred there, and it was, as we now see.

Fudge said concerning the history of the valley of Hinnom:

The valley bore this name at least as early as the writing of Joshua (Josh. 15:8; 18:16), though nothing is known of its origin. It was the site of child-sacrifices to Moloch in the days of Ahaz and Manasseh (apparently in 2 Kings 16:3; 21:6). This earned it the name "Topheth," a place to be spit on or abhorred. This "Topheth" may have become a gigantic pyre for burning corpses in the days of Hezekiah after God slew 185,000 Assyrian soldiers in a night and saved Jerusalem (Isa. 30:31-33; 37:26). Jeremiah predicted that it would be filled to overflowing with Israelite corpses when God judged them for their sins (Jer. 7:31-33; 19:2-13). Josephus indicates that the same valley was heaped with dead bodies of the Jews following the Roman siege of Jerusalem about A.D. 69-70...Josiah desecrated the repugnant valley as part of his godly reform (2 Kings 23:10). Long before the time of Jesus, the Valley of Hinnom had become crusted over with connotations of whatever is "condemned, useless, corrupt, and forever discarded." (Edward William Fudge, *The Fire That Consumes* [Houston: Providential Press, 1982], p. 160.)

We need to keep this place in mind as we read Jesus' teaching using a word referring back to this location in the Old Testament.

## The Twelve *Gehenna* Passages in Chronological Order

### Mt. 5.21-22

In Mt. 5.21-22, Jesus used *Gehenna* for the first time in inspired speech:

> Ye have heard that it was said to them of old time, Thou shalt not kill; and whosoever shall kill shall be in danger of the judgment: but I say unto you, that every one who is angry with his brother shall be in danger of the judgment, and whosoever shall say, Thou fool, shall be in danger of the hell (*Gehenna*—SGD) of fire.

As we mentioned earlier in our study of this passage, Jesus actually used the Greek word *Gehenna* for the first time in inspired writing. The word had never occurred in the Greek Old Testament, the *Septuagint*. When we read the word hell, all kinds of sermon outlines, illustrations, and ideas depicting eternal conscious torment in the spiritual realm come to the fore of our minds. None of these came to the minds of Jesus' listeners, for they had never heard the word before in inspired speech. It is very significant that the word did not occur even once in the *Septuagint*, quoted by Jesus and his apostles.

I suggest that to the Jews in Jesus' audience, Jesus' words referred merely to the valley southeast of Jerusalem. In their Old Testament background, *Gehenna* meant *a place of burning, a valley where rebellious Jews had been slaughtered before and would be again if they didn't repent, as Malachi, John the Baptist, and Jesus urged them to do.* Jesus didn't have to say what *Gehenna* was, as it was a well-known place to the people of that area, but his teaching was at least consistent with the national judgment announced by Malachi and John the Baptist. The closest fire in the context is Mt. 3.10-12, where we've seen that John announced imminent fiery judgment on the nation of Israel.

While we may not be familiar with the development of the concept of hell as eternal conscious torment in the spiritual realm, and its substitution for Gehenna by Roman Catholicism, let's be assured that the Jews who heard Jesus use the term Gehenna for the first time assuredly knew what the punishment of Gehenna was. Listen to Jeremiah's prediction of Babylonian punishment of Jerusalem in 586 BC, which the Jews of Jesus' day were assuredly familiar with (Jer. 19.1-9):

> 1 Thus says the LORD, "Go and buy a potter's earthenware jar, and take some of the elders of the people and some of the senior priests. 2 "Then go out to the valley of Ben-hinnom, which is by the entrance of the potsherd gate; and proclaim there the words that I shall tell you, 3 and say, 'Hear the word of the LORD, O kings of Judah and inhabitants of Jerusalem: thus says the LORD of hosts, the God of Israel, "Behold I am about to bring a calamity upon this place, at which the ears of everyone that hears of it will tingle. 4 "Because they have forsaken Me and have made this an alien place and have burned sacrifices in it to other gods that neither they nor their forefathers nor the kings of Judah had ever known, and because they have filled this place with the blood of the innocent 5 and have built the high places of Baal to burn their sons in the fire as burnt offerings to Baal, a thing which I never commanded or spoke of, nor did it ever enter My mind; 6 therefore, behold, days are coming, "declares the

LORD," when this place will no longer be called
Topheth or the valley of Ben-hinnom, but rather the
valley of Slaughter. 7 "And I shall make void the
counsel of Judah and Jerusalem in this place, and I
shall cause them to fall by the sword before their enemies and by the hand of those who seek their life; and
I shall give over their carcasses as food for the birds of
the sky and the beasts of the earth. 8 "I shall also make
this city a desolation and an object of hissing; everyone who passes by it will be astonished and hiss because of all its disasters. 9 "And I shall make them eat
the flesh of their sons and the flesh of their daughters,
and they will eat one another's flesh in the siege and in
the distress with which their enemies and those who
seek their life will distress them."'

When Jesus' listeners heard the word Gehenna from the lips of Jesus, they didn't think of eternal conscious torment in the spiritual
realm, or even the word hell (which wouldn't be formulated for nearly
sixteen centuries), but they thought of the slaughter the Babylonians
visited on their Jewish ancesters six centuries before. Jesus was threat-
ening impenitent Jews of his day with the same slaughter in his generation. They had seen it all before, but no one had called Gehenna hell,
and wouldn't until the 16th century AD, when it was used to threaten
European Catholics unless they purchased indulgences to protect them
from its punishment. Many European cathedrals were built with those
indulgences.

Hence John and Jesus said the wicked would be consumed with
unquenchable fire, yet we popularly read it to mean they will not be
consumed, thinking folks in hell will no more be consumed than the
burning bush was!

Let's notice the other *Gehenna* passages to ascertain more about
Jesus' use of *Gehenna.* As we do so, let's analyze each passage thus:
Does the passage teach things we don't believe about an unending
fiery hell, but which fit national judgment in *Gehenna?*

## Mt. 5.29-30

The next passage is Mt. 5.29-30, where Jesus used *Gehenna* twice
when he said:

And if thy right eye causeth thee to stumble, pluck it
out, and cast it from thee: for it is profitable for thee

that one of thy members should perish, and not thy
whole body go into hell (*Gehenna*—SGD). And if thy
right hand causeth thee to stumble, cut it off, and cast
it from thee: for it is profitable for thee that one of thy
members should perish, and not thy whole body go into hell (*Gehenna*—SGD).

In the traditional idea of hell, unending fire after the end of time,
we normally don't think of people having their physical limbs in the
spiritual realm at that time. This is not an argument, but just the realization that we don't think in terms of some people being in heaven
with missing eyes and limbs, and some in hell with all of theirs. As
William Robert West said in his excellent work on the nature of man,
"No one that I know of believes that the 'soul' shall 'enter into life,'
which he or she says is in heaven, with a hand of that soul in hell."
(William Robert West, *If the Soul or Spirit Is Immortal, There Can Be
No Resurrection from the Dead,* Third Edition, originally published as
*The Resurrection and Immortality* [Bloomington, IN: Author House,
September 2006].) Notice also that Jesus didn't mention souls pun-
ished consciously forever in a single one os these six "eye, hand, and
foot" passages.

In Mk. 9.43, *"unquenchable fire"* doesn't mean eternal fire, but
fire that you can't quench or put out. It's used of national judgment in
Ezek. 20.47-48, on Israel in Amos 5.5-6, on Jerusalem in Isa. 66.15-16,
and of Babylon's burning of Jerusalem in Jer. 21:10-14. Of course,
none of those fires were eternal; none of them are still burning!

However, these words do fit a national judgment. It would be better to go into the kingdom of the Messiah missing some members, than
to go into an imminent national judgment of unquenchable fire with all
our members. This was equivalent to John's demand that his Jewish
audience bring forth fruits worthy of repentance or receive imminent
unquenchable fire. The whole body of a Jew could be cast into the valley of *Gehenna* in the fiery judgment of which John spoke.

## Mt. 10.28

The fourth time Jesus used *Gehenna* was when he said:

And be not afraid of them that kill the body, but are
not able to kill the soul: but rather fear him who is able
to destroy both soul and body in hell [*Gehenna*—
SGD].

Again, Jesus spoke of *Gehenna* consistently with imminent national judgment on Israel. Note that he didn't say, "I will warn you whom to fear: fear the One who after He has killed the body, will punish your soul consciously eternally," as many read it. The concepts of conscious, soul, eternal, and torment are not in this passage, either. I'm afraid they are just thinking of those things as they read these verses, which say no such thing! This verse is often used to affirm that the soul of man cannot be destroyed, that we're all born with an eternal soul, and it's that soul that we think Jesus spoke of in this verse. This directly contradicts the plain language of Jesus. If the body and soul of man cannot be destroyed, the language of Jesus has no meaning whatsoever! To help us understand Jesus' teaching here, let's briefly review the Bible's teaching concerning man being a living soul. The word *soul* in the Old Testament comes from the Hebrew *nephesh,* which fundamentally refers to man's animal life, i.e., the life he shares with all animals. Hence, in Genesis 2.7, we read:

> And Jehovah God formed man of the dust of the
> ground, and breathed into his nostrils the breath of life;
> and man became a living soul.

Here, Adam consisted of (1) a physical body, composed from the earth, which was not living. However, when God gave this body (2) the breath of life, Adam was a living soul (*nephesh*). It's interesting that the term *nephesh* is applied to animals many times in that same creation chapter. For example, in Gen. 2.19, it's applied to animals: "Let the waters swarm with swarms of living creatures (*nephesh*)." In Gen, 1.21, the same word is translated *living creature:* "And God created the great sea-monsters, and every *living creature* that moves wherewith the water swarmed." In Gen. 1.24, it's again translated *animals:* "And God said, Let the earth bring forth *living creatures* after their kind, cattle, and creeping things, and beasts of the earth." In Gen. 1.30, it's translated *life:* "And to every beast of the earth, and to every bird of the heavens, and to everything that creeps upon the earth, wherein there is *life.*" Hence, the term *a living soul,* is applied to animals as well as man. They are all *living souls.*"

Since both animals and man are living souls or beings, we can read the Bible's saying that souls (*nephesh*) can be smitten with the sword and utterly destroyed, as in Josh. 11.11:

> And they smote all the *souls* [*nephesh*] that were
> therein with the edge of the sword, utterly *destroying*

them; there was none left that breathed: and he burnt
Hazor with fire.

Thus, as Israel invaded Canaan, the national judgment they were
carrying out on the inhabitants was referred to as destroying their souls
with their swords. It was not eternal conscious torment in a spiritual
realm as many imagine in Mt. 10.28. When Ed Stevens asserts, "The
physical valley of Hinnom did not affect the soul," (*Ibid.*) surely he's
forgotten these occurrences of this very thing in Joshua, and therefore
his conclusion that "therefore, gehenna must be a spiritual place in the
unseen realm in which souls are brought to everlasting ruin in the afterlife" doesn't follow at all. A similar usage of souls in the same context
is in Josh. 10.35, 39:

> ...and they took it [the city of Eglon] on that day, and
> smote it with the edge of the sword; and all the *souls*
> (*nephesh*) that were therein he utterly *destroyed* that
> day, according to all that he had done to Lachish.

> ...and he took it [the region of Debir], and the king
> thereof, and all the cities thereof; and they smote them
> with the edge of the sword, and utterly *destroyed all*
> *the souls* that were therein; he left none remaining: as
> he had done to Hebron, so he did to Debir, and to the
> king thereof; as he had done also to Libnah, and to the
> king thereof.

Likewise in Lev. 23.30, we read of the penalty for working on the
Day of Atonement:

> Whosoever *soul* [*nephesh*] it be that doeth any manner
> of work in that same day, *that soul will I destroy* from
> among his people.

In none of these examples was the word *soul* referring to an immortal part of man. Significantly, this usage is how the Jews listening
to Jesus in Mt. 10.28 and Lk. 12.4-5 would have understood such language. They knew from their Old Testament background that God
could, and had many times, destroyed both bodies and souls in various
national judgments.

The question arises, "What's to keep anyone else from carrying out
such judgments of destroying both bodies and souls?" The answer is
absolutely nothing, if they're capable of doing it. Not everyone is, and

this passage doesn't say that only God is capable, does it? We may have thought that only deity could destroy a soul because thought *soul* implied an immortal part of man. However, that wasn't what any of these passages contemplated. The same comments apply to the following passage.

## Lk. 12.4-5

This is the fifth time Jesus used *Gehenna,* when he said: Lk. 12.4-5

> And I say unto you my friends, Be not afraid of them that kill the body, and after that have no more that they can do. But I will warn you whom ye shall fear: Fear him, who after he hath killed, hath power to cast into hell [*Gehenna*-SGD]: yea, I say unto you, Fear him.

Here Jesus taught the same thing John taught in Mt. 3.10-12, that only a divine being has the power to cast someone into unquenchable fire. A human can kill you. A divine being can imminently bring an unstoppable national judgment in which a divinely ordained religion would be brought to an end. Notice also that Jesus said that one would be cast into *Gehenna* after he has been killed (Lk. 12.4-5) and that God can destroy both the soul and body in *Gehenna.*

Notice also in verse 49 that Jesus said:

> I came to cast fire upon *the earth* (Gr., *ge*, land); and what do I desire, if it is already kindled?

The fiery judgment of which Jesus spoke was not far off in time and place, but imminent and earthly. In verse 56, Jesus noted that the judgment of which he spoke was imminent, for he said:

> Ye hypocrites, ye know how to interpret the face of the earth and the heaven; but how is it that ye know not how to interpret this time?

The word for earth in both these verses is *ge,* the standard word for land or ground, not necessarily the planet, which we might think. Thayer defined the word as:

> 1. arable land, 2. the ground, the earth as a standing place, 3. land, as opposed to sea or water, 4. the earth as a whole, the world. (p. 114)

This is the word used in Mt. 2.6 (the land of Judea), Mt. 2.20 (the land of Israel), Mt. 10.15 (the land of Sodom and Gomorrah), Mt. 11.24 (the land of Sodom), Mt. 14.34 (the land of Gennesaret), Jn. 3.22 (the land of Judea), Ac. 7.3 (into the land which I shall show thee), Ac. 7.6 (seed should sojourn in a strange land), Ac. 7.11 (a dearth over all the land of Egypt), etc. Thus, Jesus again spoke of imminent fiery destruction on the land of Israel, just as Malachi and John the Baptist said he would announce.

## Mt. 18.9, Mk. 9.43-45

These verses contain the sixth, seventh, eight, and ninth times Jesus used the word *Gehenna.* These are verses like Mt. 5.29-30, which speak of it being better to enter life or the kingdom without some members of one's body rather than going into *Gehenna* with a whole body. However, we want to pay special attention to Mark's account, because in it, Jesus further described *Gehenna:*

> And if thy hand cause thee to stumble, cut it off: it is good for thee to enter into life maimed, rather than having thy two hands to go into hell, *into the unquenchable fire* [emphasis mine—SGD].

Notice that Jesus specifically said what's coming in *Gehenna-unquenchable fire.* John the Baptist said he would baptize with unquenchable fire, not necessarily fire that would burn unendingly, but which would not be quenched. Unquenchable fire is unstoppable! It's fiery destruction brought about by a divine being. In Jer. 17.27, God warned the Jews of his time of imminent fiery judgment on themselves:

> If ye will not hearken unto me...then will I kindle a fire in the gates of Jerusalem, and it shall devour the palaces of Jerusalem, *and it shall not be quenched.*

Likewise, in Jer. 7.20, Jeremiah foretold the same thing:

> Therefore, thus saith the Lord God: Behold mine anger and my fury shall be poured out upon this place, upon man, and upon beast, and upon the trees of the field, and upon the fruit of the ground, and it shall burn, *and shall not be quenched*

This unquenchable fire, brought on by the Babylonians, devoured the palaces and gates of Jerusalem during Jeremiah's lifetime, in 586 B.C.

In Ezk. 20.47-48, God promised such a national judgment on Judah:

> Hear the word of the Lord: Thus says the Lord God, Behold, I am about to kindle a fire in you, and it shall consume every green tree in you, as well as every dry tree; *the blazing flame will not be quenched,* and the whole surface from south to north will be burned by it. And all flesh will see that I, the Lord, have kindled it; *it shall not be quenched.*

Of course, Babylon fulfilled these words in the destruction of Jerusalem in 586 B.C. The fire was not quenched, but Jerusalem didn't burn unendingly from 586 B.C. on.

Likewise, in Amos 5.6, God had promised a similar judgment on the northern kingdom at the hands of the Assyrians, fulfilled in 722 B.C.:

> Seek the Lord that you may live, lest He break forth
> like a fire, O house of Joseph, and it consume with
> none to quench it for Bethel.

The unquenchable fire which consumed Israel was unstoppable, but no one believes it's still burning unendingly. Thus, when Jesus spoke of unquenchable fire in Mk. 9.43, he used language that his Jewish listeners would associate with the national judgments God had brought on nations in the Old Testament.

In fact, they had never heard such language used any other way! Of course, we have, but not from the teaching of the Bible.

Thayer mentioned the use of the word unquenchable in the Greek language by Josephus and others:

> 1. *Strabo,* the celebrated geographer, speaking of the Parthenon, a temple in Athens, says: "In this was the inextinguishable or unquenchable lamp" (*asbestos,* the very word used in Mark iiI 12, Luke iiI 17, and Mark ix. 43). Of course, all it means is that the lamp was kept constantly or regularly burning during the period alluded to, though extinguished or quenched ages ago.

2. *Homer* uses the phrase *asbestos gelos,* "unquencha-ble laughter." But we can hardly suppose they are laughing now, and will laugh to all eternity.Homer;on unquenchable

3. *Plutarch,* the well-known author of the biographies familiarly known as "Plutarch's Lives," calls the sa-cred fire of the temple "unquenchable fire" (*pur asbeston,* the exact expression of Jesus), though he says in the very next sentence it had sometimes gone out.

4. *Josephus,* speaking of a festival of the Jews, says that every one brought fuel for the fire of the altar, which "continued *always unquenchable,"* (*asbeston aei).* Here we have a union of the word supposed to mean specially endless, when in the form of aionios, with the word "unquenchable," and yet both together do not convey the idea of duration without end; for the fire of which Josephus speaks had actually gone out, and the altar been destroyed, at the time he wrote! And still he calls the fire "always unquenchable."

5. *Eusebius,* the father of ecclesiastical history, de-scribing the martyrdom of several Christians at Alex-andria, says: "They were carried on camels through the city, and in this elevated position were scourged, and finally consumed or burned in *unquenchable fire"* (*puri asbesto).* 6 Here, again, we have the very phrase employed by our Lord, and applied to a literal fire, which, of course, was quenched in the short space of one hour, probably, or two hours at the longest. All that is implied is, that it burned till it had consumed the victims. (Thayer, *Ibid.,* p. 68-69.)

These are perfect illustrations of the scriptural use and definition of the word unquenchable. Jesus used the word the way his audience had always heard it used, of something unstoppable, not endless.

## Mt. 23.15

In the tenth time Jesus used *gehenna,* he said:

> Woe unto you, scribes and Pharisees, hypocrites! for
> ye compass sea and land to make one proselyte; and
> when he is become so, ye make him twofold more a
> son of hell (*Gehenna*—SGD) than yourselves.

These Jews knew what *Gehenna* was, and Jesus and John had foretold the unquenchable fiery judgment awaiting them there. He told these Jews that they were headed for it, and the people they taught were as well. It is the same national judgment he's been speaking of thus far. It's quite a testimony to the power of the human mind that it can read things like eternal, conscious, and torment into these verses, when not one syllable of them are in the verse, isn't it?

## Mt. 23.33

Eighteen verses later, Jesus used *gehenna* for the eleventh time. Continuing in the same address, he said:

> Ye serpents, ye offspring of vipers, how shall ye es-
> cape the judgment of hell [*Gehenna*—SGD]?

Just three verses later, Jesus said, in Mt. 23.36:

> Verily I say unto you, All these things shall come up-
> on this generation.

About these same things, Jesus said in Mt. 24.34:

> Verily I say unto you, This generation shall not pass
> away, till all these things be accomplished.

Thus, Jesus gave the time element when this fiery destruction on the land would be carried out: in that generation, i.e., in the time of his dealing with the then present generation of Jews. To sum up, Jesus threatened the Jews in the environs of Jerusalem that they were headed for the valley named *Gehenna* where there would be *unquenchable fire* (Mk. 9.43) *upon his generation* (Mt. 23.36) *in his generation* (Mt. 24.34), *when God destroys the souls of those of Jesus' generation after killing their bodies* (Lk. 12.5, Mt. 10.28). We cannot make it more precise! If hell is what Jesus said it was, *hell* was the unstoppable fiery destruction of Jerusalem in 70 A.D.

Another friend of mine, Kurt Simmons (who thinks I'm taking Gehenna too literally), asserts that "it seems rather obvious (in Matt 23:33) that he is not talking about the physical valley of Hinnom outside Jerusalem." (*Fulfilled! Vol. XII, No. 2,* Winter 2017) Obvious? Is it just as obvious that Bethlehem or Jerusalem in the gospels are not those literal locations? There's just as much Bible for asserting that. Until the Roman Catholic Church came along, Gehenna meant Gehenna, yet to Kurt, it's obvious that it doesn't. He then makes a powerful-sounding argument that turns out to be a very serious blunder. Based on his assertion that Gehenna was not just the proper name of a literal location, he writes: "The Pharisees could very easily have escaped death or burial in the valley of Hinnom by moving to Rome or some other ancient city, of even by simply dying prior to the Jewish war with Rome . . . ." Kurt's a brilliant man, but *2000 years before he came up with that argument, our Lord made it clear that this was the very thing he wanted the Jews to do—trust him and get out of Judea!* He warned them to flee Jerusalem to the mountains! Our Lord told them to escape, and the faithful Jews did! Escape from Gehenna was possible! Thus, in Matthew 23:33-36, Jesus warned the Jews that their very generation (and no other) was headed for the judgment in Gehenna, and in 24:34, He said it would occur in His generation (not in any other). He warned them (not us) in 24:15-16 to watch for the sign of His coming, and flee to the mountains. In Luke 21:26, Luke's account of the same discourse, Jesus warned: "But watch ye at every season, making supplication, that ye may *prevail to escape all these things that shall come to pass*" (Luke 21:26). Kurt is right when he states that if Gehenna was the literal valley outside Jerusalem, the Jews could very easily have escaped death or burial in the valley of Hinnom. You might think Jesus was making my argument, but it's not true. I'm making His, and using Gehenna just like He was.

Kurt asserts in the next paragraph that "When Jesus asked '*how shall you escape damnation of Gehenna,*' it is clear He alludes instead to the inevitable destruction in the lake of fire." How does Kurt know this? Unfortunately, he doesn't tell us, he just asserts it. What do you, the reader, think of it? The term "lake of fire" occurs five times in the entire Bible, all in Revelation 19-20, written nearly forty years *after* Jesus spoke on Gehenna. Is it clear to you that Jesus was alluding to something no one would hear of until 40 years later? People of Jesus' time hadn't heard of the lake of fire, and no one on earth did for another forty years. It's as clear as a bell that Gehenna refers to the lake of fire to someone whose mind is permeated with Roman Catholic teaching instead of just the words of the Savior. You can be a good guy and have a mind like that. Mine was for many years, and still is on other topics. I'm just not aware of them, yet. We all have traditional "baggage" that can unknowingly color our understanding of Scripture.

Then Kurt asserts that "Gehenna is seen to be a *symbol* (emphasis Kurt's—SGD) for the lake of fire." Kurt has this exactly backward; the lake of fire is symbolic of Gehenna. The lake of fire is the symbol of the real thing, Gehenna. This is established by the following: A) the term "lake of fire" only occurs in Revelation, a book of signs and symbols (which isn't the case in any of the New Testament books in which Gehenna occurs); B) no one on earth could have possibly thought of Gehenna as a sign of the lake of fire, since that term would not be used until forty years after the last time the word Gehenna was used by our Lord. Kurt couldn't have made such an assertion either unless he had help that I think he got from you-know-where. I do think the lake of fire in Revelation *signifies* the unquenchable fiery judgment coming *on* Jesus' generation *in* his generation, but it's a sign of the real thing, Gehenna, not *vice versa*.

## Jas. 3.6

There remains but one more occurrence of *gehenna* in the Bible. It's the only time the word occurs outside the gospels, where James, writing to Jews shortly before the destruction of Jerusalem, said:

> And the tongue is a fire: the world of iniquity among
> our members is the tongue, which defileth the whole
> body, and setteth on fire the wheel of nature, and is set
> on fire by hell [*Gehenna*—SGD].

While this is the only passage speaking of *gehenna* outside the gospels, it is consistent with how Jesus defined it. James condemned misuse of the tongue, specifically in terms Jesus used the first time he used the word in Mt. 5.22, where he spoke of cursing one's brethren putting one in danger of the hell of fire (*Gehenna*—SGD). In Jas. 3.9, James said:

> Therewith bless we the Lord and Father; and therewith
> curse we men, who are made after the likeness of God:
> out of the same mouth cometh forth blessing and cursing.

Thus, the last time *gehenna* occurred in the Bible, it taught the same thing it taught in the first. Like Jesus, James uses no words like eternal conscious, torment, or spiritual realm. He merely used *Gehen-*

*na*, which his first century Jewish audience was familiar with. The Jew of Jesus' day who abused his brother with his tongue was in danger of imminent, fiery, national destruction. He was headed for unquenchable fire on his generation, in his generation.

We see the same imminence of this judgment against Jesus' generation of Jews later in James. For example, in Jas. 5.5, James mentioned a day of slaughter coming. In Jas. 5.7, he mentioned the coming of the Lord. In Jas. 5.8, he said the coming of the Lord was "at hand." In Jas. 5.9, he said "the judge standeth before the door."

## Summary of the Twelve *Gehenna* Passages

In none of these Gehenna passages do we see anything about eternal conscious torment in the spiritual realm, although we're greatly tempted to read that into them from the theologically-loaded word hell. From these twelve *Gehenna* passages, we learn that *Gehenna* would be the familiar valley on the southwest side of Jerusalem where an imminent fiery judgment was coming on the Jews of the generation in which Jesus was crucified. It was unquenchable fire on that generation in that generation. It was a national judgment against the Jews. *Gehenna* was to the Jews of Jesus' day what it was to the Jews of Jeremiah's day-where the term originated-the city dump! But it entailed all the horror of being rejected and abandoned by God to the merciless enemy who surrounded the gates and who would cause their dead carcasses to be thrown into the burning, worm-infested place. Thus, when Jesus used the term He used it in the same sense that Jeremiah did: as Jerusalem then was abandoned to Babylon's invasion, so Jerusalem of Jesus' day was about to be abandoned to Roman invasion-unless they repented. *None of these hell passages say that anyone of our day can go to hell. None of them associate hell with Satan. None of them say that Satan's domain is hell. Though they speak of men being killed and destroyed in Gehenna, none of them speak of men being tormented there.*

As we've seen, the concept of endless punishment was completely foreign to inspired writing before the Law of Moses, during the Law of Moses, and now we see it's foreign to the teaching of Jesus.

Contrast Jesus' use of hell with traditional preaching on the subject. For example, we quote a Rev. J. Furniss, who said:

> See on the middle of that red-hot floor stands a girl: she looks about sixteen years old. Her feet are bare. Listen; she speaks. "I have been standing on this red-

hot floor for years! Look at my burnt and bleeding feet! Let me go off this burning floor for one moment!" The fifth dungeon is the red-hot oven. The little child is in the red-hot oven. Hear how it screams to come out; see how it turns and twists itself about in the fire. It beats its head against the roof of the oven. It stamps its little feet on the floor. God was very good to this little child. Very likely God saw it would get worse and worse, and would never repent, and so it would have to be punished more severely in hell. So God in His mercy called it out of the world in early childhood. (J. Furniss, *The Sight of Hell* [London and Dublin: Duffy], cited by Edward William Fudge, *The Fire That Consumes* [Houston: Providential Press, 1982], p. 416.)

Charles H. Spurgeon, renowned Baptist preacher, said:

When thou diest thy soul will be tormented alone-that will be a hell for it-but at the day of judgment thy body will join thy soul, and then thou wilt have twin hells, body and soul shall be together, each brimfull of pain, thy soul sweating in its inmost pore drops of blood and thy body from head to foot suffused with agony; conscience, judgement, memory, all tortured.Thine heart beating high with fever, thy pulse rattling at an enormous rate in agony, thy limbs cracking like the martyrs in the fire and yet unburnt, thyself put in a vessel of hot oil, pained yet coming out undestroyed, all thy veins becoming a road for the hot feet of pain to travel on, every nerve a string on which the devil shall ever play his diabolical tune.Fictions, sir! Again I say they are no fictions, but solid, stern truth. If God be true, and this Bible be true, what I have said is the truth, and you will find it one day to be so. (Charles H. Spurgeon, Sermon No. 66, New Park Street Pulpit, 2:105, cited by Edward William Fudge, *The Fire That Consumes* [Houston: Providential Press, 1982], p. 417.)

Only conceive that poor wretch in the flames, who is saying, "O for one drop of water to cool my parched tongue!" See how his tongue hangs from between his blistered lips! How it excoriates and burns the roof of his mouth as if it were a firebrand! Behold him crying for a drop of water. I will not picture the scene. Suffice it for me to close up by saying, that the hell of hells will be to thee, poor sinner, the thought that it is to be for ever. Thou wilt look up there on the throne of God- and on it shall be written, "for ever!" When the damned jingle the burning irons of their torments, they shall say, "For ever!" When they howl, echo cries, "For ever!" "For ever" is written on their racks, "For ever" on their chains; "For ever" burneth in the fire, "For ever" ever reigns." (From a sermon preached in 1855, cited by Edward William Fudge, *The Fire That Consumes* [Houston: Providential Press, 1982], p. 417.)

Jonathan Edwards, famous Calvinist preacher of an earlier century, said:

So it will be with the soul in Hell; it will have no strength or power to deliver itself; and its torment and horror will be so great, so mighty, so vastly dispropor- tioned to its strength, that having no strength in the least to support itself, although it be infinitely contrary to the nature and inclination of the soul utterly to sink; yet it will sink, it will utterly and totally sink, without the least degree of remaining comfort, or strength, or courage, or hope. And though it will never be annihi- lated, its being and perception will never be abolished: yet such will be the infinite depth of gloominess that it will sink into, that it will be in a state of death, eternal death.

To help your conception, imagine yourself to be cast into a fiery oven, all of a glowing heat, or into the midst of a glowing brick-kiln, or of a great furnace, where your pain would be as much greater than that occasioned by accidentally touching a coal of fire, as the heat is greater. Imagine also that you body were to lie there for a quarter of an hour, full of fire, as full within and without as a bright coal of fire, all the while full of quick sense; what horror would you feel at the entrance of such a furnace! And how long would that quarter of an hour seem to you!And how much greater would be the effect, if you knew you must endure it for a whole year, and how vastly greater still, if you knew you must endure it for a thousand years! O then, how would your heart sink, if you thought, if you knew, that you must bear it forever and ever!That after millions of millions of ages, your torment would be no nearer to an end, than ever it was; and that you never, never should be delivered! But your torment in Hell will be immeasurably greater than this illustration represents. How then will the heart of a poor creature sink under it! How utterly inexpressible and inconceivable must the sinking of the soul be in such a case. (Jonathan Edwards, cited by A. W. Pink, *Eternal Punishment* [Swengel, PA: Reiner Publications, n.d.], cited by Edward William Fudge, *The Fire That Consumes* [Houston: Providential Press, 1982], p. 417.)

The world will probably be converted into a great lake or liquid globe of fire, in which the wicked shall be overwhelmed, which will always be in tempest, in which they shall be tossed to and fro, having no rest day and night, vast waves and billows of fire continually rolling over their heads, of which they shall forever be full of a quick sense within and without; their heads, their eyes, their tongues, their hands, their feet, their loins and their vitals, shall forever be full of a flowing, melting fire, fierce enough to melt the very rocks and elements; and also, they shall eternally be full of the most quick and lively sense to feel the torments; not for one minute, not for one day, not for one age, not for two ages, not for a hundred ages, nor for ten thousand millions of ages, one after another, but forever and ever, without any end at all, and never to be delivered. (Cited by Gary Amirault, *The Ancient Inventors and Modern Perpetrators of Hell,* p. 4.)

Did all that preaching come from the twelve *Gehenna* passages we've just analyzed? Did *any* of it? We can find none of this language of red-hot floors, dungeons, red-hot ovens, vessels of hot oil, being able to see the throne of God, brick-kilns, torture racks, chains, or great furnaces anywhere in these twelve passages that deal with the subject of *Gehenna* in the Bible. However, they are easily found in Milton's *Paradise Lost* and Dante's *Inferno.* .

Such concepts are also found in Islamic writings:

> As for the disbelievers, they know at the moment of death that they are destined for Hell. The angels beat them up on the faces and rear ends (8:50 & 47:27), order them to evict their souls (6:93), then "snatch their souls" (79:1). The Quran teaches that the disbelievers go through 2 deaths (2:28 & 40:11). They will be put to death - a state of nothingness during which they see Hell day and night in a continuous nightmare that lasts until the Day of Judgment (40:46). Hell is not yet in existence (40:46, 89:23). (Dr. Rashad Khalifa., Submission.org)

The reader may wonder, "Well, if Jesus didn't teach that the wicked presently living will finally go to hell, then what did he teach about the final destiny of the wicked?" First, we don't have to know the answer to that question to know that traditional teaching on hell is Biblically bankrupt. Second, Jesus didn't teach anything about the final destiny of the wicked, that is, at the end of time. If we're tempted to use the account of the rich man and Lazarus (Luke 16), let's recall that in this account, Lazarus, the rich man, and Abraham were all in *hades* (they couldn't be seen), and the passage doesn't address what happens after the end of time at all. Whatever the passage teaches, it doesn't deal with the final destiny of the wicked..

One other observation deserves to be made. As we've seen, the word gehenna occurs sparsely in the Bible-none in the Greek Old Testament, and only twelve times in the New Testament, eleven by Jesus, and one by James. Amazingly, the word is nowhere used in the book of Acts. Luke recorded thirty years of preaching by Paul (who claimed to have declared "the whole counsel of God") and others in Acts, yet the word is not used once. Not only does Acts not record any of the teaching on hell that we've just seen samples of, it doesn't even mention the word! The gospel being preached in Acts didn't contain such a concept at all, but it did carry a lot of preaching to Jews about the inescapable fiery judgment that was coming upon them if they didn't repent.

# Other Terminology Commonly Thought to Refer to Eternal Fiery Hell

Now we want to notice other expressions of fiery judgment which we traditionally use to describe hell. These include fire burning to *sheol,* the worm dying not, unquenchable fire, fire that is not quenched, everlasting fire, weeping and gnashing of teeth, fire and brimstone, rising smoke, no rest day or night, being cast into fire, and melting.

## Fire Consuming a Nation

In Isa. 33.10-11, Isaiah said about Assyria:

> Now I will arise, says the Lord, now I will be exalted, now I will be lifted up. You have conceived chaff, you will give birth to stubble; my breath will consume you like a fire, and the peoples will be burned to lime, like cut thorns which are burned in the fire....Who among us can live with the consuming fire? Who among us can live with continual burning?

A careful study of the Old Testament prophets shows these expressions of the Assyrians being consumed by fire, and burned to lime are expressions of national judgment upon that nation. These expressions are similar to Jesus' statement in Lk. 12.49 that he came to send fire on the land of Israel. This is also the Old Testament basis for Jesus' statement to the Jews in Jn. 15.6: :

> If a man abide not in me, he is cast forth as a branch, and is withered; and they gather them, and cast them into the fire, and they are burned.

Isaiah's language was also similar to that in Dan. 7.9-12, where Daniel foretold the judgment of the beast about to overcome the saints of the Most High:

> I kept looking until thrones were set up, and the Ancient of Days took His seat; His vesture was like white snow and the hair of His head like pure wool. His throne was ablaze with flames, Its wheels were a burning fire. A river of fire was flowing and coming out from before Him; Thousands upon thousands were attending Him, and myriads upon myriads were standing

before Him; The court sat, and the books were opened. Then I kept looking because of the sound of the boasting words which the horn was speaking: I kept looking until the beast was slain, and its body was destroyed and given to the burning fire.

This scene portrayed the national destruction of the pagan power attempting to destroy the saints of the Most High. This is the same scene described in Rev. 20.11-15:

And I saw a great white throne, and him that sat upon it, from whose face the earth and the heaven fled away; and there was found no place for them. And I saw the dead, the great and the small, standing before the throne; and books were opened: and another book was opened, which is the book of life; and the dead were judged out of the things which were written in the books, according to their works. And the sea gave up the dead that were in it; and death and Hades gave up the dead that were in them: and they were judged every man according to their works. And death and Hades were cast into the lake of fire. And if any was not found written in the book of life, he was cast into the lake of fire.

Both of these scenes depict national judgments against a nation persecuting God's saints, both have judgment scenes, both have people judged out of things written in the books, and both have those not pleasing God in the judgment being cast into a river or lake of fire. This national judgment goes with John's expressions of imminence in Rev. 1.3 ("the time is at hand"), Rev. 22.6 ("things which must shortly come to pass"), and Rev. 22.10 ("Seal not up the words of the prophecy of this book: for the time is at hand"). Those who take the early date of Revelation (A.D. 67) believe these words refer to the destruction of Jerusalem, while those who take the later date for Revelation (A.D. 90-96) believe these words refer to the destruction of the Roman Empire. Whether they refer to Jerusalem or the Roman empire, they refer to a national judgment.

## Fire Burning to *Sheol,* Consuming the Earth and Mountains

This language is generally associated with a fiery judgment at the end of time, and hell. However, in Dt. 32.22, Moses said the same about the punishment God would bring on Israel for her idolatry:

> For a fire is kindled in My anger, and burns to the lowest part of Sheol, and consumes the earth with its yield, and sets on fire the foundations of the mountains.

This·language described national judgment that caused a nation to vanish.

## Worm Dieth Not, Fire Not Quenched

While this language is generally applied to hell, it's not so used in any of the *Gehenna* passages in the Bible. In Isa. 66.24, we read of God's destruction of Jerusalem in the generation when Jesus was crucified:

> Then they shall go forth and look on the corpses of the men who have transgressed against Me. For their worm shall not die, and their fire shall not be quenched; and they shall be an abhorrence to all mankind.

This passage contains nothing about conscious suffering, much less enduring to the end of time. Yet this is the same kind of language we saw in Mk. 9.47-48, the passage where Jesus described *Gehenna* with "unquenchable fire." There Jesus said:

> It is good for thee to enter into the kingdom of God with one eye, rather than having two eyes to be cast into hell; where their worm dieth not, and the fire is not quenched.

When Jesus spoke these words, the Bible had never used such language of anything but a national judgment.

## Unquenchable Fire

Likewise, when John the Baptist and Jesus spoke of unquenchable fire, the Jews had never heard such language used of anything but a national judgment. For example, in Ezk. 20.47-48, God promised national judgment on Israel: :

> Hear the word of the Lord: Thus says the Lord God, Behold, I am about to kindle a fire in you, and it shall consume every green tree in you, as well as every dry tree; the blazing flame will not be quenched, and the whole surface from south to north will be burned by it. And all flesh will see that I, the Lord, have kindled it; it shall not be quenched.

In Amos 5.5-6, we have the same language used of national judgment on Israel again. God had promised a similar judgment on the northern kingdom at the hands of the Assyrians, fulfilled in 722 B.C.:

> Seek the Lord that you may live, lest He break forth like a fire, O house of Joseph, and it consume with none to quench it for Bethel.

In Isa. 66.15-16, 24, Isaiah spoke of New Jerusalem's enemies being burned with unquenchable fire, as he spoke of the destruction of Jerusalem by the Romans in A.D. 70:

> For behold, the Lord will come in fire, and His chariots like the whirlwind, to render His anger with fury, and His rebuke with flames of fire. For the Lord will execute judgment by fire, and by His sword on all flesh. And those slain by the Lord will be many....Then they shall go forth and look on the corpses of the men who have transgressed against Me. For their worm shall not die, and their fire shall not be quenched; and they shall be an abhorrence to all mankind.

In Jer. 21.10-12, we read of Babylon's burning Jerusalem with unquenchable fire, a national judgment fulfilled in 586 B.C.:

> For I have set My face against this city for harm and not for good, declares the Lord. It will be given into the hand of the king of Babylon, and he will burn it

> with fire. Then say to the household of the king of Judah, Hear the word of the Lord, O house of David, thus says the Lord: Administer justice every morning; and deliver the person who has been robbed from the power of the oppressor. That My wrath may not go forth like fire and burn with none to extinguish it, because of the evil of their deeds.

Again, at the time John the Baptist and Jesus used this language in the gospels, the Bible had only used it of national judgments.

## Fire That Is Not Quenched

The same thing is true of this expression. In Jer. 4.4, Jeremiah used it of the destruction of Jerusalem. In Jer. 21.12, he used it to describe the destruction of the house of David. In Amos 5.5, 6, Amos used it of the destruction of Jerusalem. In II K. 22.17, it's used of the destruction of Judah. In Isa. 34.10, Isaiah used it of the destruction of Edom, and in Isa. 66.24, he used it of the destruction of the enemies of the Messiah's people. See also Jer. 7.20, 17.27, where Jeremiah used it of the destruction of Judah, and Ezk. 20.47-48, where Ezekiel spoke of God's destruction of Jerusalem.

## Weeping and Gnashing of Teeth

These words are so often thought of as applying to people suffering unending conscious torment in hell, that it will surprise many to find that the Old Testament used this language exclusively of national judgments.

In Isa. 22.12, speaking of the time Jerusalem would be destroyed by Babylon, Isaiah said:

> Therefore in that day the Lord God of hosts, called you to weeping, to wailing, to shaving the head, and to wearing sackcloth.

See also Isa. 16.9, Jer. 9.1, and 48.32. The entire book of Lamentations contains such language as Jeremiah lamented the destruction of Jerusalem by Babylon. In the New Testament, Jas. 5.1 uses the same kind of language to describe the weeping of the rich for fear of God's imminent judgment on Jerusalem:

> Come now, ye rich, weep and howl for your miseries
> that are coming upon you. Your riches are corrupted,
> and your garments are moth-eaten.

This judgment was also imminent in Jas. 5.5-9, where the day of slaughter was spoken of as at hand, as the judge was standing before the door. John used this same language in Rev. 18.9, of the pagan kings lamenting the destruction of spiritual Babylon:

> And the kings of the earth, who committed fornication
> and lived wantonly with her, shall weep and wail over
> her, when they look upon the smoke of her burning,
> standing afar off for the fear of her torment, saying,
> Woe, woe, the great city, Babylon, the strong city! for
> in one hour is thy judgment. And the merchants of the
> earth weep and mourn over her...

On the gnashing of teeth in particular, an adversary about to kill his victim did this in Job 16.9, Ps. 35.16, Ps. 37.12, Lam. 2.16, and Acts 7.54. The Psalmist used it of gnashing of teeth by the victim in Ps. 112.10, where the psalmist said: :

> The wicked man will see and be vexed, he will gnash
> his teeth and waste away: the longing of the wicked
> will come to nothing.

Thus, when Jesus and John the Baptist issued their warnings of the impending destruction of Jerusalem, they used language that the Old Testament had only used of national destruction.

## Fire and Brimstone

In Isa. 34.9, Isaiah used this language of national judgment on Edom:

> And its streams shall be turned into pitch, and its loose
> earth into brimstone, and its land shall become burning
> pitch.

In Isa. 30.33, Isaiah used it of such a judgment on Assyria:

> For Topheth [the place of human sacrifice to Molech,
> an Assyrian god—SGD] has long been ready, indeed,
> it has been prepared for the king. He has made it deep

and large, a pyre of fire with plenty of wood; the breath of the Lord, like a torrent of brimstone, sets it afire.

Psalm 11.6 spoke of fire and brimstone on the wicked, Ezk. 38.22 used this language to speak of national judgment on Gog, a pagan nation opposed to God's people in the restoration after Babylonian captivity. In Rev. 14.9-11, John used fire and brimstone of national judgment on the empire attempting to eradicate the Messiah's people. Scripture uses this language only of national judgment.

## Rising Smoke

Isaiah used this language of national judgment against Edom in Isa. 34.10:

It shall not be quenched night or day; Its smoke shall go up forever; From generation to generation it shall be desolate; None shall pass through it forever and ever.

## No Rest Day or Night

Isaiah used this language of national judgment on Edom in Isa. 34.10, quoted above.

## Cast Into Fire

In Ezk. 5.4-5, this language described Israel being cast into the fire, in her destruction by Babylon:

And take again some of them and throw them into the fire, and burn them in the fire, from it a fire will spread to all the house of Israel...Thus says the Lord God, This is Jerusalem; I have set her at the center of the nations, with lands around her.

Thus, this expression is used consistently of national destruction.

## Unfruitful Branches to Be Burned Up

In Ezek. 19.10-14, Ezekiel used this language of the national destruction of Israel:

Your mother was like a vine in your vineyard, Planted by the waters; It was fruitful and full of branches Because of abundant waters. And it had strong branches fit for scepters of rulers, And its height was raised above the clouds So that it was seen in its height with the mass of its branches. But it was plucked up in fury; It was cast down to the ground; And the east wind dried up its fruit. Its strong branch was torn off So that it withered; The fire consumed it. And now it is planted in the wilderness, In a dry and thirsty land. And fire has gone out from its branch; It has consumed its shoots and fruit, So that there is not in it a strong branch, A scepter to rule. This is a lamentation, and has become a lamentation.

## Melt

In Mic. 1.2-7, God said he would melt Israel and Judah. In Ps. 75.3, the Psalmist used this language of the destruction of God's enemies in the Old Testament. Peter may well have used this language of the destruction of Jerusalem in II Pet. 3.10-12. Like all the other expressions, melt portrays national destruction.

In summary, this section shows that none of the language we usually associate with hell is so associated in the Bible, and most of that language was used of strictly national judgments.

# Is Hell Even a Proper Translation
# for *Gehenna?*

Having seen the concept involved in Jesus' use of *Gehenna,* that it was an unstoppable fiery punishment on his generation in his generation, we now ask whether hell is even a proper translation for *Gehenna.* Does our English word "hell" fit the concept of *Gehenna* we find in the teaching of Jesus?

## Did *Gehenna* Even Need Translating?

As we have seen, *Gehenna* was the proper name for a location just outside Jerusalem. Why did it even need translating at all? We don't translate other proper names, such as Gethsemane, Calvary, or Bethlehem, all in the vicinity of Jerusalem. People living far away from Jerusalem, say in Ephesus or Rome, might not have known what these names referred to, but residents of the environs of Jerusalem certainly did, and didn't need the word translated.

When interpreting the Bible, or any other writing, for that matter, *one of the fundamental rules is that we take a passage in its most literal sense unless something in the context forces us to interpret it otherwise.* Thus, we should take any expression as literal, or at face value, unless the evident meaning forbids it. By evidently forbidden, we mean there's evidence that forbids the idea that it should be taken literally. By evidence, we don't mean, "I just hope it's taken figuratively, or I can't figure out what this means; so therefore, it must be figurative." That's not evidence. By evidence, we mean things like the correct definition of a word or something in the context or other verses that demonstrate that it is not to be taken literally.

Applying this rule to the present case, we ask, "Is there evidence that forces us to think that *Gehenna* is anything other than the valley just outside Jerusalem? What is the evidence that Jesus' language cannot mean that?" In the absence of such evidence, Jesus simply warned the Jews in the region of Jerusalem, that unless they repented, their city was imminently to be destroyed.

A second rule for the interpretation of potentially figurative (non-literal) language is that expressions are figurative when the literal meaning would involve an impossibility. Applying this rule to the present case (the interpretation of *Gehenna*), we ask, "Does interpreting *Gehenna* literally involve us in an impossibility? Does interpreting 'Jesus as warning the Jews in the region of Jerusalem that unless they repented, their city was to be imminently destroyed' involve an impossibility?" Of course not, because historically, that is exactly what happened.

A third rule is that a passage isn't literal if the literal view places it in conflict with another. Applying this rule to the present case, we ask, "Does interpreting *Gehenna* literally place these passages in conflict with any others?" Again, the answer is, obviously not, since Old Testament prophets foretold of Jerusalem's destruction (including John the Baptist, and Jesus himself). Why didn't translators obey these rules when interpreting Jesus' teaching on *Gehenna?* Is there anything in the context that forced them to think that *Gehenna* doesn't mean exactly what it says, i.e., a physical, literal location just outside Jerusalem? Of course, people who lived far away from Jerusalem probably wouldn't have known what *Gehenna* was, any more than people outside New York City may not know about Fishkills (the proper name of their municipal dump). But no one outside the region of Jerusalem was threatened by the destruction of Jerusalem. No one in Ephesus or Rome was ever threatened with the prospect of *Gehenna* if he didn't repent. No Gentile was ever threatened with the prospect of *Gehenna* if he didn't repent. We are not threatened with the prospect of *Gehenna* if we don't repent.

As one reviewer commented, "Of all things—*Gehenna* just means *Gehenna!*"

## What Is the Origin of the English Word "Hell"?

Concerning the word "hell," the *Encyclopedia Britannica* says:

> Hell, the abode or state of being of evil spirits or souls that are damned to postmortem punishment. Derived from an Anglo-Saxon word meaning "to conceal," or "to cover," the term hell originally designed the torrid regions of the underworld, though in some religions the underworld is cold and dark. (*The New Encyclopedia Britannica, Vol. 5,* 15th edition [Chicago: Encyclopedia Britannica, Inc.], p. 813.)

Britannica's lexicographer (whose job is to define words as they are now used) correctly defined hell as it's used now as the place of punishment after death. However, notice that the word historically meant "a cover." Our word "helmet" comes from the same origin, as it covers the head. Scholars tell us this word was used in the middle ages of a farmer, who would "hell" or "cover" his potatoes to preserve them during the winter.

*Webster's Unabridged Dictionary* says:

> Hell [ME, fr. OE; akin to OE *helan* to conceal, OHG *hella,* hell, to conceal, ON *hel*] heathen realm of the dead, Goth *halja* hell, L *celare* to hide, conceal, Gk *kalyptein* to cover, conceal, Skt *sarana* screening, protecting, basic meaning: concealing. (*Webster's Third New International Dictionary of the English Language Unabridged,* editor Philip Babcock Gove, Ph.D. [Springfield, MA: Merriam-Webster Inc., 1993], p. 1051.)

Webster agrees that the Old English origin of the word means "cover." This word had nothing to do with a place of punishment or eternal torment. Those connotations came much later, just in time, we might say, to be corrupted by Roman Catholicism into its present form. To translate *"Gehenna"* (which didn't contain any meaning of eternal torment or punishment), with the word "hell" (which also didn't contain any meaning of eternal torment or punishment) isn't a translation at all, but a substitution of a man-made doctrine into a word convenient to be corrupted.

This would be like the proper noun "Palo Duro Canyon," a familiar feature in the Texas Panhandle near the author's residence. People living far away have never heard of it. If someone translated the words "Palo Duro Canyon" with a completely unrelated word, and then said that new word meant "eternal torment," it wouldn't make sense, would it? That is exactly what happened with the proper noun *Gehenna,* a location familiar with inhabitants of Jerusalem. But to then suggest that the word *Gehenna* should be translated by the word "hell," a word that has none of the meaning of the word *Gehenna,* compounds the problem. "Hell" is not a translation of *Gehenna,* any more than New York is a translation of Jerusalem.

Another example of this unjustified substitution of a completely unrelated English word for a Greek word is the word "Easter" in Ac. 12.4. The King James Version tells us that Herod arrested Peter:

> And when he had apprehended him, he put him in prison, and delivered him to four quaternions of soldiers to keep him; intending after Easter to bring him forth to the people.

The word "translated" Easter is *Pascha,* the standard word for Passover throughout the New Testament. The translators of the King James Version, all members of the Church of England, essentially the English version of the Roman Catholic Church, knew the word "Easter" didn't mean Passover, and didn't have any relation to the Passover. Rather than translate *Pascha* as Passover, they just jammed Easter into its place. The same thing happened when the translators jammed the word hell into the place of *Gehenna.* Hell is no more related to *Gehenna* than Easter is to *Pascha.*

Universalist J. W. Hanson wrote something on this subject worth considering, even though we do not agree with his theory of salvation:

> The word should have been left untranslated as it is in some versions, and it would not be misunderstood. It was not misunderstood by the Jews to whom Jesus addressed it. Walter Balfour well says: "What meaning

would the Jews who were familiar with this word, and knew it to signify the valley of Hinnom, be likely to attach to it when they heard it used by our Lord? Would they, contrary to all former usage, transfer its meaning from a place with whose locality and history they had been familiar from their infancy, to a place of misery in another world? This conclusion is certainly inadmissible. By what rule of interpretation, then, can we arrive at the conclusion that this word means a place of misery and death?"

The French Bible, the Emphatic Diaglott, Improved Version, Wakefield's Translation and Newcomb's retain the proper noun, Gehenna, the name of a place as well-known as Babylon.

Dr. Thayer significantly remarks: "The Savior and James are the only persons in all the New Testament who use the word. John Baptist, who preached to the most wicked of men did not use it once. Paul wrote fourteen epistles and yet never once mentions it. Peter does not name it, nor Jude; and John, who wrote the gospel, three epistles, and the Book of Revelations, never employs it in a single instance. Now if Gehenna or Hell really reveals the terrible fact of endless woe, how can we account for this strange silence? How is it possible, if they knew its meaning and believed it a part of Christ's teaching that they should not have used it a hundred or a thousand times, instead of never using it at all; especially when we consider the infinite interests involved? The Book of Acts contains the record of the apostolic preaching, and the history of the first planting of the church among the Jews and Gentiles, and embraces a period of thirty years from the ascension of Christ. In all this history, in all this preaching of the disciples and apostles of Jesus there is no mention of Gehenna. In thirty years of missionary effort these men of God, addressing people of all characters and nations never under any circumstances threaten them with the torments of Gehenna or allude to it in the most distant manner! In the face of such a fact as this can any man believe that Gehenna signifies

endless punishment and that this is part of divine revelation, a part of the Gospel message to the world? These considerations show how impossible it is to establish the doctrine in review on the word Gehenna. All
the facts are against the supposition that the term was
used by Christ or his disciples in the sense of endless
punishment. There is not the least hint of any such
meaning attached to it, nor the slightest preparatory
notice that any such new revelation was to be looked
for in this old familiar word."

Salvation is never said to be from Gehenna. Gehenna
is never said to be of endless duration nor spoken of as
destined to last forever, so that even admitting the
popular ideas of its existence after death it gives no
support to the idea of endless torment. (J. W. Hanson,
D.D., *The Bible Hell,* fourth edition [Boston: Universalist Publishing House, 1888. Available on World
Wide Web].)

Robert William West gave a good summary of the popular use of
the word "hell":

Hell: No such word was in their vocabulary, and they
knew of no such place. No word with the meaning that
the English word Hell has now was used, or known
about unto long after the Bible. It is not in Greek literature in New Testaments times or before, first century
writers did not use it, Josephus, or any other historian
of that time did not use it, it is not in the Septuagint. A
place where God will torment the lost forever after the
Judgment Day was not known about. the concept of
the place called hell, or the name hell is not in the bible, and does not occur in any writing of either the
Hebrews or the Greeks until long after the Bible. The
Old Testament Hebrew, or the New Testament Greek,
has no word that is even close to today's English word
"hell." How do we know about this place called hell?
Where did hell come from? It is not in the Bible. Neither is the name "hell" in the Bible. Where did it come
from? Not by faith that comes by hearing God's word.
It is from the doctrines and precepts of men [Matthew

15:9]. It was not used in the first century because it was a word that was not in their vocabulary, and a place they know nothing about. (William Robert West, *If the Soul or Spirit Is Immortal, There Can Be No Resurrection from the Dead,* Third Edition, originally published as *The Resurrection and Immortality* [Bloomington, IN: Author House, September 2006] p. 138.)

Echoing West's "No word with the meaning that the English word Hell has now was used, or known about unto long after the Bible, Dr. John Noe says:

there are no equivalent Hebrew words in the Old Testament or Greek words in the New Testament for the present-day term, concept, and eternal place of damnation variously translated (or perhaps mistranslated) as "hell." (John Noe, Ph.D., *Hell Yes/Hell No* [Indianapolis, IN: East2West Press, 2011] p. 23.)

## Clearest Proof of Roman Catholic Use of Hell vs. Gehenna

The *Roman Catholic Encyclopedia* offers the clearest proof that Roman Catholicism didn't translatet Gehenna with hell. After saying that Gehenna was "south of Jerusalem," as everyone knows, it then wonders, "Where is hell?" Obviously, they're making a distinction between Gehenna and hell! It then offers different views of where hell is:

everywhere
some far island of the sea
at the poles of the earth
the sun
the moon
Mars
beyond the confines of the universe
within the earth

It then concludes that "no cogent reason has been advanced for accepting a metaphorical interpretation in preference to the most natural meaning of the words of Scripture," which obviously suggests, why not accept Gehenna, as Jesus said? The encyclopedia continues, "hence we may say hell is a definite place; but *where it is, we do not know*," although they assuredly know where Gehenna is, and have stated such! Jesus said Jerusalem would end up in Gehenna, and Roman Catholicism substituted hell for Gehenna! It continues:

> St. Augustine says: "It is my opinion that the nature of hell-fire and the location of hell are known to no man unless the Holy Ghost made it known to him by a special revelation."
>
> St. Gregory the Great wrote: "I do not dare to decide this question. Some thought hell is somewhere on earth; others believe it is under the earth"
>
> This universal conviction of mankind is an additional proof for the existence of hell. (Even tho no one ever heard of it until the $16^{th}$ Century!)
>
> We merely call to mind the testimony of the martyrs who often declared that they were glad to suffer pain of brief duration in order to escape eternal torments; e.g. "Martyrium Polycarpi", c. ii (cf. Atzberger, "Geschichte", II, 612 sqq.).
>
> The Church professes her faith in the eternity of the pains of hell in clear terms in the Athanasian Creed (Denz., nn. 40), in authentic doctrinal decisions (Denz, nn. 211, 410, 429, 807, 835, 915), and in countless passages of her liturgy; she never prays for the damned. Hence, beyond the possibility of doubt, the Church expressly teaches the eternity of the pains of hell as a truth of faith which no one can deny or call in question without manifest heresy.

(*The Catholic Encyclopedia* (1917), Author: Herbermann, Charles George (1840-1916), Publisher: New York: ROBERT APPLETON COMPANY; Imprimatur: John M. Farley, Archbishop of New York; *Vol 7*, pp. 538-550.)

All this is fine and good, except its basis is entirely Roman Catholicism, not the words of the Savior.

# Summary of Jesus' Teaching on Hell

False theories of eternal punishment of the wicked have done un-fathomable damage in the religious realm. Untold millions of people have obeyed God purely out of fear of a false concept of hell. Other untold millions have turned their backs on God because of a false sense of hell, as described by Roman Catholic sources, and their followers in most denominations.

This study shows that when John the Baptist and Jesus used these terms, they used language familiar to the Jews whom they taught. The Jews had heard this language no other way than in scenes of national judgment. While it is easy for us to read these passages from the point of view of enduring conscious punishment, we should read them as the Jews who heard them first.

Rather than our present day beliefs about hell coming from the Bible, the caller to the radio program was right. Our beliefs come from Roman Catholic theologians. As a result of an earlier version of this material, many have asked the author to deal with the final destiny of the wicked. This larger topic is dealt with in the author's *Essays on Eschatology: An Introductory Overview to the Study of Last things.* We can see, if our conclusions are correct thus far, that the subject of the final destiny of the wicked was never part of Jesus' teaching on *Gehenna or hell. That connection was given to us courtesy of Roman Catholicism, just like it gave us purgatory, the sale of indulgences, Limbo Patrum, Limbo Infantrum, etc.*

# Comparison of Jesus' Teaching on Gehenna vs. Roman Catholicism on Hell

1. As we've seen in this study, Jesus taught that Gehenna was es-capable, while Roman Catholicism teaches that Hell is inescapable.

2. Jesus taught only one future occurrence of the punishment of Gehenna, while Roman Catholicism teaches Hell is eternal and unend-ing.

3. Jesus taught that the punishment of Gehenna was in only in his generation, while Roman Catholicism teaches it's for all generations.

4. Jesus taught that the punishment of Gehenna was a physical judgment, while Roman Catholicism teaches Hell is a spiritual judg-ment.

5. Jesus warned that the punishment of Gehenna was a regional judgment involving people in Judea, while Roman Catholicism teaches Hell is global and universal.

6. Jesus taught that mortal souls, living humans would go to Gehenna, while Roman Catholicism teaches that immortal spirits will go to Hell.

7. Jesus taught that Gehenna would be physical punishment, while Roman Catholicism teaches that spiritual punishing would be carried out on immortal spirits.

8. Jesus taught that the punishment in Gehenna was to avenge martyrs, while Roman Catholicism makes no connection to avenging martyrs in Hell.

9. Jesus taught that Gehenna was to be the end of Old Covenant Israel, while Roman Catholicism teaches nothing about Hell in relation to Old Covenant Israel.

10. Gehenna was known to Moses and the Prophets, the Roman Catholic concept of Hell is unknown to Moses and the Prophets.

11. Gehenna didn't need translating, Roman Catholicism didn't translate Gehenna, but substituted Hell for it.

12. There was no eternal conscious torment in Gehenna, like there is in the Roman Catholic concept of Hell.

13. The warnings of punishment in Gehenna originated with Jesus, the doctrine of eternal conscious torment originated in Egypt.

14. The location of Gehenna is well known, the location of Hell in the spiritual realm is unknown.

15. Photographs of Gehenna are readily available, while there are no photographs of Roman Catholicism's concept of Hell.

16. All of these characteristics of Gehenna are in the Bible, while none of Roman Catholicism's concept of Hell is in the Bible.

17. *The Roman Catholic Encyclopedia* admits that the Catholic Church knows full well where Gehenna is, but have no idea where hell is, i.e., that hell is not Gehenna, nor is it a translation for Gehenna.

18. Gehenna and Hell are not the same in any way.

For those wanting to delve into this subject further, please see Chapters 15-16, "Lazarus and the Rich Man," and "Immortality and the Afterlife" in *Essays on Eschatology: An Introductory Overview of the Study of Last Things* by Samuel G. Dawson, available at Amazon.com

# Chapter 11

# The Rich Man & Lazarus

## The Teaching of the Roman Catholic Church on the Rich Man & Lazarus

The Roman Catholic Church teaches that this account in Lk. 16.19-31 concerns the torments of hell. In the *Catechism of the Catholic Church* we read:

> 633 Scripture calls the abode of the dead, to which the dead Christ went down, "hell"—Sheol in Hebrew or Hades in Greek— because those who are there are deprived of the vision of God.480 Such is the case for all the dead, whether evil or righteous, while they await the redeemer: which does not mean that their lot is identical, as Jesus shows through the parable of the poor man Lazarus who was received into "Abraham's bosom": "It is precisely these holy souls, who awaited their Savior in Abraham's bosom, whom Christ the Lord delivered when he descended into hell."482 Jesus did not descend into hell to deliver the damned, nor to destroy the hell of damnation, but to free the just who had gone before him. (p. 164)

Jesus' teaching concerning the Rich Man and Lazarus in Lk. 16.19-31 has always been provocative. It's the main passage resorted to when striving to establish the concept of endless torturous punishment of the wicked after death. This punishment is usually thought to be in hell, though the Greek word for hell, *gehenna*, is nowhere in the passage.

Much of this story existed before Jesus taught it. Arguments have abounded for centuries on the subject of this passage, and still flourish over whether Jesus' teaching is a parable (which he doesn't call it) or reality.

My particular interest in this essay arose in response to the previous essay entitled "Jesus' Teaching on Hell." It deals with the twelve passages in the Bible actually using the word *gehenna*, eleven of them on four or five occasions by Jesus to Jewish audiences, and also one by James to a Jewish audience. In that essay, I affirmed that (1) hell is not a translation of the word *gehenna*, but a substitution, (2) *gehenna* should never have been translated at all (since it is a proper noun, like Jerusalem or Ephesus), and (3) the popular concept of hell as a place of endless punishment has no scriptural basis whatsoever.

When I first came to my present conclusions on hell, I realized that probably 80 percent of Christians obey the gospel so they won't go to a place they were never threatened with anyway. I think that demands caution in dealing with folks. I've asked a lot of people why they obeyed the gospel. Most said, "to stay out of hell;" others said, because they loved God. Still others said because they wanted to do what was right, a loving response to the love of God, etc. As a reaction to that material on hell, many readers asked, "What about Luke 16? Where does it fit in?" Most of the questions I receive concern the destiny of the wicked; more particularly with the account of the Rich Man and Lazarus.

Concerning Luke 16, let me offer the following comments from my letter to one such questioner:

> I have questions about Luke 16 myself. Here's my present understanding of it. (1) It doesn't contain the word *gehenna*, so it teaches nothing about Gehenna (and this is why I didn't discuss the passage in my original essay, "Jesus' Teaching on Hell"). (2) It doesn't teach *anything* about the final punishment of the wicked, and your preacher doesn't think so, either. I'm sure he believes it to be an intermediate punishment before the final judgment, doesn't he? So, whether I know what Luke 16 teaches or not, I know it doesn't support the popular concept of hell. (3) I'm pretty sure we use these verses to teach something that is far from the purpose of the entire chapter.

The purpose of this present work is to effectively set forth what I believe Jesus taught in this passage.

## Thc Context of Luke 16.19-31

To begin with, I suggest that the entire chapter is dealing with greed, or the love of money. To get an overall view of Luke 16, notice the five sections in it, then we'll briefly discuss the first four sections to develop the context of the fifth, concerning the Rich Man and Lazarus.

> vv. 1-8—Commendation of the Greedy Unfaithful Steward
> vv. 9-13—Jesus Applied the Story to His Greedy Audience
> vv. 14-15—The Greedy Pharisees' Reaction and Jesus' Reply
> vv. 16-18—A Faithful Steward—John the Baptist
> vv. 19-31—The Rich Man and Lazarus

Each of these five sections contains a common theme, greed: (1) the unfaithful steward acted out of greed, (2) Jesus applied this account to the Pharisees, who were lovers of money, and adhered to a common philosophy that riches imply righteousness, and (3) the end result of the Rich Man indicated that his wealth didn't work out like the Pharisees would have predicted. We'll now discuss these five sections in more detail and notice their common theme of greed.

## vv. 1-8—Commendation of the Greedy Unfaithful Steward

Jesus' telling of the unrighteous steward presents a troublesome story:

> And he said also unto the disciples, There was a certain rich man, who had a steward; and the same was accused unto him that he was wasting [squandering— NAS] his goods. And he called him, and said unto him, What is this that I hear of thee? render the account of thy stewardship; for thou canst be no longer steward. And the steward said within himself, What shall I do, seeing that my lord taketh away the stewardship from me? I have not strength to dig; to beg I am ashamed. I am resolved what to do, that,

when I am put out of the stewardship, they may receive me into their houses. And calling to him each one of his lord's debtors, he said to the first, How much owest thou unto my lord? And he said, A hundred measures of oil. And he said unto him, Take thy bond, and sit down quickly and write fifty. Then said he to another, And how much owest thou? And he said, A hundred measures of wheat. He saith unto him, Take thy bond, and write fourscore. And his lord commended the unrighteous steward because he had done wisely: for the sons of this world are for their own generation wiser than the sons of the light.

I first became aware of this passage when I was riding with an older Christian in an old pickup on a country road. He asked, "How could the Lord commend a conniving, thieving steward?" When I looked at it closely, I nearly fell out of the truck! I thought, as many do, that Jesus commended this unrighteous man, a fraud and a trickster; it presented an insuperable difficulty.

In simple terms, this story is about a master whose manager was misappropriating his money. It was such an open-and-shut case that he just called the manager in and gave him notice—told him to get his accounts together and leave. The manager didn't even contest it. Then he wondered what he would do to earn a living. He decided to cheat his master by calling in all his debtors and marking down their debts. By doing the debtors a favor, he hoped they would take care of him when he was cast out of his job.

It would be like a dentist's receptionist, who, learning she was going to be let go, called his patients and forgave half of their debts, so they would take care of her when she's out of a job. We would expect that dentist to get upset and perhaps file legal charges against her.

The question usually arises as to how the Lord could commend the unrighteous steward and use him as an example for us to follow. Not only had he already lost money for his boss, but he also deliberately cut the debts of his master's debtors. How shall we deal with this? One commentator said that no story of the New Testament has been discussed more and received more interpretations than this one. The steward has been taken to represent Pilate, Judas, Satan, Paul, and Christ himself.

Some have probably already noticed what the solution is, that it wasn't *our* Lord who commended the unrighteous steward, but *his* lord, in verse 8. *His* master commended the unrighteous steward for his clever skullduggery, even if it was directed against himself. Potentially, every person in the story is a huckster to some degree. Apparently, the unrighteous steward didn't feel any guilt for discounting his master's debts. Likewise, the debtors willingly took advantage of the unrighteous steward's plot to provide for himself at his master's expense. Even the master was worldly wise enough to appreciate the scheme, even when he was the victim!

In verse 9, Jesus said, "And I say unto you...." Notice the distinction between "his lord" in verse 8 and "our Lord" in verse 9. Jesus continued:

> ...Make to yourselves friends by means of the mammon of unrighteousness, that when it shall fail, they may receive you into the eternal tabernacles.

The mammon of unrighteousness was money. Jesus' point was this: a poor money manager finally got wise when faced with the prospect of becoming homeless. If he could use his authority over his master's money to insure that he would be provided with shelter in his old age, how much more should God's children learn how to use physical resources (though honestly) to insure that they have an eternal dwelling place? Are we that wise? Do we manage our money to God's glory, not only by looking ahead and planning for our earthly futures, but even more so in planning for our final rest in heaven?

This problem goes away quickly when we carefully read and see that it wasn't Jesus who commended the unrighteous steward, but his own master.

Some say he was granting the debtors cheap grace, forgiveness of debt that wasn't his to forgive. At least, both here and in the following section, we see that the unrighteous steward was greedy to the point of systematically stealing from his master.

In the next section, Jesus applied this story to his audience.

## vv. 9-13—Jesus Applied the Story to His Greedy Audience

> And I say unto you, Make to yourselves friends by means of the mammon of unrighteousness; that, when it shall fail, they may receive you into the eternal tabernacles. He that is faithful in a very little is faithful also in much: and he that is unrighteous in a very little is unrighteous also in much. If therefore ye have not

been faithful in the unrighteous mammon, who will
commit to your trust the true riches? And if ye have
not been faithful in that which is another's, who will
give you that which is your own? No servant can serve
two masters: for either he will hate the one, and love
the other; or else he will hold to one, and despise the
other. Ye cannot serve God and mammon.

Jesus concluded his application in verse 13, teaching that men are
incapable of serving two masters—both God and money. Literally,
men don't have *the power* to serve two masters any more than a
Volkswagen Beetle has the power to win the Indianapolis 500 Race.
Obviously, the basic point of this first section is that a man shouldn't
be a servant of money, which is greed; it matters not how little or much
money a man might possess.

## vv. 14-15—The Greedy Pharisees' Reaction and Jesus' Reply

And the Pharisees, who were lovers of money, heard
all these things; and they scoffed at him. And he said
unto them, Ye are they that justify yourselves in the
sight of men; but God knoweth your hearts: for that
which is exalted among men is an abomination in the
sight of God.

Luke specifically noted that the Pharisees were lovers of money.
They recognized that Jesus was addressing their greed, and ridiculed
his lesson, but Jesus continued to rebuke them.

The Pharisees manifested an attitude toward riches that we should
notice, because the Bible addresses it in many places. They thought
that one's riches necessarily implied he was righteous and in favor
with God. In our day, members of the Mormon church (and many
others) share this belief. In the Old Testament, Job's three friends
subscribed to it. Thus, when Job, a tremendously wealthy man at the
outset of the book, suffered great calamity and loss of wealth, his
friends automatically assumed he was not righteous but guilty of some
horrible sin. When they came to him, he expected them to comfort
him. Instead, they assailed his character. They thought they had to,
since he was evidently, in their opinion, a great sinner. So they made
speech after speech accusing him of guilt and demanding that he repent

and *restore his righteous estate.* God had told Satan Job was righteous, and made it clear that Job wasn't suffering because he was sinning.

The Pharisees shared in this philosophy. They were greedy and thought riches signified they were righteous.

## vv. 16-18—A Faithful Steward–John the Baptist

Jesus then said:

> The law and the prophets were until John: from that time the gospel of the kingdom of God is preached, and every man entereth violently into it. But it is easier for heaven and earth to pass away, than for one tittle of the law to fall. Every one that putteth away his wife, and marrieth another, committeth adultery: and he that marrieth one that is put away from a husband committeth adultery.

Several questions naturally arise at this point: Why did John the Baptist come into this passage, and why the verse on divorce, of all things?

Several years ago, when I was studying marriage, divorce, and remarriage seriously, I noticed Lk. 16.18, "Everyone that putteth away his wife and marries another committeth adultery." Most of the time we view this verse as Luke's account of Mt. 19.9 and Mt. 5.32, but this is not the case. These two teachings took place at different times, in different places, for different purposes, to different people. At first glance, it's just one verse apparently snatched out of thin air to teach something about divorce. That may be true, or it might be about something else entirely. With help from William F. Luck's book, *Divorce and Remarriage: Recovering the Biblical View* [New York: Harper & Row, 1987], I considered the context of Lk. 16.18, and it helped me with the context of the story about the Rich Man and Lazarus.

Luck observed that John was used as a contemporary contrasting example of a man who wasn't greedy, who wouldn't give cheap grace like the unfaithful steward, and knew it was not his role to forgive debts to his master without permission. In a widely-known case of the time, Josephus (*Antiquities*, Book 18, chap. 5.1, 5.4) said that Herod made a pretense at least of living under Jewish law. His family was intermarried with Simon the High Priest's family, and Herod went to

Jerusalem for feasts to offer sacrifices to God. Everybody in this story was at least claiming to live under the Mosaic Law. The Mosaic Law was why it wasn't lawful for Herod to have Herodias, although the Mosaic Law would have permitted her to remarry had she been scripturally divorced. However, Josephus said that Herodias hadn't been scripturally divorced, and she was his brother's wife, violating Lev. 20.10. Notice what John said: "It is not lawful for thee to have thy brother's wife."

John didn't forgive Herod; he didn't give cheap grace to his master's debtor. Herod couldn't buy him off, and his preaching cost him his life, as Herod had him beheaded. Unlike the unfaithful steward, he was faithful to his master to the point of death.

Verse 18 illustrates John's lack of greed. Divorce was the subject of John's preaching against Herod, not an abbreviated account of Jesus' teaching on divorce (i.e., Mt. 5.32, 19.9), but part of his discourse against greed.

Obviously, John wasn't a mercenary prophet, he didn't preach for money, and he wasn't greedy.

## vv. 19-31 - The Rich Man and Lazarus

While Jesus gave these lessons and applications on greed, he introduced the Rich Man and Lazarus. The main controversy with these verses for ages seems to be whether they constitute a parable. I've made most of the arguments on both sides of this question, so I know you can take either side and be a fine fellow. The problem is, fine fellows can be dead wrong.

Those who argue that it's a historical account of what happens after death claim that these verses are not called a parable (although others which are clearly parables are not called such, either), or that they speak of a "certain" rich man, which indicates a historical individual.

The word "certain" is translated from the word *tis*, an enclitic *indefinite* pronoun, which *may* indicate some or any person or object. The word "certain" doesn't necessarily indicate a definite person or object. A number of passages illustrate the word may mean "any old one," and not a definite one at all. For example, in Mt. 18.25ff, the parable of the talents begins with "a certain king," not speaking of any particular king, as his identity has no bearing on the story. In Mt. 22.2, the parable of the marriage feast begins with "a certain king." Who the king was matters not, nor does it matter who was getting married. The point of comparison was on something else entirely. In Lk. 7.41, we read of "a certain lender." Do we wonder who he was? We never have, because the story doesn't depend on who he was, and the indefinite nature of the pronoun permits that conclusion.

William Robert West answered the argument some make that the use of Lazarus' name proves it is a historical account of real people:

> The objection of others is that parables do not use proper names. "And he took up his parable, and said, `From ARAM has BALAK brought me, the king of MOAB from the mountains of the East: come, curse me JACOB, and come, defy ISRAEL'" [Numbers 23:7]. Not one but FIVE PROPER NAMES are used in one parable. "SATAN" [Mark 4:14] "THE SON OF MAN" [Matthew 13:37]. (William Robert West, *If the Soul or Spirit Is Immortal, There Can Be No Resurrection from the Dead*, Third Edition, September 2006, originally published as *The Resurrection and Immortality* [Bloomington, IN: Author House], p. 229.)

Thus, we see that proper names don't necessarily imply real people.

In Lk. 10.3ff, in the parable of the good Samaritan, a "certain" man went down from Jerusalem to Jericho and fell among thieves. We then read of a "certain" priest passing him by. Did you ever wonder who this Samaritan was? I doubt that you did until I just mentioned it. Now that I have, you realize it doesn't matter who he was, because his identity has no pertinence to the story, does it? Wonder who the priest was? Me neither, as it has nothing to do with the point of the story, and the use of the indefinite pronoun doesn't require that it's speaking of a historic individual at all. The parable of the pounds (Lk. 19.12ff) uses the indefinite pronoun to speak of a "certain" nobleman.

You might be thinking, "Well, if Sam doesn't think it's historical, he must think it's a parable teaching what happens after death."

I don't believe these verses are a parable, either. It's not a parable because it contains no comparison, which is the essence of a parable (lit., *para-bole*, "to throw along side" for the purpose of comparison). If we go fishing together, I'll naturally throw my fish down alongside yours to show how much better fisherman I am than you. This lack of comparison is at the basis of the plethora, no, blizzard of interpretations that people offer. Folks are trying to interpret something they think is a parable, which contains no comparison at all.

I am going to demonstrate that it's not historical, because (1) it's of pagan origin, and (2) it's not true, as we're about to see.

## Some Things to Notice About This Legend

This is the main passage in the Bible used to teach conscious suffering after death.

This is not New Testament teaching. It's a Jewish story from beginning to end. Abraham is made to say, "They have Moses and the prophets," not "They have Jesus Christ and his apostles."

No allusion to its "doctrine" exists in the rest of the New Testament.

No New Testament writer ever alluded to it—"Remember what Jesus said about the Rich Man and Lazarus."

But in this legend, "they have Moses and the prophets," yet Moses and the prophets taught none of this!

These Jews knew the point of the legend was greed.

They knew it wasn't about the state of the dead, or they would have challenged Jesus' differing with the Old Testament teaching on the subject.

This is not Old Testament teaching on the state of the dead.

No such thing as Abraham's bosom exists in the Old Testament.

No great gulf fixed exists in the Old Testament, even to keep those in Abraham's bosom out of torments!

No endless torment exists in the Old Testament.

No conversations among the dead exist in the Old Testament.

No knowledge among the dead exists in the Old Testament.

No consciousness among the dead exists in the Old Testament.

No praying to Abraham exists in the Old Testament. (Perhaps we shouldn't criticize Roman Catholics for praying to Mary!)

No Abraham hearing the prayers of the wicked exists in the Old Testament, as we presume the Rich Man to be praying to.

Nowhere is Lazarus said to be righteous.

Nowhere is the Rich Man said to be wicked.

This story is not about their character, but their economic standing.

Not a word is said about the spiritual condition of either one of them. They may both have been righteous, or wicked. As far as the legend and Jesus' use of it is concerned, it's not about religious status, but riches.

It's not about the punishment of the wicked, but about the legendary fate of a legendary rich man, and the legendary fate of a legendary poor man.

Neither the soul or the spirit of either the Rich Man or Lazarus is mentioned.

# The Pagan Origin of the Legend of the Rich Man and Lazarus

We'll see shortly that the Old Testament taught nothing like the Jewish concept of Hades, and we'll also see that before the intertestamental period, Jews didn't believe any stories like that of the Rich Man and Lazarus.However, before looking at those specific legends, let's notice some general legends about Hades and life after death.

## Legends of Hades

On the origin and spread of pagan concepts of Hades into the Jewish world between the testaments, read closely the following quotations (all cited by Al Maxey in the *Al Maxey-Thomas Thrasher Debate* available at www.zianet.com/maxey) and note their sources:

> The Greek word "hades" came into biblical use when the translators of the Septuagint [the Greek Old Testament—SGD] chose it to render the Hebrew "sheol." The problem is that hades was used in the Greek world in a vastly different way than sheol. Hades in Greek mythology is the underworld, where

the conscious souls of the dead are divided in two
major regions, one a place of torment and the other of
blessedness. This Greek conception of hades
influenced Hellenistic Jews, during the
intertestamental period, to adopt the belief in the
immortality of the soul and the idea of a spatial
separation in the underworld between the righteous
and the godless. (Dr. Samuele Bacchiocchi,
*Immortality or Resurrection? A Biblical Study on
Human Nature and Destiny*, p. 170.)

Notice that Bacchiocchi admits that we can't read anything like the
two compartments of Hades in the Old Testament. The concept arose
during the period between the close of the Old Testament and the
coming of the New, when God was silent as far as prophets were
concerned.

Look further at the finer detail of the questionable source of the
doctrine of two compartments in Hades as time between the testaments
went on:

The literature of the intertestamental period reflects
the growth of the idea of the division of Hades into
separate compartments for the godly and the ungodly.
This aspect of eschatology was a popular subject in the
apocalyptic literature that flourished in this period.
Notable is the pseudepigraphical Enoch (written c. 200
B.C.), which includes the description of a tour
supposedly taken by Enoch into the center of the earth.
In another passage in Enoch, he sees at the center of
the earth two places—Paradise, the place of bliss, and
the valley of Gehinnom, the place of punishment. The
above illustrates that there was a general notion of
compartments in Hades that developed in the
intertestamental period. (*The Zondervan Pictorial
Encyclopedia of the Bible, Vol. 3*, p. 7.)

In the intertestamental period the idea of the afterlife
underwent some development. In Jewish apocalyptic
literature Hades was an intermediate place (1 Enoch
51:1) where all the souls of the dead awaited judgment
(22:3f). The dead were separated into compartments,
the righteous staying in an apparently pleasant place

(vs. 9) and various classes of sinners undergoing punishments in other compartments (vv. 10-13). (*The International Standard Bible Encyclopedia, Vol. 2*, p. 591.)

Under the influence of Persian and Hellenistic ideas concerning retribution after death the belief arose that the righteous and the godless would have very different fates, and we thus have the development of the idea of spatial separation in the underworld, the first instance being found in Enoch. (Gerhard Kittel, *Theological Dictionary of the New Testament, Vol. 1*, p. 147.)

Nowhere in the Old Testament is the abode of the dead regarded as a place of punishment or torment. The concept of an infernal "hell" developed in Israel only during the Hellenistic period. (*The Interpreter's Dictionary of the Bible*, p. 788.)

All these scholars make the point that all these doctrines originated among pagans, particularly among Egyptians and Greeks; and later, the Jews assimilated these doctrines. These Jews couldn't have found such concepts in their Old Testaments to save their lives!

In truth, the Pharisees of Jesus' time had access to all kinds of legends like these.

J. W. Hanson, universalist, which this author is not, said:

The Jews have a book, written during the Babylonish Captivity, entitled *Gemara Babylonicum*, containing doctrines entertained by Pagans concerning the future state not recognized by the followers of Moses. This story is founded on heathen views. They were not obtained from the Bible, for the Old Testament contains nothing resembling them. They were among those traditions which our Savior condemned when he told the Scribes and Pharisees, "Ye make the word of God of none effect through your traditions," and when he said to his disciples, "Beware of the leaven, or doctrine of the Pharisees." (J. W. Hanson, *The Bible Hell* [Boston: Universalist Publishing House, 1888], p. 43.)

Consider a few examples of Hanson's from the Talmud, the authoritative body of Jewish tradition (Italics used for emphasis— SGD):

> (1) In Kiddushin (Treatise on Betrothal), fol.72, there is quoted from the Juchasin, fol.75, 2, *a long story about what Levi said of Rabbi Judah: "This day he sits in Abraham's bosom,"* i.e., the day he died.

Note that this wasn't the Bible saying anything about Abraham's bosom, but Jewish tradition. Hanson continued:

> There is a difference here between the Jerusalem and the Babylonian Talmuds—the former says Rabbi Judah was "carried by angels"; the latter says that he was "placed in Abraham's bosom."

We can't find anything in the Old Testament about anyone dying and being carried by angels to Abraham's bosom, but we can certainly find it in Jewish tradition before the time of Jesus.

> (2) There was a story of a woman who had seen six of her sons slain (we have it also in 2 Macc. vii.). She heard the command given to kill the youngest (two-and-a-half years old), and running into the embraces of her little son, kissed him and said, *Go thou, my son, to Abraham my father,* and tell him: Thus saith thy mother, Do not thou boast, saying, I built an altar, and offered my son Isaac. For thy mother hath built seven altars, and offered seven sons in one day, etc. (Midrash Echah, fol.68. 1)

> (4) We have examples also of the dead discoursing with one another; and also with those who are still alive (Berachoth, fol.18, 2—Treatise on Blessings). R. Samuel Bar Nachman saith, R. Jonathan saith, *How doth it appear that the dead have any discourse among themselves?*

> (5) Then follows a story of a certain pious man that went and lodged in a burying place, and heard *two souls discoursing among themselves.* "The one said unto the other, Come, my companion, and let us

wander about the world, and listen behind the veil, what kind of plagues are coming upon the world." To which the other replied, "O my companion, I cannot; for I am buried in a cane mat; but do thou go, and whatsoever thou hearest, do thou come and tell me," etc. The story goes on to tell of the wandering of the soul and what he heard, etc.

(6) *As to "the great gulf,"* we read (Midrash [or Commentary] on Coheleth [Ecclesiastes], 103. 2), "God hath set the one against the other (Ecc. vii. 14) that is Gehenna and Paradise. How far are they distant? A hand-breadth." Jochanan saith, "A wall is between." But the Rabbis say "They are so even with one another, that they may see out of one into the other."

Of course, a lot of these expressions about Abraham's bosom, angels taking the righteous there, conversations between the dead, sending children to make requests of Abraham, etc., seem familiar to us now. Assuredly, had we lived under the Old Testament, we would never have heard such concepts in inspired teaching.

Alan Burns, author of *The Rich Man and Lazarus*, commented on these quotations:

The traditions set forth above were widely spread in many early Christian writings, showing how soon the corruption spread which led on to the Dark Ages and to all the worst errors of Romanism. The Apocryphal books (written in Greek, not in Hebrew, Cents.i. and ii. B.C.) contained the germ of this teaching. That is why the Apocrypha is valued by Traditionists, and is incorporated by the Church of Rome as an integral part of her Bible. (All these quotations are from Alan Burns, *The Rich Man and Lazarus* [Santa Clarita, CA: Concordant Publishing Concern, n.d., available at www.concordant.org].)

In my earlier work, "Jesus' Teaching on Hell," we comment extensively on the origin of the concept of eternal torment and the outright substitution (not translation) of the word *hell* for the Greek *gehenna* to create the Roman Catholic concept of hell which was unknown to the Old Testament, the teaching of Jesus, or the New Testament.

Thus, between the Egyptians and Greeks originating the concept of conscious unending torment, a part of Hades, then Roman Catholicism adapting it in about the 14th century and substituting (not translating) the word "hell" for Gehenna in English translations, it's difficult to wade through all the debris and recover the Bible's teaching on the punishment of the wicked. Shortly, we'll see that Jesus took a then-current pagan legend, that of the Rich Man and Lazarus, and used it to show the greedy Pharisees that even according to their own legend, the possession of riches didn't ensure God's approval. However, first, let us consider the origins of the specific legend of the Rich Man and Lazarus.

## Legends Concerning the Rich Man and Lazarus

Concerning the origin of the account of the Rich Man and Lazarus, J. F. Witherell wrote in his 1843 book *Five Pillars in the Temple of Partialism Shaken and Removed*:

> It may be proper to remark in this place, that this story was not original with the Saviour, but was simply used by him to illustrate his subject. The story was probably familiar to his hearers and our Saviour for that reason took occasion to make a practical application of it. In "Paige's Selections," we find the following from Dr. Whitby—"That this is a parable, and not a real history of what was actually done, is evident (1) Because we find this very parable in the Gemara Babylonicum whence it is cited by Mr. Sheringham, in the preface to his Joma. (2) From the circumstances of it, viz. The rich man's lifting up his eyes in hell, and seeing Lazarus in Abraham's bosom, his discourse with Abraham, his complaint of being tormented with flames, and his desire that Lazarus might be sent to cool his tongue; and if all this be confessedly parable, why should the rest, which is the very parable in the Gemara, be accounted history!"—end footnote Annot in loc. (J. F. Witherell, *Five Pillars in the Temple of Partialism Shaken and Removed* [Concord: Published at the Balm of Gilead Office, 1843], Placed into

electronic format by Gary Amirault [Hermann, MO: Tentmaker Ministry, January 1997].)

While I doubt that "this very parable" is found in the Gemara Babylonicum, I would agree that the essential story is there, and that it had been adapted by the Greeks and Jews, and Jesus adapted it further for his use in Luke 16.

Thomas B. Thayer, in his classic *The Origin & History of the Doctrine of Endless Punishment*, ascribed the legend to the same origin:

> It must also be remembered that this is only a parable, and not a real history; for, as Dr. Whitby affirms, "we find this very parable in the Gemara Babylonicum." The story was not new, then, not original with Christ, but known among the Jews before He repeated it. He borrowed the parable from them, and employed it to show the judgment which awaited them. He represented the spiritual favors and privileges of the Jews by the wealth and luxury of the rich man, and the spiritual poverty of the Gentiles by the beggary and infirmity of Lazarus; and while the former would be deprived of their privileges and punished for their wickedness, the latter would enjoy the blessings of truth and faith. *The Jews accepted this picture of Abraham's bosom very much like many Christians accept the idea that the Apostle Peter supposedly sits at the Heavenly Pearly Gates, with the ledger of the faithful dead, and the keys of admission to bid them enter.* (Thomas B. Thayer, *The Origin & History of the Doctrine of Endless Punishment* [Boston: Universalist Publishing House, 1855], p. 57.)

Al Maxey, a minister in churches of Christ who has written and debated this subject extensively, cited several sources to this same effect in the *Al Maxey-Thomas Thrasher Debate* available online at www.zianet.com/maxey.

> It seems appropriate to reopen this question and ask: Where should the origin of this parable be placed? (*The Anchor Bible Dictionary, Vol. 4*, p. 267). *Eerdmans Dictionary of the Bible* informs us that "much of the study of the parable of Lazarus and

Dives (Latin: 'rich man') in the 20th century has focused on possible literary antecedents." (pp. 796-797.)

This parable is not theology. It is a vivid story, not a Baedeker's guide to the next world. Such stories as this were current in Jesus' day. They are found in rabbinical sources, and even in Egyptian papyri." (The *Interpreter's Bible, Vol. 8*, p. 290.)

Similar stories existed in Egypt and among the rabbis; Jesus could easily have adapted this tradition to his own purpose. (*The Jerome Biblical Commentary*.)

This parable follows a story common in Egyptian and Jewish thought. This parable does not intend to give a topographical study of the abode of the dead, it is built upon and thus confirms common Jewish thought. (*International Standard Bible Encyclopedia, Vol. 3*, p. 94.)

*The Catholic Encyclopedia, Vol. 1* (online version) states that the imagery of this parable "is plainly drawn from the popular representations of the unseen world of the dead which were current in our Lord's time."

Jesus told this story to reinforce the fact that the riches of the Pharisees were not necessarily a sign of God's approval. Some interpreters suggest that the kernel of the story was a popular story of those times and possibly derived from an Egyptian source. (New Commentary on the Whole Bible, based on the classic commentary of Jamieson, Fausset, and Brown.)

Josephus (a Jewish historian, c. 37-100 A.D.), in his work Discourse to the Greeks Concerning Hades (in which he notes that the concept of a soul being created immortal by God is "according to the doctrine of Plato"), presents a very similar story to that of our Lord's, including many of the same figures Jesus employed. Yes, he may have borrowed from the

Lord's parable, but it is equally possible both were aware of such stories current in their culture.

Finally, Maxey (*Ibid.*) cited several other references on this point:

Several good reference works document and describe in some detail a good number of these stories that our Lord may have adapted to His own needs. (*Eerdmans Dictionary of the Bible*, p. 797; Dr. James Hastings, *Dictionary of Christ and the Gospels, Vol. 2*, p. 18; *The Interpreter's Bible, Vol. 8*, p. 289; *The Anchor Bible Dictionary, Vol. 4*, p. 267; Edersheim's *The Life and Times of Jesus the Messiah, Book IV*, pp. 280-281; Dr. Samuele Bacchiocchi, *Immortality or Resurrection? — A Biblical Study on Human Nature and Destiny*, pp. 174-176.)

Then he concluded:

My own personal conviction is that Jesus used or adapted a popular folktale well-known to His hearers for the purpose of conveying, by a means they would best comprehend and most easily remember, an eternal truth.

The obvious eternal truth was that riches do not assure a successful end.

Dr. James Hastings, in his famous *Dictionary of Christ and the Gospels*, wrote:

Jesus was accustomed to speak the language of His hearers in order to reach their understandings and hearts. And it is noteworthy how, when He employed Jewish imagery, He was wont to invest it with new significance (James Hastings, *Dictionary of Christ and the Gospels, Vol. 2*, p. 18.)

Sidney Hatch, in his book on conditional immortality, wrote:

In the story, then, of the Rich Man and Lazarus, Jesus has put them down with one of their own superstitions. He used their own ideas to condemn them. It is simply a case of taking what others believe, practice, or say, and using it to condemn them. "Since the elements of the story are taken from the Pharisees' own traditions, they are judged out of their own mouths." (Sidney Hatch, *Daring to Differ: Adventures in Conditional Immortality*, p. 91.)

## If the Story Were Pagan, Didn't Jesus Still Endorse Its Teaching?

If Jesus' use of this legend were the only example in his ministry, this question might have some validity to it, but consider that Jesus (and New Testament writers, as well) used a number of such allusions to pagan concepts. For example, in Mt. 10.25 and 12.24-27, Jesus answered charges that he was working miracles by the power of Beelzebub, the Philistine god of flies. When Jesus mentioned Beelzebub, he said:

> It is enough for the disciple that he be as his teacher, and the servant as his lord. If they have called the master of the house Beelzebub, how much more them of his household!

> But when the Pharisees heard it, they said, This man doth not cast out demons, but by Beelzebub the prince of the demons. And knowing their thoughts he said unto them, Every kingdom divided against itself is brought to desolation; and every city or house divided against itself shall not stand: and if Satan casteth out Satan, he is divided against himself; how then shall his kingdom stand? And if I by Beelzebub cast out demons, by whom do your sons cast them out? therefore shall they be your judges.

When Jesus referred to Beelzebub, do you suppose he knew the legend about Beelzebub was false, but still endorsed its teaching? Surely not. He was not trying to teach about Beelzebub to answer their argument. He was showing that even if they were right about the existence and activity of Beelzebub, they were still wrong about his miracles, and that their argument was no good.

Likewise, when Jesus spoke of the god of Mammon in Mt. 6.24, he wasn't endorsing Mammon's teaching or admitting his existence. As in the case of the Rich Man and Lazarus, he was using a legend that was popular in his time and place as an illustration we might use in our own teaching to illustrate his point.

Recall Thayer's comment earlier about the Jews' acceptance of this legend:

> The Jews accepted this picture of Abraham's bosom very much like many Christians accept the idea that the Apostle Peter supposedly sits at the Heavenly Pearly Gates, with the ledger of the faithful dead, and the keys of admission to bid them enter. (*The Origin & History of the Doctrine of Endless Punishment* [Boston: Universalist Publishing House, 1855], p. 57.)

Jeremy Lile, a preacher in churches of Christ who has studied and written extensively on this subject, has pointed out that Paul also used pagan sources as illustrations of his point:

> Jesus was not alone in this. Paul likewise borrowed from myth to suit his purposes. In Acts 17:26-29, Paul, using the alter 'To an unknown god' as a segue, stood before the Athenians in the Areopagus and said:

> From one man ['the unknown God'] made every nation of the human race to inhabit the entire earth, determining their set times and the fixed limits of the places where they would live, so that they would search for God and perhaps grope around for him and find him, though he is not far from each one of us. *For in him we live and move about and exist*, as even some of your own poets have said, '*For we too are his offspring.*' So since we are God's offspring, we should not think the deity is like gold or silver or stone, an image made by human skill and imagination.

> The first portion of verse 28, in italics, is a quote from Epimenides; a Cretan philosopher, poet and prophet. The second portion of verse 28, also in italics, is from the *Phaenomena* of Aratus. In their original contexts, both of these lines refer to Zeus. Paul hijacked the poets praise of Zeus and applied those lines to the God of Israel, the "unknown God." Of course, Paul was not confirming the existence of Zeus by quoting poets who lauded the Olympian's virtues. No one ever accuses

him of such. Why is Jesus different? Surely, Jesus was
not substantiating Grecian notions of the underworld
(which had been diffused into Judaism) by using such
themes in a parable about Israel. Both Jesus and Paul
used myth to suit their purposes—yet neither apply the
stamp of *truth* to myth. They used myth to illustrate
the truth. (Jeremy Lile *Otherworld Journey: The
Origins of Hell in Christian Thought*,
PlanetPreterist.com)

Suppose you overheard me admonish someone in sin, "If you think
Peter's going to welcome you in the pearly gates with this kind of
behavior, you've got another think coming." Would you deduce that I
accept and endorse the doctrine that Peter actually sits at pearly gates?
Most people would recognize that I spoke in terms of a popular
folktale or legend we know about Peter's admitting people to heaven.

James MacKnight, the well-known Scottish Presbyterian
commentator, realized Jesus' use of pagan sources, when he wrote:

It must be acknowledged, that our Lord's descriptions
(in this parable) are not drawn from the writings of the
Old Testament, but have a remarkable affinity to the
descriptions which the Grecian poets have given.
They, as well as our Lord, represent the abodes of the
blessed as lying contiguous to the region of the
damned, and separated only by a great impassable
river, or deep gulf, in such sort that the ghosts could
talk to one another from its opposite banks. The
parable says the souls of wicked men are tormented in
flames; the Grecian mythologists tell us they lie in
Phlegethon, the river of fire, where they suffer
torments. If from these resemblances it is thought the
parable is formed on the Grecian mythology, it will
not at all follow that our Lord approved of what the
common people thought or spake concerning those
matters, agreeably to the notions of the Greeks. In
parabolical discourses, provided the doctrines
inculcated are strictly true, the terms in which they are
inculcated may be such as are most familiar to the ears
of the vulgar, and the images made use of such as they
are best acquainted with. (James MacKnight, cited by

Thomas B. Thayer, *The Origin & History of the Doctrine of Endless Punishment*, p. 60.)

Notice that MacKnight said, "Our Lord's descriptions are not drawn from the writings of the Old Testament." In our essay "Jesus' Teaching on Hell," we've investigated the writings of Moses and the prophets on this subject, and they nowhere taught endless torment.

## The Relationship of Jesus' Teaching to the Old Covenant

Jesus, a faithful rabbi correctly interpreting and applying the Law of Moses to the Jews of his age, promised he wouldn't teach them anything different from that law. In Mt. 5.19-20, in discussing the law and the prophets, he said:

> For verily I say unto you, Till heaven and earth pass away, one jot or one tittle shall in no wise pass away from the law, till all things be accomplished. Whosoever therefore shall break one of these least commandments, *and shall teach men so* [Emphasis mine—SGD], shall be called least in the kingdom of heaven: but whosoever shall do and teach them, he shall be called great in the kingdom of heaven.

Do we think Jesus pronounced such woe on those who didn't teach what Moses and the prophets taught, and then taught differently himself? It's interesting that on the subject of divorce and remarriage, most people think he taught something just twelve verses later in Mt. 5.31-32, that was different from what Moses taught, after giving this warning in Mt. 5.20. Do we think he contradicted himself just seconds after pronouncing this woe? How about on our current subject, the state of the dead? After promising to be true to Moses and the prophets, did he then teach something directly contradictory to Moses and the prophets on our present subject?

Either the Old Testament teaching on the subject was true, or the legend of the Rich Man and Lazarus was true, but they both certainly cannot be true.

Now that we've seen the origin of legends like that of the Rich Man and Lazarus, we notice that these legends are not true, but that Jesus was merely taking a popular traditional teaching of the Pharisees, itself taken from Greek and Egyptian origins, and using this (about to be seen) false legend against them in teaching them about the perils of greed, or of trusting in riches.

## The Legend of the Rich Man & Lazarus Isn't True

I affirm that it's not true for this reason: The Old Testament's teaching on the status of the dead is taught in verses like these:

> For there is no activity or planning or wisdom in Sheol where you are going. (Eccl. 9:10)

> The dead do not know anything, nor have they any longer a reward." (Eccl. 9:5)

Further, it is declared of man:

> His breath goeth forth, He returneth to his earth. In that very day his thoughts perish. (Ps. 146.4)

and,

> In death there is no remembrance of Thee. In the grave who shall give Thee thanks? (Ps. 6.5)

Had we lived in the Mosaic Age, and someone asked us about the state of the dead, what would we have told them? Surely we would have told them exactly these things, would we not? We'd have said that the dead don't plan, they don't exercise wisdom, they're not active, and they don't know anything. And we'd have been correct, for that's exactly what the Bible says.

However, when we come to the Rich Man and Lazarus, should we then throw all that overboard and accept down to the smallest detail on what happens after death (even though we don't believe a lot of those details ourselves) a legend of highly dubious origin? Why not accept it as pagan teaching assimilated by the Jews between the testaments, as it contradicts everything the Old Testament taught about the consciousness, memory, etc. of the dead?

If this is true, then as we've noted, Jesus was teaching in the entire chapter, Luke 16, against greed to Pharisees who needed that very teaching. In the course of his teaching, Jesus used a story pervasive in their time to illustrate that wealth didn't indicate one was righteous, or that he would have good fortune.

# Conclusion

We've seen why the account of the Rich Man and Lazarus is in Luke 16, in the context of Jesus' teaching on greed to greedy Pharisees. It has nothing to do with the fate of anyone, righteous or wicked, after death. It has nothing to do with the final destiny of the wicked. Any understanding of the chapter that doesn't account for the context of the entire chapter falls short. In the Rich Man and Lazarus, Jesus merely used a story current in their time to illustrate that just because one was rich (whether righteous or unrighteous), that didn't guarantee a favorable outcome. Therefore, love and trust in riches was not a wise course to choose through life.

# Chapter 12

# Immortality & The Afterlife

In the preceding chapters on the resurrection, the return of Christ, Jesus' teaching on hell, and the Rich Man and Lazarus, we cleared away a great amount of doctrinal debris concerning the last things and the afterlife. As we're about to demonstrate, this leaves us with something very simple.

## The Popular Chart on the Afterlife

The following figure illustrates the popular position concerning what happens after death. Notice that the chart addresses four stages of being: life on earth, what happens when we die, what happens when Christ returns; and finally, our eternal resting place.

### Earth

The realm of life on earth is divided where one is either in Christ through obedience to the gospel or lost as a citizen of the world.

### Hades

At death, the popular position is that one's body returns to the dust and his spirit goes to Hades, either into paradise (or Abraham's bosom) or into torments. A great impassable gulf separates these two places.

All this is supposedly based on Jesus' account of the Rich Man and Lazarus in Lk. 16.19-31. As we saw in the previous chapter, this interpretation disregards the context of the entire chapter in Luke, contradicts plain Old Testament teaching on the state and activity of the dead, and ignores the origin of this story as entirely within Egyptian and Greek paganism. Jesus didn't teach on the state of the dead, but built upon the theme of the chapter—greed. In the course of warning the Pharisees about their conduct, he used a street legend popular in his time that didn't teach truth on the state of the dead. Similar to Solomon's proverb to answer a fool according to his folly, Jesus used this story to show that even according to their popular legend, the Pharisees (who were lovers of money, Lk. 16.14), like Job's three friends, were wrong if they thought that prosperity assured them of a right relationship with God.

# Where Are the Dead?

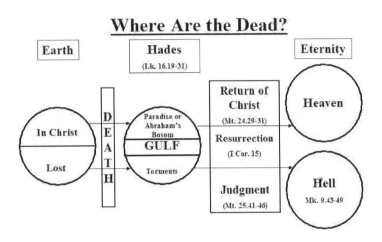

## The Return of Christ, the Resurrection, and the Judgment

The next part of the popular chart illustrates the return of Christ, normally referred to as "The Second Coming." We saw in previous chapters that Jesus taught that his return and the judgment would occur while some of his disciples were still alive (Mt. 16.27-28). In the Olivet Discourse, we noted how his return would occur in Jesus' own generation (Mt. 24.29-31, 34) and the judgment would take place within that same context (Mt. 25.41-46). We also explored how the resurrection of Israel of which Paul spoke in I Corinthians 15 was fulfilled at the destruction of Jerusalem (Daniel 12).

While we agree that the return of Christ, the resurrection, and the judgment were to take place at the same time, this chart shows the resurrection taking place, not as revealed earlier at the destruction of Jerusalem in AD 70, but at some time in our future.

# Further Discussion on the Imminent First-Century Judgment

Since we've already discussed the returning of Christ and the resurrection fully, let's take this opportunity to discuss the concept of an imminent first-century judgment mentioned so often in the Bible.

## Daniel 12.1-7

We begin with Dan. 12.1-2, which speaks of the resurrection and judgment of Israel:

> Now at that time Michael, the great prince who stands guard over the sons of your people, will arise. And there will be a time of distress such as never occurred since there was a nation until that time; and at that time your people, everyone who is found written in the book, will be rescued. "And many of those who sleep in the dust of the ground will awake, these to everlasting life, but the others to disgrace and everlasting contempt.

Notice that the judgment is implied by the fact that some are raised to their reward, and some to punishment. As for the time element, we see in vv 6-7, where Daniel asked:

"How long will it be until the end of these wonders?" And I heard the man dressed in linen, who was above the waters of the river, as he raised his right hand and his left toward heaven, and swore by Him who lives forever that it would be for a time, times, and half a time; and as soon as they finish shattering the power of the holy people, all these events will be completed.

This shattering of the power of the holy people refers first to the holy people, Israel, and the shattering of their power, the Mosaic Law and it's temple services. This is even more clear in verse 11, speaking of the "the time that the regular sacrifice is abolished, and the abomination of desolation is set up." This, of course, can refer to nothing other than the destruction of Jersualem. Even Jesus referred to this prophecy of the abomination of desolation of Daniel in Mt. 24.15 ("When therefore ye see the abomination of desolation, which was spoken of through Daniel the prophet..." and affirmed that "This generation shall not pass away, till all these things be accomplished...") connecting it to the destruction of Jerusalem and the temple.

Thus, Daniel foretold the destruction of Jersualem and the judgment of the Jews in Dan. 12.1-2, 6-7 in AD 70.

## Mt. 16.27-28

Here Jesus, speaking to his disciples, said:

> For the Son of man shall come in the glory of his Father with his angels; and then shall he render unto every man according to his deeds. Verily I say unto you, there are some of them that stand here, who shall in no wise taste of death, till they see the Son of man coming in his kingdom.

Notice three things about this passage. First, Jesus refers to his coming in glory (like Mt. 24.30, 25.31, in his generation). Second, at that time he will execute judgment, by rending to every man according to his deeds. Third, it will happen in the lifetime of some of his disciples. Either this judgment was fulfilled in his generation, or there are some mighty old Jews (to whom he was preaching) that haven't seen his coming nor the judgment yet, and Jesus falsely prophesied, thereby justifying his own execution.

Many times, folks are tempted to say that this prophecy was fulfilled at the transfiguration a few days later. That would be a stupendous prophecy, wouldn't it, to say that some in his audience would be alive a few days later? Even atheists have made prophecies more impressive than that! Big deal! Second, the transfiguration had no element of judgment in it at all. Thus, the fulfillment of this prophecy was more than a few days off, and, as Daniel had prophesied, the judgment was to take place at the destruction of the temple, when the power of the holy people was completely shattered.

## Mt. 25.31-33, 41

The next passages to notice concerning an imminent first-century judgment are in the Olivet discourse. In Mt. 25.31-33. We say it's imminent because it's part of the same discourse as Matthew 24. The judgment spoken of here is the same as that announcing the destruction of Jerusalem in that chapter. Speaking of the judgment coming on Israel, Jesus said:

> But when the Son of man shall come in his glory, and all the angels with him, then shall he sit on the throne of his glory: and before him shall be gathered all the nations: and he shall separate them one

from another, as the shepherd separateth the sheep from the goats; and he shall set the sheep on his right hand, but the goats on the left.

Several details need to be noticed in this passage. First, this speaks of Jesus' judgment of the Jews, again, in his generation (Mt. 24.34). Second, his coming in glory is the same coming spoken of in Mt. 24.30, which speaks of "the Son of man coming on the clouds of heaven with power and great glory," about which Jesus said in verse 34:

> Verily (truly—SGD) I say unto you, This generation shall not pass away, till all these things be accomplished.

We must all ask ourselves: Was Jesus really speaking "truly" when he said that, or not? If he wasn't lying or mistaken, his coming in glory came in his generation, did it not? This is the same coming in glory he spoke of on the same occasion to the same people, on the same subject, in Mt. 25.31-33. Again, unless Jesus was lying or mistaken, all the things of which he spoke were fulfilled in his generation. Thus, no partial fulfillment with a complete fulfillment after two thousand years would fill the bill. Those believing in only a partial or dual fulfillment of "all these things" in his generation don't really believe that all of them were fulfilled in Jesus' generation. Jesus affirmed that nothing ever like the destruction of Jerusalem had ever happened, and it wasn't going to happen again.

Third, in Mt. 25.41, Jesus says, "before him shall be gathered all the nations." Someone will legitimately say, "Mt. 25.32 says "nations." How can a judgment which involves nations speak of just a national judgment on Israel?" This is a notable objection until we realize that the land of Israel comprised many nations. We normally think of Israel of Jesus' time as one nation, but not so. For example, the Jewish historian Josephus referred to the nation of the Samaritans, the nation of the Galileans, and the nations of Idumea, Perea, Trachonitis, Iturea, and Abilene. Judea was spoken of as a distinct nation, with a king of its own. The Greek term *ethnarch* (literally, "ruler of a nation") described the rulers of these nations.

This agrees with Jesus' own usage in Mt. 24.7, where He said:

> For nation shall rise against nation, and kingdom against kingdom

Jesus spoke of many nations in that region, with Jews in all, which would be affected by the Roman invasion of the land. In Lk. 21.25-32, Luke quoted Jesus:

> And there shall be signs in sun and moon and stars; and upon the earth distress of nations, in perplexity for the roaring of the sea and the billows . . . This generation shall not pass away, till all things be accomplished.

Accordingly, "all the nations" is speaking of Old Covenant Israel, who received Christ's judgment on the nations of Palestine at the hands of the Roman armies in AD 70.

### Ac. 17.30-31

Having seen that both Daniel and Jesus foretold his judgment on Israel in the generation in which Jerusalem was destroyed, we now turn to the teaching of Paul on this same subject in Ac. 17.30-31. Speaking to the philosophers at Athens, he said:

> The times of ignorance therefore God overlooked; but now he commandeth men that they should all everywhere repent: inasmuch as he hath appointed a day in which he will [lit., "about to"—SGD] judge the world in righteousness by the man whom he hath ordained; whereof he hath given assurance unto all men, in that he hath raised him from the dead.

Thus Paul wasn't speaking of a judgment which hasn't occurred after two millennia yet, but one that was "about to" take place.

### Jas. 5.9—the judge is standing at the door

Significantly, James said to Jewish Chrisitans that this judgment was so near that:

> Murmur not, brethren, one against another, that ye be not judged: behold, the judge standeth before the doors.

**Rev. 11.18, 14.7, 18.20, 20.12—in the context of "the time is near, shortly to come to pass."**

A number of passages in Revelation, in the context of fulfillment being "at hand" (1.3, 22.10) and "shortly to come to pass" (1.1, 22.6), thus also speak of the imminence of the judgment.

## Rev. 11:18

> And the nations were wroth, and thy wrath came, and the time of the dead to be judged, and (the time) to give their reward to thy servants the prophets, and to the saints, and to them that fear thy name, the small and the great; and to destroy them that destroy the earth.

## Rev. 14:7

> and he saith with a great voice, Fear God, and give him glory; *for the hour of his judgment is come:* and worship him that made the heaven and the earth and sea and fountains of waters.

## Rev. 18:20

Rejoice over her, thou heaven, and ye saints, and ye apostles, and ye prophets; for God hath judged your judgment on her.

## Rev. 20:12

> And I saw the dead, the great and the small, standing before the throne; and books were opened: and another book was opened, which is (the book) of life: and the dead were judged out of the things which were written in the books, according to their works.

Thus, all these passages speaking of the judgment are in a context of imminence. Do we believe in their imminent fulfillment? Before answering casually, recall that in conclusion on an imminent first-century judgment, we noticed Mt. 5.17-18, where Jesus said:

> Think not that I came to destroy the law or the prophets: I came not to destroy, but to fulfil. For verily

> I say unto you, Till heaven and earth pass away, one
> jot or one tittle shall in no wise pass away from the
> law, till all things be accomplished.

Here, Jesus plainly teaches that none of the Mosaic law would pass away until all of it had been accomplished, including the teaching of the prophets. However, popularly, we believe that all of the law of Moses has been done away, and only part of it has been fulfilled. Is that what Jesus said, or did he say none of it would pass away until all of it had been fulfilled? Clearly, if the judgment prophesied in Dan. 12 was not fulfilled at the destruction of Jerusalem, then all of the Mosaic Law is still in effect! The only other alternative is that Christ was a false prophet, and his death sentence was valid according to the Mosaic Law itself.

Now, find a judgment at the end of time, realizing that the Bible nowhere uses the term "end of time," or at the last days of the Christian age, which has no end!

## The Wicked Being Sent to hell

By way of review, in Jesus' teaching, the substitution (not translation) of hell comes from *gehenna*, and in every single one of the twelve times the word is used in the New Testament, Gehenna is the proper name of an area on the south side of Jerusalem, where the inhabitants of the city would be destroyed in the first century. No one outside of Judea was ever threatened with *gehenna*. Instead, Roman Catholicism transformed that imminent punishment upon the rebellious Jews of Jesus' generation into a general eternal conscious torment of all the wicked at the end of time. Thus, this part of the chart of the popular position is Biblically bankrupt, as well.

Before we construct a chart based only on Bible teaching, we want to examine a fundamental question on the nature of man. Many teach that man is a dual being, a physical body with an inborn immortal spirit, and that from birth, man is immortal and eternal. This immortality is said to be innate at birth and is unconditional. It doesn't depend on whether man is righteous or wicked. *Unconditional immortality* is the most popular view of the nature of man, and entire systems of the destiny of man build on this doctrine: what happens to man at death, the nature of the resurrection, the return of Christ, the judgment, and his eternal destiny.

## Immortality: Innate or Conditional?

Is immortality really unconditional? We generally hear that Adam was created immortal, not subject to death, and that because of Adam's sin, he died physically, as did his descendants.

But was Adam created immortal, not subject to physical death? It appears not. Let's briefly review the Bible's teaching concerning man being a living soul. The word *soul* in the Old Testament comes from the Hebrew *nephesh,* which fundamentally refers to man's animal life, i.e., the life he shares with all animals. Hence, in Genesis 2.7, we read:

> And Jehovah God formed man of the *dust* of the ground, and breathed into his nostrils the *breath* of life; and man became a *living soul.* [emphasis mine— SGD]

Here, Adam consisted of (1) a physical body, composed from the earth, which was not living. However, when God gave this body (2) the breath of life, Adam became a living soul (*nephesh*). It's interesting that the term *nephesh* is applied to animals many times in that same creation chapter. For example, Gen. 2.19 says: "Let the waters swarm with swarms of living creatures (*nephesh*)." In Gen, 1.21, the same word is translated *living creature:* "And God created the great sea-monsters, and every *living creature* that moves wherewith the water swarmed." In Gen. 1.24, it's again translated *animals:* "And God said, Let the earth bring forth *living creatures* after their kind, cattle, and creeping things, and beasts of the earth." In Gen. 1.30, it's translated *life:* "And to every beast of the earth, and to every bird of the heavens, and to everything that creeps upon the earth, wherein there is *life.*" Hence, the term *a living soul,* is applied to animals as well as man. They are all *living souls.*

Not only were Adam and all the living creatures *living souls* before Adam sinned, but they were all subject to death before he sinned. After his creation outside the garden, God placed Adam in the garden and gave him access to the tree of life to sustain his life. This fact tells us that he wasn't immortal, but subject to death before he sinned. Some suggest that even the fact that Adam had to eat at all, much less of the tree of life, before he sinned, shows that he was mortal (as much so as all other living creatures) before he sinned. Would he not have starved to death had he not eaten? If not, why did God arrange for him to eat anything at all? When he sinned, he lost access to the tree of life, "lest he stretch out his hand, and take also from the tree of life, and eat, and live forever" (Gen. 3.22).

God forbade Adam to eat of the tree of the knowledge of good and evil, saying in Gen 2.16-17:

> From any tree of the garden you may eat freely; but from the tree of the knowledge of good and evil you shall not eat, for in the day that you eat from it you shall surely die.

Obviously, Adam didn't die physically the day he ate from the tree of knowledge, but hundreds of years later. However, he did die in the sense of being separated from God by his sin the day he ate, and he knew it. Suddenly, his relationship with God changed. He became fearful of approaching God, and attempted to hide from him. This broken relationship with God was Adam's sin-death.

Notice some conclusions thus far concerning whether Adam was immortal. First, Adam didn't die physically because of sin. The physical death of Adam and his descendants was not a punishment for Adam's sin, any more than the physical death of any other *living creatures* was punishment for Adam's sin. Like all others of Adam's descendants, you and I will die physically, but not because of Adam's sin. We die physically for the same reason Adam did. We're mortal, and we lack access to the tree of life.

Second, Jesus was resurrected from the dead to remedy the effect of Adam's sin (Rom. 5.12-21, I Cor. 15.22, 45), which was not physical death. Adam wasn't immortal because he was subject to death both before and after he sinned. Nor are we immortal. Christ's resurrection provides the remedy for Adam's spiritual death—his separation from God.

Though the concept of the dual nature of man predated him, the Greek philosopher Plato was most influential in propagating it. Henry Constable, author of *Duration and Nature of Future Punishment*, explains how Plato argued that every soul is immortal by nature, denying that any soul can ever become extinct or pass out of existence. How?

> In the very terms in which the punishment of the wicked is asserted in the New Testament! When the latter says the soul shall die, Plato says it shall not die; when the latter says it shall be destroyed, Plato says it shall not be destroyed; when the latter says it shall

perish and suffer corruption, Plato says it shall not
perish and is incorruptible. The phrases are the very
same, only that what Plato denies of all souls alike the
New Testament asserts of some of the souls of men.
(Henry Constable, *Duration and Nature of Future
Punishment, 6th ed.* [London: Edward Hobbs, 1886] p.
42)

## What Does the Bible Say About Immortality of the Soul?

William Robert West, in his book *If the Soul or Spirit Is Immortal,
There Can Be No Resurrection from the Dead*, answers the question
this way:

What does the Bible say about immortality of the
soul? Nothing. Together soul and spirit are used
almost 1100 times in the King James Version, but not
one time is immortal even used in the same verse with
either one. Immortal and immortality are in the Old
Testament 0 times, in the New Testament, immortal
one time, immortality five times, all by Paul. (William
Robert West, *If the Soul or Spirit Is Immortal, There
Can Be No Resurrection from the Dead, Third Edition,*
September 2006, originally published as *The
Resurrection and Immortality* [Bloomington, IN:
Author House], p. 76.)

While we bandy about quite handily the terms immortality,
immortal soul, and immortal spirit, no Bible writer ever used the term
immortal soul or spirit. However, Paul spoke about immorality. In I
Tim. 1.17 and 6.16, he said that "only God has immortality." In II Tim.
1.10, he said that Christ "abolished death and brought life and
immortality to light through the gospel." Did we need to have
immortality brought to light if we all had it from birth since Adam and
the Old Testament taught it?

In Rom. 2.5-9, Paul referred to an imminent judgment and revealed
what will be given both to the righteous and the wicked:

...but after thy hardness and impenitent heart treasurest
up for thyself wrath in the day of wrath and revelation
of the righteous judgment of God; who will render to
every man according to his works: to them that by

> patience in well-doing seek for glory and honor and
> incorruption, eternal life: but unto them that are
> factious, and obey not the truth, but obey
> unrighteousness, shall be wrath and indignation,
> tribulation and anguish, upon every soul of man that
> worketh evil, of the Jew first, and also of the Greek...

Thus, the righteous are promised four things: (1) glory, (2) honor, (3) incorruption, and (4) eternal life. The word incorruption comes from the same Greek word as immortality, and is so translated in the King James, New American Standard, New King James, and New International versions.

Likewise, the wicked are also promised four things: (1) wrath, (2) indignation, (3) tribulation, and (4) anguish.

Notice especially that the righteous are promised immortality. They weren't born immortal, else why would they seek it?

In addition, Paul said that at the resurrection "this mortal must put on immortality" (I Cor. 15.53), and "this mortal shall have put on immortality" (I Cor. 15.54). Why would we need to put it on then if we've all had it from birth? If Romans 2 and I Corinthians 15 teach nothing more, they teach that a man does not possess immorality prior to the resurrection.

## A More Scriptural Chart on the Destiny of Man

The figure below displays a more scriptural view of the destiny of man after all the proof-texts on the popular view have been dealt with and discarded as being used out of context. In this analysis, while alive on earth, each person is either in Christ through his obedience to the gospel or he's lost. When the righteous man dies, he goes to be with Christ where he is happy and resting, Rev. 14.13. He doesn't go to a warehouse (with "Hades" on the sign out front) for thousands of years awaiting a future return of Christ, a resurrection, and the judgment. Christ returned in AD 70 in the destruction of Jerusalem. Hades was destroyed in the first century according to Rev. 20.13-14. John said these events were to be fulfilled at a time that was "at hand" and "shortly to come to pass."

When a person dies outside of Christ, this figure doesn't show him going anywhere. Instead, as the Old Testament taught, and as we would have believed had we lived under the Old Testament, there is no wisdom, no knowledge, no thought, no memory of God, and no thanks of God for the dead. Furthermore, he is destroyed, and no more (Eccl. 9.5, 10, Ps. 6.5, 34.16, 37.20, 35-38). These passages are not the flawed combative rantings like those of Job's three friends, but solemn statements of the psalmist David.

## Where Are the Dead?

## Notice What's Not on This Chart

This chart is significant, not only for what it contains, but also more especially for what it does not contain.

No future return of Christ–See "The Olivet Discourse"

No conflagration of the planet–See "II Peter 3"

No future resurrection of physical bodies out of holes in the ground–See "I Corinthians 15 and the Resurrection of Israel"

No future simultaneous judgment of all men

No warehouse where souls wait for thousands of years for the return of Christ and the resurrection

No consciousness, memory, planning, knowledge, thanks, or wisdom by the wicked after death

No Abraham's Bosom–See "The Rich Man and Lazarus"

No conscious torment awaiting the wicked–See "Jesus' Teaching on hell"

# Frequently-Asked Questions

## Aren't You Encouraging People to Sin?

Question: The question arises in the minds of many, "If one does not teach that the wicked will be punished with unending suffering in a Devil's hell, aren't you encouraging people to sin?"

Answer: First, as we noticed in the chapter on hell, there is no passage that describes a "Devil's hell," i.e., that denotes it as Satan's abode. We get that strictly from Roman Catholic tradition.

Second, if both Old and New Testaments are silent on the concept of unending torment, do we need to contrive such a doctrine to make folks live right? As we've seen, that's exactly why the doctrine was concocted in the first place, first in Egypt, then among the Greeks, from where Roman Catholics appropriated it into their teaching.

God assures us in Heb. 2.2 that under the Old Covenant, which knew nothing of the popular concept of hell, that "every transgression and disobedience received a just recompense of reward," and yet the only just recompenses we find under the Law are temporal physical punishments. Do we need to concoct further punishments to pile on top of those God thought were just and sufficient, or can we trust that God knew what he was doing? Have not Roman Catholics encouraged lawlessness among many millions when they invent additional punishments to put on men that God never conceived of, thereby becoming lawless themselves? If we continue to add to God's just and sufficient punishments, won't we be encouraging lawlessness?

We might consider what punishment we'll suffer for teaching false doctrine whose origin is within Egyptian and Greek paganism, and finding fruition within Roman Catholicism. What is a just punishment for preaching a doctrine that millions recoil from as being unjust and then rejecting the Gospel? This has nothing to do with my motive in pursuing this study. I've taught Roman Catholic doctrine on this subject for more years than I've rejected it. If it's in the Bible, I'll continue to teach it, regardless if everyone in the world rejects it. If it's not, and we refuse to study the subject for fear that we might be removing a reason many people become Christians, then whose blood do we have on our shoulders?

Question: What about Hitler? Are you saying that he'll receive no future judgment and punishment, even after he killed millions?

Answer: The Old Testament spoke of monstrous rulers as evil as Hitler, and they received physical death. Hebrews 2.2 says that every trespass and disobedience received a just recompense of reward, with no interminable conscious torment even mentioned. Do we believe that, or should we help God out by piling more punishment on top of what God ordained? Who has the superior sense of justice, God or us?

Question: What about Samuel being called up from the dead? Doesn't his case indicate that the dead are conscious?

Answer: I Samuel 28 gives the account of Saul, who was in rebellion to God at the time and pursuing the lawful king David. Due to his rebellion, God wasn't communicating with Saul, so he sought out a medium and spiritist (Heb.—a ventriloquist), whom God had outlawed in the land. Under the Mosaic Law, all such seeking the dead was strictly forbidden (Lev. 19.31, 20.6). This woman is variously called the Witch of Endor, or a spiritist.

Opinions of what happened in this chapter range from the entire incident being fraudulent to the view that God intervened in this lady's séance to communicate to Saul. I lean toward the first view; but in any case, ventriloquists depend on fraud. God had already refused to communicate with Saul due to his evident lack of trust in what God had said earlier.

Thus, at the hand of this ventriloquist, the Bible says that Samuel spoke to Saul, i.e., in the way that ventriloquists work, not in reality. If we're going to affirm the consciousness of the dead, surely we should pursue more reliable evidence than the performance of a fraudulent spiritist to the ungodly Saul or pagan legends from Egypt, shouldn't we?

Question: When Jesus' disciples saw Moses and Elijah at the transfiguration, and heard them speaking, doesn't that indicate that the dead are conscious?

Answer: Jesus' disciples saw Moses and Elijah *in a vision.* Jesus said they saw *a vision* ("tell the vision to no man," Mt. 17.9), not reality. We cannot use something unreal to teach a reality, can we?

Question: When Jesus said that "God is the God of Abraham, Isaac, and Jacob; God is not the God of the dead, but of the living," wasn't he implying that Abraham was not dead, but alive?

Answer: Not at all, for Abraham was dead! Other passages teach it, but most importantly, that Abraham was dead is taught in these very verses. The text is Mt. 22.31-32, where Jesus said:

> But as touching the resurrection of the dead, have ye
> not read that which was spoken unto you by God,
> saying, I am the God of Abraham, and the God of

Isaac, and the God of Jacob? God is *not* the God of the
dead, *but* of the living. [Emphasis mine—SGD]

One who makes the above argument to show that Abraham was
not dead, but alive, fails to recognize the presence of an ellipsis in this
passage, the "not—but" construction modifying a common verb.

To appreciate fully Paul's teaching, we must understand a figure of
speech, called "ellipsis," which he used here as well as many times
elsewhere in his writings. Ellipsis simply means "words left out,"
which the writer wants the reader to supply. All people in all languages
use ellipsis. When we tell Junior, "Shut the door," we omit the subject,
but he understands that we speak to him.

The particular type of ellipsis in this verse is identifiable by the
occurrence of "not" and "but" as initial words in dependent clauses
that modify a common verb. If we don't recognize this figure of speech
the hundreds of times it occurs in the New Testament, we will teach
false doctrine about each one of them, as we'll make the "not" phrase
an absolute negative. The most basic example we find in the New
Testament is I Pet. 3.3-4, where Peter instructed Christian women:

> Whose adorning let it *not* be the outward adorning of
> braiding the hair, and of wearing jewels of gold, or of
> putting on apparel; *but* let it be the hidden man of the
> heart, in the incorruptible apparel of a meek and quiet
> spirit, which is in the sight of God of great price.

Some of our Pentecostal friends, who don't recognize this figure of
speech, use this verse to prohibit their women from wearing gold
jewelry and having their hair done. They claim, "The Bible plainly
says, let it not be the outward adorning of braiding the hair, and of
wearing jewels of gold." They are not so hard on Peter's next phrase,
though, "or putting on of apparel." Was Peter also prohibiting women
from wearing apparel? Of course not, and they shouldn't bind an
interpretation on others which they are not willing to obey themselves.
If they don't believe their argument enough to obey it consistently,
why should we?

Note that the "not" clause and the "but" clause both modify the
verb "to let." Peter, in effect, said, "not only, but also," with emphasis
on the "also" phrase. In other words, Peter taught, "let your apparel be
*not only* the outward, *but also* the inward, and *especially* the inward."
Christian women should put more emphasis on their inward clothing of
a meek and quiet spirit than they put on their physical clothing.

We find a similar basic example in Jn. 6.27, where Jesus told his listeners:

> Work *not* for the food which perisheth, *but* for the food which abideth unto eternal life.

Notice again the "not . . . but . . ." construction with the common verb "to work." One who doesn't spot this ellipsis could say, "The Bible says not to work for physical food." His interpretation would conflict with other passages: "If any will not work, neither let him eat," (II Thes. 3.10). If one recognizes the figure of speech Jesus used, he'll not make an absolute prohibition out of the "not" phrase. Then he can correctly understand that Jesus taught that we should work for both physical and spiritual food, and put the emphasis on the spiritual.

Literally, this is saying, "not only-but also" with emphasis on the "also" phrase. The New Testament contains hundreds of ellipses, and someone will take every one of the "not" statements as an absolute negative, as is done in the above question. (For further discussion of ellipsis, please see Chapter 17, "Ellipsis: Speaking Where the Bible Is Silent" in the author's *How to Study the Bible: A Practical Guide to Independent Bible Study*.)

Applying this tool for interpreting ellipsis to Jesus statement gives us:

> God is *not only* the God of the dead, *but also* (and *especially*) of the living.

Thus, in Mt. 22.31-32, Jesus was not affirming that Abraham was alive or immortal when he said this at all, but dead, teaching, "God is *not only* the God of the dead (including Abraham), *but also and especially of the living.*" The argument advanced in this question is just another example of misinterpreting the "not" part of an elliptical statement as an absolute negative.

To further corroborate this conclusion, in Rom. 14.9, Paul says:

> For to this end Christ died and lived (again), that he might be Lord of both the dead and the living.

## Conclusion

In concluding this chapter, we've seen that the popular view of the afterlife is sorely lacking, consisting mainly of proof-texts with concepts "cut and pasted" together with little regard for the context of any of the passages used. Looking closer at the issue of man's immortality, we've seen that, contrary to the Roman Catholic view, immortality is conditional; it's a reward to the righteous, not an innate property of man's nature. Finally, we hope we've presented a more accurate picture of the destiny of man.

In summary, it appears that Roman Catholicism, that concocted the concept of man being created with an immortal spirit, then had to make sure of the location of that spirit from then on. Thus, they concocted the concept of hell, a place to store the spirits of the wicked eternally, and then interpreted the legendary basis of The Rich Man and Lazarus to have a temporary storage place until the judgment, and finally, appropriated the judgment spoken of in the last days of Israel to be at the end of time, again, a term not found in scripture.

# Chapter 13

# Summary and Conclusions

In this study we have seen that the Bible knows or says nothing about a supposed end of time, tho it does affirm that there's no end to the messianic age. Men have invented those concepts, and moved many last times events down to those points. Since Roman Catholicism has done that with all the elements of eschatology we've discussed in this volume, none of their concepts have any Bible basis, and any concepts of theirs we agree with don't either.

Opposed to that, the Bible does speak about the last days and the end of the Mosaic age, and specifies that the end of the Mosaic age would bring about the return of Christ, the judgment, the passing of the old heavens and earth, the Mosaic covenant world, the resurrection of Old Covenant saints, and the destruction of Old Covenant Israel at Gehenna, as seen in the following table of these events.

**Event: The End of Time**
Roman Catholicism teaches? Yes
Bible teaches? No

**Event: The Return of Christ at the End of Time**
Roman Catholicism teaches? Yes
Bible teaches? No, at the End of the Mosaic Age

**Event: The Judgment at the End of Time**
Roman Catholicism teaches? Yes
Bible teaches? No, at the End of the Mosaic Age

**Event: Heavens & Earth Pass Away at the End of Time**
Roman Catholicism teaches? Yes

Bible teaches? No, at the End of the Mosaic Age

**Event: Resurrection at the End of Time**
Roman Catholicism teaches? Yes
Bible teaches? No, at the End of the Mosaic Age

**Event: Eternal Conscious Torment at the End of Time**
Roman Catholicism teaches? Yes
Bible teaches? No, the Jews punished at Gehenna at the End of
the Mosaic Age

For further study on these topics, please refer to the author's
*Essays on Eschatology: An Introductory Overview of the Study of Last
Things*, available from Amazon.com. This book has one chapter for
each paragraph of I Corinthians 15, totaling over 100 pages, and
another 100 pages on the theme of imminent judgment in the New
Testament.

# Bibliography

*Anchor Bible Dictionary.* Cited in *Al Maxey-Thomas Thrasher Debate* available online at www.zianet.com/Maxey.

Augustine, *City of God, Book IV*, p. 32, cited by Thomas B. Thayer, *Origin & History of the Doctrine of Endless Punishment.* Boston: Universalist Publishing House, 1855.

Amirault, Gary *The Ancient Inventors and Perpetrators of Hell*, www.tentmaker.org.

Bacchiocchi, Dr. Samuele. *Immortality or Resurrection? A Biblical Study on Human Nature and Destiny.* Cited in Al Maxey-Thomas Thrasher Debate available online at www.zianet.com/Maxey.

Burns, Alan. *The Rich Man and Lazarus.* Santa Clarita, CA: Concordant Publishing Concern, n.d. Cited in *Al Maxey-Thomas Thrasher Debate* available online at www.zianet.com/Maxey.

*Catechism of the Catholic Church Second Edition.* Washington, DC: United States Catholic Conference, 2000.

Dawson, Samuel G. *Essays on Eschatology: An Introductory Overview of the Study of Last Things*, Third Edition. Bowie, TX: SGD Press, 2016.

Dawson, Samuel G. *Fellowship: With God and His People: The Way of Christ Without Denominationalism* Second Edition. Amarillo, TX: Gospel Themes Press, 2004.

Dawson, Samuel G. *The Teaching of Jesus: From Sinai to Gehenna, A Faithful Rabbi Urgently Warns Rebellious Israel,* Third Edition. Bowie, TX: SGD Press, 2013.

Dawson, Samuel G. *Denominational Doctrines: Explained, Examined, Exposed*, Second Edition. Amarillo, TX: SGD Press, 2010.

Dawson, Samuel G. *How to Study the Bible: A Practical Guide to Independent Bible Study.* Amarillo, TX: Gospel Themes Press, 2005.

Dawson, Samuel G. *Revelation Realized: Martyr Vindication from Genesis to Revelation.* Bowie, TX: SGD Press, 2016.

Dawson, Samuel G. *What Is Wrong with Most Churches of Christ and How They Can Avoid Extinction.* Amarillo, TX: Gospel Themes Press, 2006.

Edwards, Jonathan. cited by A. W. Pink, *Eternal Punishment* Swengel, PA: Reiner Publications, n.d., cited by Edward William Fudge, *The Fire That Consumes.* Houston: Providential Press, 1982

Eusebius, Pamphilus. *The Ecclesiastical History,* translated by C. F. Cruse, Philadelphia: J. B. Lippincott and Company, 1869.

Frost, Samuel. *Exegetical Essays on the Resurrection.* Xenia, OH: Truth Voice Publishing, 2004.

Frost, Samuel. *Misplaced Hope: The Origins of First and Second Century Eschatology.* Colorado Springs, CO: Bimillennial Press, 2002.

Furniss, J. *The Sight of Hell.* London and Dublin: Duffy, cited by Edward William Fudge, *The Fire That Consumes.* Houston: Providential Press, 1982.

Fudge, Edward William. *The Fire That Consumes.* Houston: Providential Press, 1982.

Hanson, J. W. D.D. *The Bible Hell,* fourth edition. Boston: Universalist Publishing House, 1888. Available on World Wide Web.

Hastings, Dr. James. *Dictionary of Christ and the Gospels.* Cited in *Al Maxey-Thomas Thrasher Debate* available online at www.zianet.com/Maxey.

Hatch, Sidney. *Daring to Differ: Adventures in Conditional Immortality.* Cited in Al Maxey-Thomas Thrasher Debate available online at www.zianet.com/Maxey.

*International Standard Bible Encyclopedia.* Grand Rapids: William B. Eerdmans Publishing Co., 1979.

*Interpreter's Bible.* Cited in Al Maxey-Thomas Thrasher Debate available online at www.zianet.com/Maxey.

James, Timothy A. *THE MESSIAH'S RETURN, Delayed? Fulfilled? or Double-Fulfillment?* East Liverpool, OH: Northeast Ohio Bible Institute, 1982.

*Jerome Biblical Commentary.* Cited in Al Maxey-Thomas Thrasher Debate available online at www.zianet.com/Maxey.

Josephus, Flavius. *Complete Works.* Translated by William Whiston. Grand Rapids: Kregel Publications, 1960.

Kittel, Gerhard. *Theological Dictionary of the New Testament.* Grand Rapids: Eerdmans, 1974.

Lile, Jeremy. *Otherworld Journey: The Origins of Hell in Christian Thought*. PlanetPreterist.com.

Luck, William F. *Divorce and Remarriage: Recovering the Biblical View*. New York: Harper & Row, 1987.

Maxey, Al and Thrasher, Thomas. *Al Maxey-Thomas Thrasher Debate* available online at www.zianet.com/Maxey.

Maxey, Al. "The Consuming Fire, Examining the Final Fate of the Wicked in Light of Biblical Language," *Reflections #46*, June 6, 2003.

Mosheim, John Lawrence, D. D., *Institutes of Ecclesiastical History Ancient and Modern*. New York: Robert Carter & Brothers, 1861.

*New Commentary on the Whole Bible*. Cited in Al Maxey-Thomas Thrasher Debate available online at www.zianet.com/Maxey.

Packer, J. I. *"Fundamentalism" and the Word of God*. Grand Rapids, MI: William B. Eerdmans Publishing Co., 1958.

Simmons, Kurt. *Fulfilled! Vol. XII, No. 2*, Winter 2017, pp. 6-7.

Spurgeon, Charles H. Sermon No. 66, New Park Street Pulpit, 2:105, cited by Edward William Fudge, *The Fire That Consumes*. Houston: Providential Press, 1982.

Stanley, Floyd Irvin *As A Lamb Slain, A Unique Commentary on the Book of The Revelation* Rogers, AR: F. I. Stanley, 1985.

Stevens, Ed. *Fulfilled! Vol. XI, No. 2*, Summer 2016 issue, pp. 10-11

Thayer, George Henry. *Greek-English Lexicon of the New Testament*. Grand Rapids: Zondervan Publishing House, 1962.

Thayer, Thomas B. *The Origin & History of the Doctrine of Endless Punishment*. Boston: Universalist Publishing House, 1855.

*The Catholic Encyclopedia*. Charles George Herbermann (1840-1916). New York: ROBERT APPLETON COMPANY; Imprimatur: John M. Farley, Archbishop of New York, 1917.

*The New Encyclopedia Britannica, Vol. 5*, 15th edition Chicago: Encyclopedia Britannica, Inc.

Vine, W. E. *Expository Dictionary of New Testament Words*. Grand Rapids: Fleming H. Revell, 1966.

*Webster's Third New International Dictionary of the English Language Unabridged*, editor Philip Babcock Gove, Ph.D. Springfield, MA: Merriam-Webster Inc., 1993.

West, William Robert. *If the Soul or Spirit Is Immortal, There Can Be No Resurrection from the Dead*, Third Edition, originally published as *The Resurrection and Immortality*. Bloomington, IN: Author House, September 2006.

Witherell, J. F. *Five Pillars in the Temple of Partialism Shaken and Removed.* Concord: The Balm of Gilead Office, 1843. Placed into electronic format January 1997 by Gary Amirault. Hermann, MO: Tentmaker Ministry.

Young, Robert. *The Holy Bible, Consisting of the Old and New Covenants; Translated according to the Letter and Idioms of the Original Languages.* Edinburgh: George Adam Young & Co., 1863. Revised edition 1887. Third edition 1898. Reprinted frequently under the title, *Young's Literal Translation.*

*Zondervan Pictorial Encyclopedia of the Bible.* Cited in Al Maxey-Thomas Thrasher Debate available online at www.zianet.com /Maxey.

# Scripture Index

# Topic Index

230 Topic Index

# *Revelation Realized:*
## *Martyr Vindication from Genesis to Revelation*

### Samuel G. Dawson
*502 pp with indexes*

We believe you'll think this is the most common sense and understandable view of Revelation you've ever read. Dawson begins with Jesus' promise to avenge the blood of all the martyrs from Abel to Zechariah on the Jerusalem of his generation, within his generation.

The theme of the vindication of martyrs begins with the death of Abel and permeates the entire Bible through the history of Old Covenant Israel, the prophets, the gospels, the New Testament epistles, and right into the last book of the Bible, where it reaches its climax and fulfillment. This theme demands that Revelation was written in the late 60s AD, just before the imminent destruction of the great harlot city, Jerusalem, where the Lord was crucified, having warned the wicked and perverse generation of their destruction and the vindication of the martyrs in his generation

The theme of the vindication of martyrs begins with the death of Abel and permeates the entire Bible through the history of Old Covenant Israel, the prophets, the gospels, the New Testament epistles, and right into the last book of the Bible, where it reaches its climax and fulfillment. This theme demands that Revelation was written in the late 60s AD, just before the imminent destruction of the great harlot city, Jerusalem, where the Lord was crucified, having warned the wicked and perverse generation of their destruction and the vindication of the martyrs in his generation

Imminently readable, true to the text, and appealing to common sense, see if this commentary on Revelation doesn't finally enable you to confidently grasp this important book. we think it's the most consistent view of the book written from the early date point of view!

**Consider copies for yourself, others, and for class study.**
**We think you'll be glad you did!**

*Samuel G. Dawson's books are available at Amazon.com*

# Essays on Eschatology:
## An Introductory Overview of the Study of Last Things

### Samuel G. Dawson

*598 pp with indexes*

Eschatology, the study of last things, is concerned with time. Futurists believe that much of eschatology is still future. Because of the imminence statements in the gospels and epistles, preterists (including the author) believe all of the last things (the return of Christ, the judgment, and the resurrection) were all fulfilled in Jesus' generation.

This volume deals with the importance of time to God and His faithfulness in fulfillment of prophecies concerning time. Major topics discussed are the Olivet Discourse, II Peter 3, and Paul's preaching and teaching on the resurrection.

One major section of this book deals with the afterlife: Hell, the Rich Man & Lazarus, and immortality. Another deals with the faithless foundation of dispensational premillennialism. A last collection of topics includes The Importance of the Old Testament to Christians, Zionism, and Frequently-Asked Questions.

*Samuel G. Dawson's books are available at <u>Amazon.com</u>*

# How to Study the Bible:

## A Practical Guide to Independent Bible Study

### Samuel G. Dawson

*446 pages with comprehensive indexes*

## A tradition-challenging publication without denominational bias!

This book begins with a chapter on "Jesus' Call for Disciples" that demonstrates what it means to be a true disciple or student of God's word, rather than just a spectator sitting in a pew.

Another chapter explores "The Importance of the Old Testament to New Testament Christians," while it exposes many of our unfounded prejudices against the Old Covenant.

A great help is a list of "Old Testament Passages Quoted in the New Testament," which points us to the inspired commentary on those prophetic verses.

Also, the 42-page "Outline of the Bible" provides a valuable tool for grasping the overall view and context of the Bible and is a fascinating read in itself.

Other items of importance are a strategy for both individuals and churches to use in teaching and studying all of the books and topics of the Bible in a timely fashion and an analysis of how all of us have two reservoirs of Bible knowledge: topical and book-by-book.

When one Christian used the material to teach a class, the elders asked him to repeat the class the next year.

Although written by a serious non-denominational Bible student, preacher, and teacher of nearly 40 years, this book is not for the professional Bible scholar or theologian. It is for the independent Bible student who would like to know more of the Bible's teaching without a denominational slant or dependence on a professional.

In recent years, the availability of helpful reference works has exploded, as have resources on the Internet. As modern Bibles and the religious world are becoming more premillennialistic and Calvinistic, the emphasis on online easy-to-use Bible aids helps today's student remain true to God's word-for-word inspired text. You can take advantage of these new opportunities for yourself.

This book brings the Bible to life and makes it relevant for today. Lessons progress from examining basic attitudes toward the Bible to choosing a dependable translation to rules for interpretation to dealing with difficulties in the Bible.

### *Samuel G. Dawson's books are available at*
### *amazon.com*

# Marriage, Divorce & Remarriage
### *The Uniform Teaching of*
### *Moses, Jesus & Paul*

## Samuel G. Dawson

This book brings the Bible to life and makes it relevant for today. Lessons progress from examining basic attitudes toward the Bible to choosing a dependable translation to rules for interpretation to dealing with difficulties in the Bible. Not only will you learn how to study the Bible, but you'll also come away with good, basic Bible knowledge from all the examples given in the book.

This groundbreaking material differs from others on the subject in that it proves that Moses, Jesus, and Paul all taught the same thing about divorce and remarriage. Most efforts on this issue don't deal with Moses' teaching in the Old Testament; and thus, they take Jesus' and Paul's teaching out of the context of explaining divorce and remarriage to the Jews: "men who understood the law" (Rom. 7:1). By studying the consistencies between what Moses, Jesus, and Paul taught, as one preacher explained, "Sam has finally cracked the nut on MDR." Undoubtedly, this work will aid other serious students in their quest for truth and open up new avenues for study.

## THIS BOOK DEALS WITH THE ISSUES!

*Is sexual intercourse a right or a condition of marriage?* • *In the Bible, betrothal was marriage.* • *What is civil government's interest in marriage?* • *Common-law marriage in the Bible.* • *Is fon-dling sexual intercourse?* • *Why were most adulterers in OT not stoned to death?* • *Is the Sermon on the Mount OT or NT teaching?* • *Two problems that must be worked.* • *What are the three ways a person can commit adultery?* • *Does God hate all divorce?* • *Is there a guilty party in Mt. 5.32 or Mt. 19.9?* • *Can an unjustly put-away person put away a fornicating spouse?* • *Four questions that lead to a solution of every situation.* • *Church limitations in dealing with divorce.* • *Fellowship.* • *Can a local church study these issues for itself? If not, let's not hear any more about local church autonomy.*

# Christians, Churches, & Controversy:
## Navigating Doctrinal & Personal Clashes

### Samuel G. Dawson

An eighteenth century Scottish poet wrote concerning war: "Rash, fruitless war, from wanton glory waged, is only splendid murder."

An older preacher used this quotation when he wrote concerning a particularly brutal doctrinal attack on another elderly preacher by a group of younger, treacherous preachers. While many controversies among Christians and churches aren't this vicious, many Christians and congregations simply don't know how to navigate personal and doctrinal clashes; and thus, do more harm than good. Such situations expose some noble and naïve souls to some pretty treacherous Christians. Yet, many Christians consent to much worse than Saul did at Stephen's stoning while "consenting to his death" by just holding the coats of the stone-throwers.

Most members, whose jobs aren't even on the line, refuse to ratchet up their courage to be bothered by congregational problems and decisions. They may just want difficulties handled by the congregational leaders so they can avoid being involved. Consequently, many Christians go blithely on, consenting through ignorance to mistreatment of others that goes on behind the scenes.

### This book is not for you if:

- You're not a serious student of the Bible
- Your concept of Bible study is listening to your teacher go through a quarterly class book
- Your concept of being a Christian consists mainly of "going to church"
- You depend on the preacher to do your studying for you
- You're in a denomination where all the thinking is done at the top
- You're an elder who is afraid for the congregation to study controversial subjects

### Ideal for: Individual Study, Preaching, Elders

*Samuel G. Dawson's books are available at* <u>amazon.com</u>

# The Teaching of Jesus
*From Sinai to Gehenna: A Faithful Rabbi*
*Urgently Warns Rebellious Israel*

520 pages
Samuel G. Dawson

**This Book Will Change Your View of Jesus'**
**Teaching and the Entire New Testament as It**
**Exposes Many of Our False Concepts**

This work begins with a study of covenant concepts in the Bible, the reign of God prior to the coming of Christ, and the sophisticated expectations God has always had of non-covenant people. After demonstrating that forgiveness of sins existed under the Mosaic Law, the author develops the preaching of John the Baptist and Jesus as an urgent attempt to turn the Jewish nation back to God through faithful obedience to the Mosaic Law in order to avoid imminent national destruction.

The Sermon on the Mount is viewed, not as a contrast between the Mosaic Law and the teaching of Christ, but as Jesus correctly interpreting Moses to the Jews of his day. Thus, every syllable of that sermon is Old Testament teaching. That most of that teaching is also contained in the New Covenant is demonstrated.

The parables of Jesus are then briefly analyzed, showing that each one of them is first related to the attempted reform of the Jews by Jesus. The theme of the relative importance of one's treatment of his fellowman over his formal religious service is traced throughout the Old and New Covenants. The study of *The Teaching of Jesus* concludes as Jesus concluded it, with a study of his pronouncement of imminent national destruction in Matthew 24.

*Samuel G. Dawson's books are available at <u>amazon.com</u>*

# Samuel G. Dawson

A physics and mathematics graduate from Texas Tech University, Samuel G. Dawson did research in celestial mechanics and intercontinental missile guidance in the aerospace industry before preparing to preach the gospel of Christ. In twenty-two years of full time public teaching, he did extensive live call-in radio work daily for eight years and participated in a number of religious debates. Sam's scientific background has given him an inquisitive, logical, and thorough approach to the scriptures and a reputation for making Bible students re-think teaching they've taken for granted.

Sam drew on decades of experience working with local congregations to write:

*Fellowship: With God and His People: The Way of Christ Without Denominationalism* covers the nature of fellowship with God in the universal church and with other Christians in local churches with no denominational allegiance, since no denominations existed in the New Testament.

*Denominational Doctrines: Explained, Examined, Exposed* carefully documents and explains popular denominational doctrines such as Calvinism, the Sabbath Question, Dispensational Premillennialism, Modern-Day Tongue-Speaking, Indwelling of the Holy Spirit, Baptism, Jehovah's Witnesses, Mormonism, and Theistic Evolution.

*Marriage, Divorce, & Remarriage: The Uniform Teaching of Moses, Jesus, & Paul* demonstrates how Moses, Jesus, and Paul all taught the same thing about this controversial subject, concluding with many practical solutions of unscriptural divorce and remarriage situations.

*The Teaching of Jesus: From Sinai to Gehenna: A Faithful Rabbi Urgently Warns Rebellious Israel* shows how many people take Jesus' teaching out of the context of the people he preached to and misapply it to our day. For instance, every syllable of the Sermon on the Mount is from the Mosaic Law, and how Jesus correctly interprets it to the Jews of his day. Most of it, but not all, of his teaching will be repeated in the New Covenant.

*How to Study the Bible: A Practical Guide to Independent Bible Study*, helps students be faithful students of the Scriptures, and avoid depending on professionals for their Bible knowledge.

*Christians, Churches, & Controversy: Navigating Doctrinal & Personal Clashes* affirms the teaching of Jesus that how we treat our fellow man is more important than our formal religious service, and how such clashes should be dealt with.

*Essays on Eschatology: An Introductory Overview of the Study of Last Things* affirms the Bible's teaching that "last things" are the last days of the Mosaic covenant, not the last days of history or the Christian age, which has no end. The Lord's imminent return, resurrection, and judgment are covered in the Old Testament, the gospels, and the New Testament epistles are all covered in detail.

*Revelation Realized: Martyr Vindication from Genesis to Revelation* covers the theme of martyr vindication from Abel, the first martyr, through Deuteronomy 32 where Moses foretells the destruction of Jerusalem for its making martyrs of the prophets, through Isaiah and others of the prophets, into the gospels, where Jesus announces further judgments on Jerusalem for martyring him, his apostles and saints in his generation, through the New Testament epistles, and finally into Revelation, where the great harlot city of spiritual Babylon, where he was crucified, was announced and carried out.

All these books are available on Amazon.com

Made in the USA
San Bernardino, CA
14 May 2019